DON'T USE YOUR WORDS!

Don't Use Your Words!

Children's Emotions in a Networked World

Jane Juffer

NEW YORK UNIVERSITY PRESS
New York

NEW YORK UNIVERSITY PRESS
New York
www.nyupress.org

© 2019 by New York University
All rights reserved

References to Internet websites (URLs) were accurate at the time of writing. Neither the author nor New York University Press is responsible for URLs that may have expired or changed since the manuscript was prepared.

Library of Congress Cataloging-in-Publication Data
Names: Juffer, Jane, author.
Title: Don't use your words! : children's emotions in a networked world / Jane Juffer.
Description: New York : New York University Press, [2019] | Includes bibliographical references and index.
Identifiers: LCCN 2018037668| ISBN 9781479831746 (cl : alk. paper) | ISBN 9781479833054 (pb : alk. paper)
Subjects: LCSH: Emotions in children. | Television and children. | Mass media and children.
Classification: LCC BF723.E6 J84 2019 | DDC 155.4/124—dc23
LC record available at https://lccn.loc.gov/2018037668

New York University Press books are printed on acid-free paper, and their binding materials are chosen for strength and durability. We strive to use environmentally responsible suppliers and materials to the greatest extent possible in publishing our books.

Manufactured in the United States of America

10 9 8 7 6 5 4 3 2 1

Also available as an ebook

CONTENTS

Introduction: "Run Over by a Unicorn" 1

1. Affective Intensity and Children's Embodiment 33

   PART I. POLITICAL SUBJECTS 55

2. The Production of Fear: Children at the
   U.S.-Mexico Border 61
3. "I Hate You, Dunel Trump": Anger or Civility? 83
4. "Criss-Cross Applesauce": Keeping Control
   in the Classroom 107

   PART II. KIDS' TELEVISION, FROM PROBLEM SOLVING
   TO SIDEWAYS GROWTH 137

5. TV's Narratives for Emotional Management 142
6. The Steven Universe, Where You Are an Experience 173

   PART III. THE LIMITS OF DIGITAL LITERACY 201

7. *Minecraft*'s Affective World Building 205
8. From Memes to Logos: Commercial Detours in the
   Game of *Roblox* 232

Conclusion: "Shame on You Killers, Shame on You" 255

Acknowledgments 261
Notes 263
Bibliography 271
Index 279
About the Author 285

Color photos appear as an insert following page 162.

Introduction

"Run Over by a Unicorn"

"What if you could see your feelings, and they were chasing you?" says the child. "Which one would be fastest?" I ask. "Quickness," he responds. "But is that a feeling?" I ask. "Of course. I feel quick this morning. Sometimes I feel slow." And another morning, upon waking, he comments, "I feel like I've been run over by a unicorn."
—Ezra, six years old

The scene in the therapist's office goes something like this: she points to the chart on the wall with its rows of faces typifying different expressions—happy, sad, hopeful, angry, frustrated, scared; there are almost 50 faces represented. Then she asks the seven-year-old to point to which face best describes how he is feeling. The idea, she explains to the parent, is if children can "put a label on it, they can begin to manage their emotions." Children often respond bodily when they are feeling out of control, she adds: they may hit or scream or run away. If they can name the feeling, they may be able to respond with their words rather than their bodies. The child, however, is not convinced. He studies the chart for a few minutes, then responds, "How I'm feeling is not there." She asks what he is feeling. "Irritated," he says, sighing. "Can I go now?"

The gap in expression between adult and child is at the heart of this book. My goal is not to close the gap but to let it remain, to perhaps even widen it, in the interest of allowing children a semi-autonomous space in which to express themselves. I do not dispute the importance of therapy for some children, nor the need for a language children can use to help them navigate the world. I am convinced, however, that this language, often taught by the most well-intended adults, fails to capture children's affective intensities even as it valorizes the realm of emotional expression. In fact, the very objective of "naming one's emotions" in the interest of controlling one's body almost certainly dampens the intensity and range of the feelings and their expression, especially their expression through the body. Self-regulation becomes "appropriate" bodily comportment. "Extreme" emotions should be subsumed, with happiness and "niceness" the goal. In the language of problem solving that has become central to television programming for young children, the "problem" that needs to be solved is the emotion that threatens social order. "Being run over by a unicorn" would not be considered a viable expression.

Media for children is one of the primary sites for the production of this therapeutic discourse. It is also one of the primary sites available to kids for creating alternatives to the management of emotions. This negotiation, this struggle, drives this book. On one side, the discourse of "emotional intelligence" across educational, therapeutic, and media sites aimed at young children valorizes the naming of certain emotions in the interest of containing affective expressions that don't conform to the normative notion of growing up. On the other side, kids, through the appropriation of these media texts and the production of their own culture, especially on the internet, resist these emotional categorizations, creating an "archive of feelings"[1] that this book compiles and analyzes. This archive sheds light on the conditions that make it hard for children to be heard and understood, which has significant implications for a range of policy arenas. What does it feel like to be a kid?[2] Why do so many policy makers, parents, and pedagogues treat feelings as something to be managed and translated?

The therapeutic influence on media produced for kids is sometimes derived directly from the private-sector counseling world; there exists what Stuart Hall would call an "articulation," bringing together the sites of children's television, therapy, parenting, and elementary education.[3] For example, three Nickelodeon preschool shows—*Ni Hao, Kai-Lan*; *Blue's Clues*; and *Wonder Pets*—used the consulting services of a therapist named Laura G. Brown to advise them in creating the characters and the stories. Nickelodeon's 2007 press release announcing the premiere for *Ni Hao, Kai-Lan*, a show featuring a five-year-old Chinese American girl, described Kai-Lan as an "emotionally gifted child who is driven to understand the world and how things are linked together both physically and emotionally" (quoted in Hayes 2008, 42). A recent article in *Psychology Today* is headlined "Can TV Promote Kids' Social-Emotional Skills? Help Your Child or Student Learn Positive Social-Emotional Lessons from TV" (2014). Its authors, academics Claire Christensen and Kate Zinsser, draw on and quickly redirect the familiar concern that television causes kids to be violent: "As a parent or educator, you've heard it before: violent TV creates violent children. But, what about TV shows that depict getting along with others, solving problems, or handling emotions constructively? If kids can learn to fight from the Teenage Mutant Ninja Turtles, can they also learn to share from Daniel Striped Tiger?" Their answer is yes—if the shows feature characters with strong "socioemotional skills" such as sharing and if parents engage their children in conversation about what is being represented. They should ask questions such as "Did you see Dora cooperate with Boots? Why did she do that? How did it make Boots feel?" and "You look nervous. Do you want to try taking deep breaths like Rabbit did?"

The therapeutic approach puts a new spin on the title of Marie Winn's influential 1977 *The Plug-In Drug*, in which she lamented television's addictive effects on children and urged parents to regain control of the powerful medium. Television is still a drug, but now it's a helpful drug, like the stimulants used to treat kids with attention deficit hyperactivity disorder (ADHD). In fact, one executive in the children's television industry, in response to the criticism that television can become addictive to children, said, "Everything is fine as long as the dosage is right. It's prescription drugs being given without a prescription. If you take too much, you get a stomachache. If you take the right amount, your headache is gone" (quoted in Hayes 2008, 15). Receiving the right dosage makes children more, not less, socially adjusted.

And the television industry more profitable. The focus on feelings is beginning to overshadow the industry's desire to show the educational value of television, a goal that has characterized research on television since PBS introduced *Sesame Street* in 1969. For example, when Disney launched its Disney Jr. channel in 2013, it told *The New York Times* that "its research indicated that mothers were less interested than they used to be in programs that promote academic goals. What matters more now . . . is emotion-based storytelling that captures attention long enough to teach social values and good behavior" (Barnes and Chozick 2013). These values and skills, in turn, help the child to be a better learner and, ultimately, a successful adult.

Films for children have become similarly preoccupied in the last decade. Take, for example, the highly successful *Inside Out*, released by Pixar in 2015. Set inside the brain of an 11-year-old girl named Riley, the film tells the story of her family's move from Minnesota to San Francisco as her father begins a new job. Although we sometimes get Riley's point of view, we rely primarily on the five characters inside her brain, each of whom represents different emotions: Joy, Sadness, Anger, Fear, and Disgust. As Riley begins to negotiate her new home and school and realizes how much she misses her old home, friends, and hockey team, the emotions jockey for position, with Joy desperately trying to maintain the control she enjoyed up to this point and politely trying to sideline Sadness, whose role nobody appreciates or even understands. Initially, Joy succeeds, and Riley pluckily makes the best of a difficult situation, with her parents thanking her for being such a good sport.

Gradually, though, it becomes clear that Riley is struggling. Despite Joy's best efforts, Sadness creeps in, gradually touching Riley's core memories—and because these memories reside deep in Riley's brain, no one in the "real" world initially recognizes that Riley is not actually happy, least of all her parents, who seem completely clueless. Riley cries at school in front of her new classmates, gets angry when Skyping with her old friend as the latter recounts a hockey team victory and describes a girl who is seemingly taking Riley's place, and storms off the hockey court during tryouts for a new team. Joy and Sadness later journey through Riley's brain to try to recover some of the core happy memories that Sadness has "corrupted," only to discover that it's OK to be sad. In fact, Sadness transforms from a frumpy, absent-minded girl into a heroic, articulate figure, the emotion who needs to be acknowledged by both Riley and her parents in order for her to be happy in her new home, and, importantly, to avoid the excessive outbursts she experienced at school and the hockey arena.

Inside Out speaks to both children and the adults who care for them: for children, emotions are so real that they are like little people inside your brain, controlling how you feel and act even though you don't realize it. By naming these emotions and emphasizing the complexity of children's lives, the film respects kids even as it reassures them that their emotions, while sometimes inexplicable, are really on their side. For adults, the film not so subtly tells them to recognize that children are complicated subjects, capable of a wide range of emotions, and that our job is to help them identify those feelings rather than demeaning or ignoring them. Ultimately, Riley and her parents happily resolve their differences and end the film as a peacefully contained nuclear family. The fact that the film ends with everyone getting along goes beyond the generic requirement for a happy ending; it also speaks to the assumption that kids, while they experience a range of emotions, should ultimately be cheerful. This goal is exactly what therapist/consultant Laura Brown expressed as her mission in designing kids' programming: "In America, happiness is the goal. It's in our Constitution. So we set out to create as many calm, happy moments as there are excited, happy moments" (quoted in Hayes 2008, 116).

I analyze these conditions through a two-pronged approach. First, how is the young child—roughly ages five to nine—constructed in U.S. media and school curriculum debates? What subject positions are made available? Drawing on work by scholars in the fields of cultural studies, media studies, and childhood studies—and locating their intersections—I reconstruct these subject positions insofar as they relate to emotions. Because cultural production is always shaped, even as it reshapes, economic and other policy realms, I begin the book by describing several relevant policy arenas and the manner in which they shape children's lives. These include immigration policy regarding refugee children; the electoral victory of Donald Trump and kids' responses to that; and educational policy, especially the debates around standardized curricula such as No Child Left Behind and Common Core. At each of these sites, I show how adults provide the language they deem suitable for kids to use in expressing their feelings, thus instantiating a powerful kind of conformity in the name of individual expression. I then situate kids' television programming in relation to these policies, showing some overlap and also some divergence. In each of these arenas, I focus on the production of a kind of emotional intelligence that expects children to speak in the (rational) language of adults, even as it assumes they are not fully capable of doing so.

Second, what texts have kids produced that resist these efforts at emotional management, illustrating their affective intensities and range?

I analyze and include a variety of kinds of cultural production by kids: original drawings by Central American refugee children; letters written and pictures drawn by kids in response to the Trump victory; observations of a Montessori classroom; tweets from a Syrian child; Tumblr fanart; kids' television reviews from Common Sense media; and kids' dance moves and memes that circulate on YouTube. I also analyze the commentary of kids playing two popular video games, *Minecraft* and *Roblox*, as well as their YouTube tutorials. The second half of the book illustrates how kids communicate with each other across these media by cross-referencing memes, songs, and movements; in so doing, they construct a common vernacular that departs from normative conceptions of proper expression. This vernacular is less about the naming of emotions and more about moving through space, constructing homes, and caring for pets. Kids share these experiences with each other, illustrating the "spreadability" of internet texts, to use the phrasing of Henry Jenkins and Sam Ford, or the way users can "share content for their own purposes" (2013, 3). These purposes, I argue, involve the production of a kids' community based on affect. Affect does not name an emotion; rather, it points to a movement, an inhabiting of the body that defies categorization. "Feelings" are much more akin to affect than are emotions because "feelings" capture the way a body actually feels, physically, when experiencing something; "emotions," by contrast, tend to sublimate these bodily feelings to language. In the next chapter, I elaborate in detail, using Brian Massumi's theory of affect, how affect differs from emotion. This affective realm is so important to archive because kids—especially younger ones—are not in a position to organize as a group for greater power, dependent as they are on adults for basic life necessities and mobility.

The first half of the book illustrates this affective range, even as it demonstrates how difficult it is for some kids to access the kinds of media, such as the internet, that allow them to connect with each other. The drawings of kids recently released from immigration detention centers, for example, testifies powerfully to a longing for home and a sense of belonging—feelings that are not captured in the language of the immigration system. Artwork by kids after Trump's victory illustrates their justified anger and rejection of his definition of national belonging, in contrast to the lessons in civics and polite letter-writing that some teachers were encouraging. Cumulatively, I hope that the many examples of kids' texts in this book speak both to their heterogeneity and different levels of privilege as well as to their common situation as subjects whose various forms of expression are rarely taken seriously. Although I can make no definitive claims about the transformations that might occur if kids' expressions were not dismissed, I feel confident asserting that we would no doubt live in a much different world than we do now.

Be Happy

The power of positive thinking defines a normative U.S. ideology, as Barbara Ehrenreich (2009) argues; she distinguishes between hope, which she says is considered an "emotion, a yearning, the experience of which is not entirely within our control," and optimism, a "cognitive stance, a conscious expectation, which presumably anyone can develop through practice" (4). One must practice positive thinking, and not only will that make one feel happier, but it will—we are told by psychologists and others—improve "health, personal efficacy, confidence, and resilience" (5). This provides us with the illusion of control—though it is a powerful illusion—and the devaluation of hope as a less productive "feeling."

This belief in the power of optimism as a cognitive realm that can be controlled (unlike the emotion of hope) also defines the discourse of emotional intelligence—seen as a specific set of skills that can be taught to children, much as math skills are, in order to build their resilience in the face of any one of a number of difficult situations, from bullying to poverty to learning difficulties. It also has entered schools; educational experts have developed "emotional literacy programs"—in the tens of thousands—across the country. As *New York Times* reporter Jennifer Kahn describes the concept in a September 11, 2013, article:

> The theory that kids need to learn to manage their emotions in order to reach their potential grew out of the research of a pair of psychology professors—John Mayer, at the University of New Hampshire, and Peter Salovey, at Yale. In the 1980s, Mayer and Salovey became curious about the ways in which emotions communicate information, and why some people seem more able to take advantage of those messages than others. While outlining the set of skills that defined this "emotional intelligence,"

Salovsey realized that it might be even more influential than he had originally suspected, affecting everything from problem solving to job satisfaction: "It was like, this is predictive!"

The goal, thus, is to figure out how to measure emotional intelligence in much the same way as academic intelligence is measured, so as to maximize the potential for future successes.

Academic psychology departments have contributed to this push for measurement of emotions. A 2016 article in *Psychology Today* titled "The Most Important Thing We Can Teach Our Children" describes a lecture given by Marc Brackett, director of the Yale Center for Emotional Intelligence, on a program that center developed for schools called RULER. Says the article's author, Lisa Firestone,

> RULER is an acronym that stands for *R*ecognizing emotions in self and others, *U*nderstanding the causes and consequences of emotions, *L*abeling emotions accurately, *E*xpressing emotions appropriately and *R*egulating emotions effectively. The program has been shown to boost student's emotional intelligence and social skills, productivity, academic performance, leadership skills and attention, while reducing anxiety, depression and instances of bullying between students. RULER creates an all-around positive environment for both students and teachers, with less burnout on both ends.

Like a ruler, the program becomes a tool of measurement and precision, making ambiguous realms such as emotions more clear-cut.

Within the discourse of emotional intelligence, children's self-determination is valorized, but this valorization occurs within regimes of governance that are highly managed for specific purposes. "Self-regulation" positions the self for success within a normative vision of what counts as success. As Nikolas Rose describes it, "Childhood is the most intensively governed sector of personal existence. In different ways, at different times, and by many different routes varying from one section of society to another, the health, welfare, and rearing of children have been linked in thought and practice to the destiny of the nation and the responsibilities of the state" (1999, 121). This is not, to be clear, the suppression and subsumption of children's identities as if they were important only in terms of what they represent;

rather, this is the encouragement of the *expression* of children's rights, including their rights to emotional expression, in the interest of a more vital public body. "Health" includes emotional health, achieved by successfully managing emotions, in the interest of "normal" development and "successful" citizenship. For those children considered to be on the margins or outside of normative citizenship, such as the Central American children seeking refuge in the U.S. whom I discuss in chapter 2, the forms of governance are more intense and punitive, and less about incorporation.

Yet children resist. By "resist," I don't mean that kids actively oppose adult control (though that may happen), for this would entail seeing them only in relation to adults, which is exactly not my point. Rather, kids have their own ideas and forms of expression that are not easily managed. In this book, I argue that media for young children provides a space of both management and resistance, the latter both intentional and inadvertent. The world of the internet has spawned multiple and dispersed sites of creativity; even relatively young kids can quite easily produce their own fanart, memes, and YouTube videos as well as remixing other texts. In gaming, kids construct their own spaces, often connecting with other kids in communities defined through both mutuality and competition. All of these sites, individually and networked, are places of intensely affective experience, where kids deploy nonverbal modes of expression such as images/memes, music, and movements (such as the "dab"). Kids collaborate without adult intervention, in their own language—a language that is often dismissed as nonsense or immature but that actually constitutes a complex web of intertextual references that an adult would likely have a difficult time understanding.

Some kids more easily access the internet than others, and its mode of reproduction and circulation makes it an apt venue for appropriation and community. However, I am not positing the internet as the utopian alternative to more conventional forms of expression, such as drawing, coloring, Play-Doh, and Legos, since all of these media include a refusal (or simply a lack of desire) to name, pin down, and categorize one's emotions. Drawings by Central American children just released from detention (chapter 2) and artwork by kids responding to the election of Donald Trump (chapter 3) reveal that it is too reductive to attempt to distill a range of feelings into a single emotion. These texts also illustrate the manner in which well-meaning adults attempt to mediate kids' expressions so as to manage them for certain purposes that may not be in the kids' best interests. Some teachers and parents, for example, used the presidential election to teach kids a civics lesson, encouraging them to emphasize kindness and manners through letter writing rather than expressing outright anger and fear.

Adults are not always evil or misguided, however, and they play a necessary role for the age group that is my focus in this book—the five- to nine-year-olds who are in their early years of schooling and exposure to forces outside the home, while still heavily shaped by the domestic sphere. In each chapter on different cultural realms, I show how adults can best facilitate kids' expressions when they provide the structures that allow for independence and autonomy, then step back and let kids take over. This happens, for example, with the Central American kids, as activists provided them the space in which to draw anything they wanted, and by some teachers and artists who provided spaces for kids reacting angrily to Trump's victory.

Drawing on insights gleaned from disability studies, I argue here for a valorization of alternative forms of expression. Within disability studies, scholars writing specifically about autism and other diagnoses "on the spectrum" of neurological differences have been arguing for an acceptance of "neurodiversity" rather than a diagnosis and treatment. Is there a disorder here? Or, rather, is there a different way of thinking based on differences in the structure of the brain that should be valued rather than treated? E. Kay M. Tisdall notes the similarities between the fields of disability and childhood studies

> Like children versus adults, disabled people have been positioned theoretically as being non-able bodied, with the comparison continuously against a mythical gold standard of "normal"—failing to recognize, for example, that most people have impairments at some point in their lives and capacities vary widely. . . . Children and disabled people have been treated as "lesser" because they are positioned as dependents on adults or carers/able-bodied people respectively. This ignores the realities of people's interdependencies and the different types of "work" done (whether paid or unpaid). It ignores contributions made by children and disabled people in their personal and more public lives. (2012, 183)

The assumption that only certain people are dependent, in other words, allows for certain norms to be produced and consolidated—norms such as the one that defines growing up as the gradual subsumption of feelings within rational communication.

My goal is not to demonize therapy or homogenize it; in fact, I speak to the potential of music therapy below. Clearly, I do not have enough evidence to claim that therapy does not help some kids, nor would I want to pursue that argument, because therapy should not be used as a scapegoat. It is part of the larger picture in which normative emotional expression is produced. I do want to ask: what is sacrificed via this cultivation of proper emotions? How might emotions be misunderstood as they are distilled into recognizable categories? The naming of Anger, Joy, Disgust, and Fear, for example, privileges certain emotions over others and assumes that these are distinct categories that exist somewhat independently from each other.

Furthermore, what is the realm of expression that cannot or should not be named in normative terms? What alternative kinds of expression are available? This is an especially important question for younger children, for whom adults are particularly prone to speak for/on behalf of because of their assumed immaturity. Their relationship to language is much less linear and direct; their expression of feelings lies more in different kinds of speech, or in music, drawing, running, jumping, and so forth. The question "What do you think that means?" or "How does that make you feel?" is met by a quizzical look. The directive to "use your words" may produce even more frustration. Because children's bodies are different (and different from each other as well as from older kids and adults), their feelings will be different, and differently expressed.

The pleasure lies in the excessive. These excesses can be found as children navigate their way through other media forms, connected to but sometimes quite distinct from adult productions. I show in this book how children can produce their own "archives of feeling," to use Ann Cvetkovich's phrase, as they talk about television on social media, create their own fan fiction and fanart, and play video games such as *Minecraft*. Cvetkovich defines her project as "an exploration of cultural texts as repositories of feelings and emotions, which are encoded not only in the content of the texts themselves but in the practices that surround their production and reception" (2003, 7). She uses this idea to explore queer cultural production, a realm that she says has not been considered worthy of archiving because of its ephemerality, performativity, and affective engagement. Her materials, she says, "emerge out of cultural spaces—including activist groups, women's music festivals, sex toy stores, and performance events—that are built around sex, feelings, and trauma. These publics are hard to archive because they are lived experiences, and the cultural traces that they leave are frequently inadequate to the task of documentation" (9).

Young children—as much if not more than any other subculture—lack a "conventional archive" as well as the ability to organize, formally or informally. They belong, ostensibly, in the home, defined by their families. Perhaps this is one reason Cvetkovich does not think to even mention children in *An Archive of Feelings*; with no archive to recover, even in ephemeral terms, children seem not to count as archivable subjects, authors of cultural texts that can be recovered in the fashion that Cvetkovich does for her queer subjects and texts.[4] Children's culture is more likely to be truly ephemeral—clay sculptures, Lego trucks, chalk drawings on the sidewalk, angels in the snow. It is harder to analyze the emotional content of such ephemeral texts in part because they simply do not persist in any concrete, documentable way.

Yet kids' culture is not unlike any other form of culture insofar as it is produced within specific, structural conditions—conditions that shape the culture, much as the culture will reshape the conditions. Raymond Williams's (1977) notion of "structures of feeling" is a useful supplement to the "archive of feelings." He critiques the binaries that Marxism relies on—structure/feeling, material/subjective, social/personal, past/present. Rather, says Williams, the weight and force of institutions is felt through the embodied, affective experiences of everyday life; these immaterial forces are, in turn, constitutive of the institutions. While we tend to describe social structures and institutions as if they are finished, says Williams, they are not: they are moving and in process—they are "structures of feeling." As that phrase means to suggest, feelings—usually associated with amorphousness—do in fact have a structure:

> We are talking about characteristic impulses, restraint, and tone; specifically affective elements of consciousness and relationships: not feeling against thought, but thought as felt and feeling as thought, practical

consciousness of a present kind, in a living and interrelating continuity. We are then defining these elements as a "structure": as a set, with specific internal relations, at once interlocking and in tension. (132)

The structure of feeling is both spatial and temporal. The present, Williams says, is "not only the temporal present, the realization of this and this instant, but the specificity of present being, the inalienably physical, within which we may indeed discern and acknowledge institutions, formations, positions, but not always as fixed products, defining products" (128). It is in the "inalienably physical" that we can discern these structures of feeling: what enables a child, within the conditions and routines of everyday life, to express herself in a way that has a shaping influence on those conditions and routines? The structures of feeling are shaped by and reshape both time and place; for instance, a cultural production such as a *Minecraft* world or the theme song to a favorite television show can create a temporary home, as an affective, embodied, felt place.

At one level, I am simply trying to record here some of the ways in which children express themselves; in fact, if this was not an academic book in which I was compelled to make an argument, I would be tempted to simply let these different texts speak for themselves. At moments, I do exactly that, letting kids' monologues during gaming stand on their own for at least a short period of time, for example. I acknowledge that when I turn to analysis, I am contributing to the idea that kids need some kind of adult mediation in order to be heard and understood.

At another level, though, I believe that compiling an archive of feelings and analyzing it can shed light on the conditions that make it hard for children to be heard. What does it feel like to be a kid? Although I can no longer know what that feeling is, and there is no one, universal feeling, I can guess—from many years of mothering, volunteering in schools, and consuming hundreds of hours of kids' media. I can guess: it is both intensely fun and intensely scary to inhabit fully one's body and yet not ever to be fully in control of what happens next. Cvetkovich argues that trauma derives not just from catastrophic events such as the Holocaust or war but also from ongoing and everyday experiences— "insidious trauma," as she calls it. These everyday events, these encounters with racism, sexism, and homophobia, are in the realm of "felt experiences," which, she says, should not be dismissed simply because they are not as identifiable or widely recognized as something like surviving a genocide is. She seeks to analyze the structural causes of these everyday feelings as an alternative to more individualized approaches such as therapy: "Once the causes of trauma become more diffuse, so too do the cures, opening up the need to change social structures more broadly rather than just fix individual people" (33).

One could argue, using this definition, that being a child is a traumatic experience, insofar as it involves everyday acts of being socialized into spheres that one might not understand, spoken to and directed in a language that only partially makes sense, and compelled to move one's body in ways that make one feel out of place. Furthermore, the pressure to learn how to perform one's gender and sexuality could be seen as traumatic; as Cvektovich notes, referring to Judith Butler's work, "Even though Butler doesn't name it as such, the normalization of sex and gender identities can be seen as a form of insidious trauma, which is effective precisely because it often leaves no sign of a problem" (46). Some children, in addition, experience the physical and mental violence of war, migration, and deportation.

Lessons in socialization are perceived to be a necessary part of growing up; indeed, they are elements of "successful" maturation. Thus, they leave no trace in part because they are not articulated as problems. Says Cvetkovich, "Trauma can be unspeakable and unrepresentable and because it is marked by forgetting and dissociation, it often seems to leave behind no records at all" (7). When an event is experienced as traumatic, she adds, it often cannot be "articulated in a single coherent narrative" (2). It would seem that children, especially younger children, may experience events as traumatic without having the language to articulate them as such to adults who—precisely because they see the events as normal—are not looking for signs or asking the right questions. If children are "acting out" in various ways, their "problems" are likely to be seen as individual, at which point they may be sent to a therapist, who will attempt to identify the feelings that are getting in the way of the child's happiness, successful performance, or sociability. Rarely are the problems seen as systemic and institutional, for this would require a serious questioning of the very structures that are supposed to be helping the child succeed.

At the point of naming, we encounter another dilemma: does the identification of children's feelings become a form of archiving that in turn becomes institutionalized, and threatens to then become part of the problem? Cvetkovich seeks to create an archive of alternative realms of experience that does *not* become institutionalized but rather remains at a somewhat ephemeral level in order to retain its affective force. While, on the one hand, she wants to make visible these ephemeral productions, she also wants to "keep as open as possible the definition of what constitutes a public in order to remain alert to forms of affective life that have not solidified into institutions, organizations, or identities" (9). Children—as much if not more than any other subculture—are not often perceived in terms of either publics or counterpublics; they are, frankly, not even perceived as potential political agents, as I show in part I of this book. The texts I analyze demonstrate, however, that kids are savvy and creative, able to discern politics such as Trump's, and to form communities that function as alternative spaces when they have access to the technologies that enable communication.

"Growing Sideways"

The fields of education, child psychology, and therapy have combined over the years to produce a notion of normative development—roughly stated, the belief that children proceed through more or less similar stages based on a biological maturation process. While still influential today, the model has also been widely critiqued for its universalizing and essentializing notions of childhood as well as its propensity for reproducing norms such as heterosexuality that are implicit in the notion of stages of development. This model, when integrated into school curriculum, lends itself to the belief that children should "naturally" be ready to learn certain skills at certain ages, regardless of context, leading to problematic definitions of normalcy, as critics in the field of pedagogy such as Liselott Mariett Olsson have argued:

> Learning processes are considered to be inherent, natural and biological phenomena that follow predetermined stages. Through scientific theories of developmental psychology, the child's development is possible to predict, prepare, supervise, and evaluate according to predefined standards.

> This is a child that learns in a completely de-contextualized way, its development is set from the very beginning and when the child does not develop according to the predefined schema there is something essentially wrong with the child. (2009, 34)

This model establishes the teacher and/or parent as the authority who is interested not in what the child desires but in what he or she lacks: "The pedagogical challenge lies in giving the right support at the right moment for the child to develop properly. The child's response to this developmental help then indicates whether the child is following the normal curve of development or not. What the teacher is looking for is the lack of proper development; she/he is functioning as a detector of lack, an observer of error" (35). The child lacks, in other words, what the adult possesses, and what the adult assumes the child needs in order to "grow up."

This notion of growing up relies on an adult concept of time, argues Kathryn Stockton in *The Queer Child* (2009); she proposes an alternative: "How, we should ask, are children depicted as conceiving their relation to the concept 'growing up'? Are they shown as (un)wittingly making strange relations when they anticipate how they will participate in adult time?" (15). Why should growth be perceived in linear terms? Why not sideways, asks Stockton, explaining that

> growing sideways would likely be an apt phrase for what recent cognitive science recognizes as the brain's growth (throughout a person's lifetime) through the brain's capacity to make neural networks through connection and extension. Hence, "growing up" may be a short-sighted, limited rendering of human growth, one that oddly would imply an end to growth when full stature (or reproduction) is achieved. By contrast, "growing sideways" suggests that the width of a person's experience or ideas, their motives or motions, may pertain at any age. (11)

Here Stockton importantly notes the constructedness of the models of linear development that assume a steady progression of maturity as one's body grows. This linear development is not in fact inherent but rather socialized as part of the normative conception of growing up—one which involves the channeling of what is actually a more naturally occurring divergent thinking (the "brain's capacity to make neural networks through connection and extension").

Most importantly for my purposes, the normative model of development assumes a movement from affective responses to linguistic control to bodily "self-management." The normative thus names the ability to regulate one's emotions in a socially acceptable fashion. This is considered an important skill for young children to learn; however, it also requires varying degrees of conformity to a set of rules of conduct and adherence to authority, allowing for only a limited amount of questioning and creativity. It also assumes that language can accurately capture emotions, and that adults can provide the proper language for children to use. In doing so, however, these models do not merely describe but rather impose a way of thinking and feeling on children that shapes their sense of the world, often in normative ways—with the goal of "doing well," "cooperating," and "attaining one's goals," all of which feed in to concepts of citizenship, consumerism, and national identity.

We arrive at the conundrum that poststructural theory identified: there is no outside to language. Affect studies offers some provisional escape routes, as I will argue in chapter 1, but we will always come back to language, especially in the context of a book such as this one. Still, it is worth the effort to identify the gaps and moments in which language, or at least a particular kind of language, is not the primary mode of bodily expression. A brief turn to the field of music therapy provides one such moment.

Music therapists build their practice on the recognition that the brain processes music differently than it does language. David Hussey (2003), a specialist in children's mental health, explains that "music has the potential to bypass the defensive operations of the higher cortical functions of the brain and move directly to the limbic system where emotions are processed. Music is also thought to stimulate right-brain functioning, which is associated with imagination and feelings, especially feelings of sadness." Music therapy is especially effective with children who are not verbally adept; this lagging in verbal skills could be due to an early trauma that occurred at the same time as verbal skills were developing, says Hussey. Lacking in language skills, some children are reluctant to try forms of talk therapy because it can just increase frustration and impede the relationship between therapist and child. As Hussey summarizes:

Research has found that early trauma affects the developing nervous system, causing chronic states of over-arousal in traumatized children. Music is an ideal way to help these children self-regulate and soothe as it creates a middle ground between over-arousal and numbness and helps the child to experience a state of stability (Montello, 1999). The immediate success that children experience in the music therapy setting can provide a boost to self-esteem and create a successful, nonthreatening environment in which the therapist can help the child to decrease symptoms of arousal or disinhibition.

Once the child feels more comfortable, he or she may be more demonstrative, indicating through his or her body what she is feeling. An observant therapist can read the body rather than listen to words:

> During music therapy sessions the therapist uses deep reflective listening to try and understand the client's experiences. The therapist listens to and observes the client, the client's playing, and the music that the client and therapist co-create. This sensitive listening includes attention to the somatic experiences, or sensations in the body, of the therapist and to other thoughts and impressions that arise. These impressions are not censored in the way they might be in social interactions in everyday life but are allowed to be experienced and felt, coming into conscious awareness so they can be thought about and reflected upon in order to increase awareness of clients' experiences. With many clients these experiences of the therapist are not able to be relayed back to them in words because they may not be able to comprehend language, or these experiences are not able to be discussed because the client may not be able to understand or reflect on these impressions. Therefore these experiences are discussed in supervision sessions, and are used by the therapist to deepen their awareness of the life world of the client, and the thoughts, impressions, and experiences of that world. (Hussey 2003)

The last stage of the process demonstrates the inevitable return to language, which also restores the hierarchy of therapist-client that ostensibly dissipated during the musical exchange. This return does not negate, however, the possibility that the client will have benefited from a form of communication that did not rely on language but on affective exchanges that use a different part of the brain than does language.

Such an approach avoids the problem I described at the beginning of this chapter—the often awkward ascribing of a single word to a complex set of feelings. This effort artificially fixes emotions, as if they were static entities that can be identified and addressed. By contrast, music therapy calls upon the idea that music is constantly flowing, capturing affective responses that are also in movement. There are different schools of thought within music therapy, and here I am drawing on an approach called the Nordoff Robbins method, which is based on linking

> the therapeutic potency of music to the congruence between the dynamic, kinetic qualities of musical form and the qualities of human emotions and physiological functions (Pavlicevic 1997). Ansdell (1995) describes the "pulses and tones, tensions and resolutions, phrasing of actions, bursts of intensity, repetitions and developments" that characterize physiological processes, coordinating the components of each of the body's systems and coordinating these systems with each other (p. 8). Pavlicevic (1997) observes that "the ebb and flow, tensions and relaxations in music resemble the ebb and flow, tensions and relaxations of human feeling" (p. 32). Music does not capture emotions as static entities, but rather conveys the processes of their unfolding and transformation over time. (Guerrero, Marcus, and Turry 2015)

This emphasis on flows and intensities is similar to what I describe in chapter 7, on *Minecraft*, in which kids' engagement with the game is characterized by "phrasing of actions, bursts of intensity, repetitions, and developments." This stands in contrast to the attempt to match a physiological sensation, such as a racing heart, to a recognized emotion, such as anger, to a specific experience, and ultimately, to the "appropriate" response. This attempt invariably requires the child to distance herself from her own body; in order to understand better her feelings, she must see herself as others see her and provide a singular name for what then becomes a fixed moment in time. By contrast, music therapy attempts to dissolve the distinction between inner and outer, especially as clients and therapists improvise together: "Through the dynamic form of an improvisation, qualities of expression are intimately linked with qualities of experience, rather than being 'an *external* display of ... internal, categorical emotional states such as joy, anger, sadness, and so on'" (Guerrero, Marcus, and Turry 2015).

While I have not focused on music in this book, I have chosen texts that demonstrate this idea of the "dynamic form of an improvisation," which in their dynamism dissolve the distinction between inner and outer. This dynamism better captures how kids feel—their affective intensities—as I illustrate in texts including drawings, YouTube videos, fanart, memes (which often include music, as I discuss in chapter 8), and gaming. While it is not possible to avoid completely the linguistic naming of emotions, it *is* possible to identify cultural productions that rely on images (drawing or photographic) or different kinds of language, such as nonlinear narrations or "nonsense" words. These different forms of communication can become a common vernacular for a community. The more kids, especially younger kids, can form communities, albeit virtual ones, the more likely they will be to define the terms of their everyday lives. This control is enhanced because they are communicating laterally, with other kids, rather than mediating their expressions through adults. These venues of expression allow for passionate, engaged, affective responses that are also (usually) attentive to other kids' feelings.

The Field of Childhood Studies

Historically, the study of young children has occurred primarily in the academic disciplines of education, social work, and psychology, where they are often considered objects of study rather than active subjects, lumped together in the universal category of "children." Chris Jenks links this ongoing naturalization to "the ideology of development," which, he says, "has remained relatively intact" (2005, 4), along with the attendant concepts of maturation and socialization—all of which "leave the actual child untheorized; they all contrive to gloss over the social experience that is childhood" (7). "Childhood," says Jenks, "receives treatment as a stage, a structured process of becoming, but rarely as a course of action or a coherent social practice" (8). Children matter only insofar as they are seen as future adults, and their socialization is necessary in order to negate the threat of the child as disorder, argues Jenks.

Young children are not even considered as objects of study in many other disciplines and fields, including my primary field of cultural studies. The underlying assumption here is that children do not figure as interesting topics of academic work until they become teenagers and thus "resistant" cultural producers in their own right; hence, there is a fair amount of attention paid to "youth," going back to the seminal work at the Centre for Contemporary Cultural Studies in the area of teens' subcultures, but not to younger children. As David Buckingham notes in his cultural studies work on children, "children were almost entirely absent from the empirical research conducted at Birmingham" (2008, 220).[5] Furthermore, research on media and children, says Buckingham, "continues to be dominated by conventional approaches drawn from developmental psychology, social psychology and communication studies" (221). "Conventional" refers to their empiricist approaches—the attempt to prove exactly what effects media is having on children, who are not seen as actual viewers but rather as abstract subjects, measured by universalist theories of how "normal" children develop (as in Jean Piaget's influential work).

The relatively new interdisciplinary field of childhood studies offers important correctives to the academic elisions and assumptions about children.[6] Perhaps most central to these correctives is the valorization of children as subjects, with different degrees of agency, shaped differently across time and space rather than adhering to a universal model of development. As three founders of the field—Allison James, Chris Jenks, and Alan Prout—put it in their 1998 *Theorizing Childhood*, "the rise of childhood agency" signals

> the transition from "the child" as an instance of a category to the recognition of children as particular persons. . . . In sociology, this has been codified in the "new paradigm" (James and Prout 1990b), as a call for children to be understood as social actors shaping as well as shaped by their circumstances. This represents a definitive move away from the more or less inescapable implication of the concept of socialization: that children are to be seen as a defective form of adult, social only in their future potential but not in their present being. (6)

Recognizing children as social actors often leads researchers to incorporate their voices in the research project; presumably, these interviews and direct engagement mean that the researchers are getting closer to "the truth" of kids' experiences. However, as Allison James argues in a 2007 essay, while this incorporation of kids' voices had become commonplace in anthropology, it did not necessarily mean that the work had led to any less mediated access:

> Although children's words quoted in research reports may be "authentic"—in that they are an accurate record of what children have said—it remains the case that the words and phrases have been chosen by the researcher and have been inserted into the text to illustrate an argument or underline a point of view. The point of view being presented is, therefore, the view of the author, not that of the child; furthermore, the author inevitably glosses the voices of children as part of the interpretive process. (265)

Using kids' words to validate research as "authentic" and "child-centered" has become commonplace in policy analysis and within the NGO community, says James, but it can actually reinforce normative models rather than dismantle them. For example, in a study James and two colleagues did of family court advisers in England, they found that although the advisers' specific duty was to represent children's interests to the court by speaking to kids and finding out what they wanted, in fact the researchers imposed their own views of what was in the children's best interests, using quotes or glosses of the quotes to support their views. James summarizes:

> Besides mediating children's voices as a form of protection, it was also the case that what children said might be translated by practitioners in accordance with what they, as adults, felt was "normal" and "acceptable" for children. And, in making such judgments, it was to traditional models of child development that scale children's competence in relation to age that the practitioners turned. And this was despite their ready acknowledgement that such generalizations about "children" might not apply in individual cases. (267)

One alternative, says James, is to observe kids' interactions and communications as they occur naturally in their everyday lives (268). This observation is in fact what I have attempted in this book, as I collect, describe, and record kids' cultural productions, both in the context of their "real," everyday lives, and in the context of online artistic creations and gaming conversations. Of course, this does not erase my mediating influence, but it does allow some autonomy to the representations.

There is an additional reason to the ones James describes for not relying on interviews or direct questioning of kids, and that is in some sense the entire focus of this book: the inadequacy of language for capturing feelings. I do not, in other words, think children's agency can be linked directly to their ability to represent themselves in a language that commands adults' attention. "Voice" is a problematic concept, says the disability studies scholar Tisdall, pointing to another connection between disability and childhood studies:

> The metaphor of "voice" may reproduce the very understandings that marginalize children: the voice as the property of a rational, articulate, knowledgeable individual, capable of speaking for herself (see Tisdall and others, 2009). Focusing on voice privileges comprehensible verbal utterances over other forms of communication, which risks excluding children and young people who communicate little or not at all through speech or who remain silent or laugh in response to a researcher's questions. . . . It excludes other forms of communication from drawing to role play to observation, which are popular methods to engage with a diversity of children, but tend to be translated into text for analysis and presentation. This privileges text over other forms of communication. (185)

"Other forms of communication" include, for me, drawings, fanart, free-flowing narration of games, memes, and YouTube videos. These texts do not exist in isolation from each other but rather form a complex intertextual web of meaning—what I am calling a common vernacular—that connects kids even though they may not share the same physical location.

Why Tell Stories?

This kids' vernacular is not driven by storytelling or narrative in the conventional sense; it defies the very notion of a "story time." Why, after all, do we (adults and academics) automatically assume that stories matter to kids—both in the sense of telling them stories and of urging them to tell us their stories? These stories are supposed to take the shape of a beginning-middle-and-end narrative; to return to Stockton, the narrative imposes an adult sense of time. This idea of mastery aims to help kids "make sense" of situations, to see things in a cause-and-effect kind of way. The child must learn the consequences of certain actions, and a narrative helps them piece together how scenarios play out. This goal is further enhanced through the construction of a protagonist with whom the child is assumed to identify (hence, for example, the concern with diversity in television programing—with creating characters for all children to identify with).

This paradigm was powerfully critiqued by Jacqueline Rose in her 1984 *The Impossibility of Children's Fiction*. Rose is often and favorably cited for her argument that adults mediate all forms of children's fiction; as she puts it, "there is no child behind the category children's fiction, other than the one which the category itself sets in place, the one which it needs to believe is there for its own purposes" (10–11). However, what gets less attention is Rose's critique of narrative. The genre of children's fiction has been produced, she says, by a shift in the form of storytelling, from the "conspicuous narrating voice" of 18th-century fables and fairy tales, in which the adult motivation was blatant, to the absorption of "adult intention" into the story. "The ideal work lets the characters and events speak for themselves" (60), with the goal being to let the child immerse himself or herself in a pleasurable world, without thinking about the constructedness of the story. Says Rose,

> The development of narrative in children's books has gone hand in hand with an apparent reduction in its pedagogic function and an increasing stress on the child's own pleasure. However, given the way that this form of narrative is almost always described in terms of its ability to secure the identification of the child with the story . . . the idea that the narrative is progressive per se seems to me to be highly questionable. (62)

It is "questionable," Rose goes on to argue, because "fiction becomes a central tool in the education of the child," with the imperative that literature "be taught to the child according to a notion of competence or skill" (63). The "acquisition of fictional competence" is supposed to occur in a series of stages, what Rose calls "that march into rationality that dominates one particular conception of the development of a child," namely, she says, the Piagetian notion of development—the "gradual acquisition of motor and sensory development in the child" (64).

Narrative is not inherently conformist, then, but rather becomes so when it is linked to essentialized notions of child development, in which deviations from the norm are considered just that—deviations in need of correction. This unexamined linkage is exactly what happens in another important text on children's cultural production, Marsha Kinder's 1991 *Playing with Power in Movies, Television, and Video Games*. Kinder relies on narrative analysis; as she writes:

> Narrative maps the world and its inhabitants, including one's own position within that grid. In acquiring the ability to understand stories, the child is situated as a perceiving, thinking, feeling, acting, speaking subject within a series of narrative fields—as a person in a family saga, as a spectator who tunes in to individual tales and identifies with their characters, and as a performer who repeats cultural myths and sometimes generates new transformations. Ever since television became pervasive in the American home, this mass medium has played a crucial role in the child's entry into narrative. My study explores how television and its narrative conventions affect the construction of the subject. (2)

To her credit, Kinder recognizes that narrative shapes children *as* children—not as adults. To theorize this particularity, she turns, however, to Piaget, and does exactly what Rose cautions against, assuming a steady "march" from age 18 months through adolescence through four phases of cognitive growth related to their mastery of language, arriving ultimately at "formal thought" and the "completion of reflective intelligence" (quoted in Kinder 1991, 8). Kinder also uncritically deploys Piaget's notion of "equilibration," which, she says, "he defines as 'a sequence of self-regulations whose retroactive processes finally result in operational reversibility'" (8). The goal is for the child to be able to perform an operation and then reverse it, to understand the logic of going forward and backward; as Piaget puts it,

> A mental operation is reversible when, starting from its result, one can find a symmetrically corresponding operation which will lead back to

the data of the first operation without these having been altered in the process.... If I divide a given collection of objects into four equal piles, I can recover the original whole by multiplying one of my quarters by four: the operation of multiplication is symmetrical to that of division. Thus every rational operation has a corresponding operation that is symmetrical to it and which enables one to return to one's starting point. (quoted in Kinder 1991, 8).

Clearly, this formulation relies on a linear growth model, in which divergent thinking (those wandering neural pathways of creativity) needs to be redirected into more efficient and straightforward ways of thinking. The model also relies on a universal child, who—no matter where or when—is expected to demonstrate proper growth in the same fashion as all other children.

If narrative is not inherently conformist, when is it deployed in critical fashion? I would argue this happens in situations like that described by Sarah Projansky in her work on girls as critical readers of media texts. After spending the bulk of her *Spectacular Girls* (2014) analyzing media representations of mainly adolescent girls, she turns to an ethnography of third graders. Her goal, she says, is to shift from "girl as media representation" to "girl as media critic" (182). She shows that girls often respond critically to the media panic assumptions about them, rejecting the idea, for example, that they automatically desire to look like celebrity girls. Projansky came to this conclusion by observing the third graders in her ethnographic sample, being careful, she says, to "speak to/with rather than co-opt" her subjects (185). She did not try to teach them how to read media critically—a common goal of media literacy projects—but rather took note of the ways they were already reading critically. She also let them refuse her requests for writing samples as proof of their analytical skills: "Even when I asked them to do so [write a media analysis essay] in a variety of different ways, they both implicitly and explicitly refused. Thus they made it impossible for me to simply 'publish' their work, and they asserted the specificity of their (non-writing) voices from day one" (185).

Projanksy looks for "analytical skills the kids already had," which she finds in their "ability to notice details, their thoughtful questions, their pleasure in creating their own stories and drawings, and their concerns about gender difference" (194). However, even with her respect for the autonomy of the kids' expressions, Projanksy cannot help but look for aspects that she finds important to critical reading: "many students implicitly employed genre and/or narrative analysis when describing details, although they did not label it as such" (195). She notes how one student created her own "analytical vocabulary in order to express her ideas about narrative structure and tone" (194). She says in response to another student, "Right. It was a key narrative element that moved the story forward." With this student, she is especially interested in how the girl did not find in the story the same moral that Projansky did but rather focused on the structure of the story, on how it was told. Yet it seems that Projansky still finds in the girl's reading something that confirms her thesis—that girls read critically—and that this critical ability rests in the skills of narrative analysis. As Projansky observes, "she focused on her understanding of the narrative structure, which of course is a key aspect of scholarly media criticism" (196).

I do not want to argue that third graders are not in fact analytical; clearly, they are capable of critical insights that will overlap with academic insights. However, by valorizing this realm, Projansky downplays other reactions that are not predicated on criticism as articulated through narrative; she enters this study already having decided that she would look for analysis as proof of girls' ability to think critically about media texts. Other reactions, more affective responses, are not considered within the realm of critical responses. She asks no questions (at least none that are mentioned) about feelings, emotions, or affective responses to the media. The cognitive is valued over the feeling realm, reifying a mind/body binary.

By contrast, I seek ways to avoid that binary, difficult as it is within a profession and, indeed, a society that value verbal acuity. What kinds of expressions emerge from kids' everyday lives? I have incorporated some examples from my younger son's life as well as numerous accounts of kids in classrooms, kids playing games online and making fanart, and kids loving memes and making YouTube videos. I have tried to be constantly aware of the gap between my thoughts, my language, my desires and those of the kids. I have not assumed that my sense of time and place are superior to theirs. I have tried to stop asking those predictable questions that impose an adult sense of time, such as "How was your day?" and "What do you want to be when you grow up?"

Even as I have incorporated the experiences and exchanges of individual children, I have put these individuals within a much broader social context. Thus, while my focus is media, media consumption never takes place in a vacuum. As Buckingham puts it, "people are never only audiences; and 'audiencing' is merely a part of their broader social experience" (224). The question becomes how to delineate which elements of the "broader social experience" are most relevant for understanding kids' media consumption as it intersects with emotional expression. I answer that question in the first section of the book, where I analyze three policy arenas that affect kids: immigration policy, electoral politics, and educational policy. This section also demonstrates the different conditions that shape kids' lives, showing both what kids in the U.S. have in common and how they differ across space given particular experiences with legal status, for example, or racialization (post-Trump, especially). While my focus is on the U.S., I recognize that some conditions cross borders, shaping kids' emotional expressions in places ranging from Syria to Central America.

Organization of the Book

Chapter 1 establishes my theoretical framework, using Brian Massumi's theory of affect to elaborate the differences between emotions and affect. This chapter also reviews some of the media studies literature on children to show how my argument is both indebted to and departs from this scholarship. I also argue here for attending to children's physiological differences from adults, while at the same time not positing an essentialized category of children.

The remainder of the manuscript is divided into three sections, with two or three chapters in each part. Each section begins with a short preface explaining the chapters in that section. The first part, "Political Subjects," argues that kids' affective responses to political situations demonstrate their engagement in various political issues (despite the fact that kids are not often perceived to be capable of articulating political positions). I begin this section with the story of Bana al-Abed, a seven-year-old Syrian girl who gained international attention through her tweets in 2016 while her home in Aleppo was being bombed. Many of the tweets expressed her immediate, bodily reactions to the violence while it was going on, like this one on September 24, 2016: "200 died yesterday and today whose next? I'm very afraid tonight." She was both lauded and criticized, and much of the latter had to do with skepticism about her use of technology to take a political position.

The first full chapter in this section (chapter 2) analyzes the situation of Central American children seeking refuge in the U.S.; for them, the gap between adult impositions and their own experiences means that their feelings—namely, their fears of bodily harm—are not taken seriously as they proceed through the immigration system seeking relief from deportation to dangerous homelands. I present as well an exhibit of drawings by children just released from detention to illustrate an alternative range of feelings.

In chapter 3, I analyze the discourse of civility—which goes under the name of "niceness" in elementary schools—as it appears in kids' letters to Trump during the presidential campaign and immediately following the election. In this version of the emotional intelligence paradigm, teachers and parents advocate writing letters as an exercise to help kids process and name their emotions in a manner that makes them feel like they can do something within the system. These "proper" modes of expression inevitably involve conforming to standards and rules, especially of bodily regulation. I then turn to examples of kids' artwork from three locations in which teachers gave kids the opportunity to say and especially draw whatever they wanted; in these cultural productions, I find a much greater affective range, illustrating feelings of anger, fear, and hatred in a manner that does not adhere to the discourse of niceness.

Chapter 4 analyzes how the discourse of emotional intelligence intersects with national curriculum efforts such as No Child Left Behind and Common Core, as well as how these discourses play out in an actual kindergarten classroom. Emotional management dovetails with physical regulation to teach young children how to manage themselves for their own success; I show how this involves the expression rather than suppression of emotions and thus intersects with neoliberal notions of self-management. This chapter lays the groundwork for my argument about educational media, showing how kids' television programming prepares kids for a successful school experience.

The second section, "Kids' Television, from Problem Solving to Sideways Growth," argues that much programming for younger children on

Nick Jr., Disney Jr., and PBS encourages them to manage their emotions and limit their affective, bodily responses through a focus on problem solving. These shows also advocate empathy and tolerance, teaching kids how to recognize and respond to others' feelings. Many shows segue from emotional management to an appreciation of difference, thus contributing to the wider discourse of diversity management. In a stark shift from the years when television was seen as harmful to children's development, many therapists now urge parents to use television to help their children learn prosocial behavior. However, television is far from homogenous, and I also present some exceptions to this emphasis on management. A genre of what I call "sideways growth" encourages kids to defy proper behavior, to revel in their bodies, and to occupy spaces of intensely affective pleasure. These shows interrupt the linear narratives that characterize problem-solving approaches and thus introduce the idea of alternative modes of communication.

The Cartoon Network series *Steven Universe* extends this genre in several ways, demonstrating that it is possible for television programming to valorize neurodiversity. In chapter 6, I argue that the show and its fandom speak to the creativity of kids who occupy precarious positions in the contemporary U.S. because they are members of blended, mixed-race, mixed-legal-status, and/or gender-nonconforming families. I analyze what kids say in their reviews of the show, many of which describe the range of feelings the program encourages. The show's hero is a young boy whose superpowers are explicitly linked to his ability to express (rather than control) his emotions. Kids also say they love the show because it allows them to process mixed identity categories in complex ways, especially through the show's notion of "fusion," in which characters who are emotionally in accord with each other fuse into a hybrid identity. This fusion is illustrated in numerous examples of fanart that I present, focusing on Tumblr as a social media platform that has marketed itself as a safe space for young people (and here my focus is tweens) who are struggling with depression and loneliness.

The third section, "The Limits of Digital Literacy," argues that the internet and gaming offer considerable potential for kids' affective expression, a realm that has been largely ignored in the valorization of digital literacy and its focus on technological skills. In chapter 7, I argue that the popular game *Minecraft* exhibits a Deleuzian kind of becoming, in which subjects are constantly maneuvering and experimenting as they construct their own worlds as well as collaborative spaces. Because the game has sprawled across technologies and led to the creation of so many spin-off products, it provides a unique space for seeing how children construct themselves through their relationship to this broadly defined "text." In addition to the games and their products, I rely on commentary by children: my son Ezra, his friends, and YouTube users, all of whom contribute to the construction of an "archive of feelings" that is largely unregulated by adult efforts to name and govern. This archive is also part of the construction of a community of kids who, although often not physically in the same space, form social relationships. In chapter 8, I extend this analysis to another popular game, *Roblox*, which also serves as the basis for community building. However, in the *Roblox* world, kids' movements through the various game spaces are frequently interrupted by images of the consumer world, such as fast-food signs and branded logos. While the movement is somewhat similar to the *Minecraft* world, consumerism shapes a different kind of space for kids' expressions.

The reader will find an occasional story from my younger son, since he was between the ages of four and nine while I was beginning to think about and then writing this book. These observations are both the most mediated and the least mediated of all my sources—the former because they occur within the subjective space of my home, shaped by my ongoing research and ideas about "how kids feel." They are less mediated, however, because they were most often written down almost in the moment they occurred, as direct observations of what Ezra said or did. I attempt to leave out the interpretation, though they acquire another level of meaning when I transfer them from my notes into this book. Still, I want to end this introduction with some of Ezra's thoughts about being biracial to illustrate (and here is my mediation) the complexity of his feelings:

> EZRA: I feel black. Black in my mind. Black in my body. Black in my soul. Not black as in bad, you know, but just black.
> ME: That's great. You're proud to be African American. You should be.
> EZRA: But I also feel scared.
> ME: Why?

EZRA: (looking at me skeptically) Really? You don't know?
ME: Trump?
EZRA: Don't say his name! I told you to never say his name!
(Silence.)
EZRA: Is he going to come to Ithaca and kill me?
ME: No, sweetie, he would never do that.
EZRA: Just get me my boxing gloves. I'm going to sleep with them on tonight.

1

Affective Intensity and Children's Embodiment

It is bedtime, and I tell him, "It makes me so happy to see you happy. It's also OK to be sad, and then I feel sad, but that's OK. Everybody gets sad." And he says, "When you feel scared, I feel brave. And now I'm hungry, I'm just hungry."
—Ezra, five years old

Brian Massumi, one of the most influential theorists of affect in the humanities, begins his "The Autonomy of Affect" (1995) with a reading of a study by German researchers on cognition and television. The impetus for the study was a short cartoon that aired on German television that prompted complaints from parents who said the story scared their children. Here is Massumi's description of the cartoon: "A man builds a snowman on his roof garden. It starts to melt in the afternoon sun. He watches. After a time, he takes the snowman to the cool of the mountains, where it stops melting. He bids it good-bye, and leaves" (83).

In an attempt to understand why the story purportedly frightened the children, the research team gathered a group of nine-year-olds, attached wires to their bodies to measure their physiological responses, and added two versions to the original—one with a "factual" voiceover and one with an "emotional" voiceover that included "at crucial turning points words expressing the emotional tenor of the scene under way" (83). The children were asked to rate the versions on a scale ranging from pleasant to unpleasant as well as to rate individual scenes on a happy-sad scale. Here's what the researchers found: "the factual version was consistently rated the least pleasant and also the worst remembered. The most pleasant was the original wordless version, which was rated just above the 'emotional' version. And it was the emotional version that was best remembered." Interestingly, the "sad scenes were rated the most pleasant, the sadder the better" (84).

The findings of the study seem striking, on at least two counts. One, the facts that were used to presumably clarify what was happening and alleviate the children's fears were not well received or remembered, suggesting that they had little effect. Two, perhaps the children were not initially afraid at all and their parents misinterpreted their reactions or were reluctant to understand that sadness can in fact be pleasant. Cumulatively, then, the study suggests to me the inadequacy of words such as "pleasant," "unpleasant," "happy," and "sad" as well as the gap between adult forms of communicating (the need for facts) and children's.

My interpretation can be supported by Massumi's elaboration of affect, especially regarding the distinctions between emotions and affect. Massumi comments that the researchers seemed uncertain what to make of the results; "their only positive conclusion was the primacy of the affective in image reception." Strangely, however, Massumi seems uninterested in the age of the subjects; only once does he refer to them as children, commenting that the children's rating of the "sad" scenes as "pleasant" "suggests" that "in some kind of precocious anti-Freudian protest, the children were equating arousal with pleasure" (84). As he goes on with his argument about affect, there is no follow-up to this comment or to the question of how age might shape affective responses, nor to the question of why the parents assumed their children were scared by the original, wordless story when in fact the children rated it as the "most pleasant." One wonders why he did not pursue these compelling questions, since he begins the article with a focus on children: what might this considerable gap between parents and children reveal about the embodiment of affect? How do bodies at different stages of physical and cognitive development respond differently from how adults might respond? As Ezra's quote above indicates, how do children's feelings manifest themselves in their bodies much as does a physical sensation such as hunger?

In this chapter, I use Massumi's theory to set up my theoretical framework for the rest of the book, emphasizing the distinction between affect (with which I associate "feelings") and emotions. This distinction proves useful for understanding how the discourse of emotional intelligence relies on teaching children to manage their emotions by suppressing their bodily feelings. Since Massumi's essay was published in 1995, "affect studies" has developed as its own area and attracted a great deal of attention in the loosely defined field of cultural studies precisely because of this focus on intensity over cognition. However, I can find no essays that deal specifically with children, and only a few scattered references to kids. One might fathom (though disagree with) the bias against children in other academic areas, such as literature or philosophy, where the assumption is that children are not worthy of academic study because their language is too simplistic, their cultural productions not worthy of analysis, and their thoughts far from complex. They are "too emotional." Yet it would seem that this very stereotype might draw scholars of affect to children, in order to both disprove the stereotype and further deconstruct the emotions/rationality binary as it governs all subjects. Sara Ahmed, for example, notes that "emotion has been viewed as 'beneath' the faculties of thought and reason. To be emotional is to have one's judgement affected: it is to be reactive rather than active, dependent rather than autonomous. Feminist philosophers have shown us how the subordination of emotions also works to subordinate the feminine and the body" (2004, 3). And, we could add, the child and the body, for children, as much as if not more than women, have been defined as irrational creatures governed by their emotional "outbursts." Yet Ahmed—one of the most prolific and frequently cited theorists to focus on affect and emotions—never attends to children as specific subjects.

This elision of children within affect studies is also linked to another tendency within cultural and media studies: the valorization of the text as a site from which to read meaning. In this chapter, I analyze this tendency within media studies of children, arguing that this textual focus prioritizes cognition over feelings. Texts tell stories, which, as I argued in the introduction, become the vehicle for socialization into the valorized realm of articulation and communication. Not just any language but a particular kind of linear language is linked to skills of critical reading and analysis—skills that are embedded not only in academia but also in parental and pedagogical spheres—really, any site of learning. I acknowledge my own limitations here—as an academic trained in the humanities with no expertise in biology or health, my own inclination is to turn to texts as a way of understanding the world. And while texts matter to kids as well, they do not likely matter in the same way, especially to younger kids. The question becomes, then, how to understand media texts as sites for kids' affective expression. The last half of my book provides many examples of these expressions; here I provide the rationale and the theory for looking for them, for constructing an "archive of feeling."

"Winding Boulevards"

Much work about affect and embodiment has not really been about the body—even though affect purports to ground itself in the body. This is Elspeth Probyn's argument in *Blush: Faces of Shame*, published in 2005: "In more than a decade's work that speaks of embodiment," she asks, "what have we seen beyond the repetition of 'the body,' 'corporeality,' or 'embodiment'?" (20). She adds that "we have tended to overly privilege the body's cultural meanings and have not really tried to tell the psychosomatic body's stories" (41). Drawing on the work of Silvan Tomkins to more fully capture the physiological, Probyn focuses on shame to illustrate that "affects are innate and compel us to see the human body as a baseline in all human activity" (28). Diverging from identity politics' emphasis on difference, Probyn argues that "in some ways, we all share more than we don't, although of course—and often with good cause—we tend to fixate on what separates us" (22). Focusing on what all humans share could, Probyn suggests, go some distance toward erasing the binary distinctions that are produced by yet also reproduce power differentials: man/women, gay/straight, black/white.

Precisely for these reasons, however, attention to the "innate" prompts suspicion about universalizing across time and space, says Probyn: "Essentialist or ethnocentric epithets hover in the air" (28); feminists in particular may fear a return to essentialist beliefs that have tied women to their bodies. These fears may explain why even some scholars of emotions distance themselves from the physiological, looking instead to the cultural and social structuring of emotions. For example, the editors of *Emotions: A Cultural Studies Reader* (2009) come down decidedly on the side of the social construction of emotions. In their introduction, Jennifer Harding and Deirdre Pribram acknowledge that "bodily states are vital to producing emotional states," but emphasize that "the imperative to interpret and name bodily sensation as emotion must be learned and is bound up with socio-cultural meanings and social relationships" (8). They describe their approach as constructing "a culturalist formulation

[that] does not focus on the biological individual" (12) but rather on "specific structures of feeling—that is, the emotions different categories of subjects are permitted to experience and express at any historical juncture, and how both individuals and collectives are brought into being through specific articulations of emotion" (13).

Similarly, Sara Ahmed rejects the idea that emotions are interior to the body; interiority, she argues, reverts to an individualized and psychological model of emotions—devoid of the social and cultural realms. The idea that emotions are exterior to the body, imposed on a subject from the outside, is equally reductive, says Ahmed: "Emotions are not simply something 'I' or 'we' have," says Ahmed. "Rather, it is through emotions, or how we respond to objects and others, that surfaces or boundaries are made: the "I" and the "we" are shaped by, and even take the shape of, contact with others" (10). She tracks "how emotions circulate between bodies, examining how they 'stick' as well as move" (4). Ann Cvetkovich says her objects of analysis are texts, something she acknowledges could be seen as a limitation: "For a book on emotions, which argues that emotions cannot be separated from bodily sensations, this book may seem very orientated towards texts" (12). However, she argues that her "close readings of texts" illustrate how "'figures of speech' are crucial to the emotionality of texts . . . the emotionality of texts is one way of describing how texts are 'moving,' or how they generate effects" (13).

Yet this insistence on the structural, material, and textual over the bodily and the non-discursive ignores a significant realm of expression—that which cannot be analyzed through textual effects or structural positioning. The search for meaning in texts is a common practice in cultural studies, with its emphasis on various theories of "social construction." Lawrence Grossberg addresses this tendency in his work on music and affect, where he argues that while the "identity and effects of any cultural practice" are important to analyze, they are not exhaustive: "And while I have never wanted to deny that cultural practices enable us to 'make sense' of the world and our experiences, I do want to contest the reduction of sense-making to cognitive meaning and interpretation, and the model of culture as somehow standing apart from another plane that it interprets. I have argued that cultural practices always operate on multiple planes, producing multiple effects that cannot be entirely analyzed in the terms of any theory of ideology, consciousness, or semiotic"

(1997, 6). In other words, the positioning of "culture" as a practice apart from any other practice allows cultural critics to claim to understand the world through their readings of cultural texts. These readings invoke ideology, consciousness, and semiotics to interpret how the texts make meaning for their consumers, within particular conditions. By contrast, Grossberg asks, what is produced when we abandon the need to "make sense" of a text?

Affect offers a way to attend to bodily responses without devolving into essentialized claims about biology, an argument eloquently made by Anne Fausto-Sterling in her influential *Sexing the Body* (2000). For example, attending to the sexed body—hormones, chromosomes, genitalia, etc.—is crucial if we are in fact to understand and intervene in how women, and others, inhabit our bodies and live our desires, as well as to deconstruct binary differences between, for example, "male" and "female." As Fausto-Sterling demonstrates, it is completely arbitrary for bodies to be divided into two sexes—five would more adequately capture the complexity of the human body. To deconstruct male/female, thus, requires at least some knowledge of how things like hormones work, even as one also acknowledges that seemingly scientific observations do not exist separately from "political, social, and moral struggles about our cultures and economies" (5). These struggles in turn become "quite literally embodied, incorporated into our very physiological being" (5). The nature versus nurture binary diverts us from understanding that the two are inseparable, says Fausto-Sterling, citing Elizabeth Grosz's analogy of the Möbius strip, in which "the body and the mind come into being together" (24).

Similarly, I argue, it is imperative to attend to children's biological differences from adults and from each other, at different ages and in different locations, even as we pursue the manner in which these biological differences are entangled with "political, social, and moral struggles." Societal ideas (which of course differ across "societies") about "childhood" shape childhood itself, taking on material form in children's everyday lives; kids' brains and bodies take shape in response to pedagogical imperatives such as "emotional intelligence." Yet because "growing up" is believed to occur through a "normal" series of developmental stages, this entanglement of the biological and the social is not perceived as a problematic process but rather as the best way for children to mature.

Thus, it is considered only healthy and proper for children to learn how to name their emotions. Little consideration is given to the possibility that such naming shapes the brain in a manner that shuts down non-normative ways of seeing and experiencing the world.

How, then, do we attend to differences in body and brain development without invoking essential, universal truths about "children" or imposing a developmental model? Clearly, children are physically different from adults; also, three-year-olds are very different from 15-year-olds, who are different from 25-year-olds. As Alison Gopnik, a cognitive psychologist and philosopher, writes in *The Philosophical Baby* (2009), "Children aren't just defective adults, primitive grown-ups gradually attaining our perfection and complexity. They have very different, though equally complex and powerful, minds, brains and forms of consciousness, designed to serve different evolutionary functions" (9). Here is how she describes a young child's brain (her research focuses on children five and under, whom she calls, in a kind of shorthand, "babies"):

> Babies' brains seem to have special qualities that make them especially well suited for imagination and learning. Babies' brains are actually more highly connected than adult brains; more neural pathways are available to babies than adults. As we grow older and experience more, our brains "prune out" the weaker, less used pathways and strengthen the ones that are used more often. If you looked at a map of the baby's brain, it would look like old Paris, with lots of winding, interconnected little streets. In the adult brain, those little streets have been replaced by fewer but more efficient neural boulevards, capable of much more traffic. Young brains are also much more plastic and flexible—they change much more easily. But they are much less efficient; they don't work as quickly or as effectively. (11–12)

As Gopnik further explains, the prefrontal cortex, "a part of the brain that is uniquely well developed in human beings, and that neuroscientists often argue is the seat of distinctively human abilities," is far less developed in a child. This is the site of "thinking, planning, and control," of rationality, so to speak; it may not be completely formed until one's midtwenties (12). It is "especially involved in inhibition—"it actually helps shut down other parts of the brain, limiting and focusing experience, action, and thought" (13). It helps us make decisions and act efficiently; however, its downside, says Gopnik, is that it can squelch imagination and learning—to the extent that these require one to be open to multiple possibilities. Some studies show, says Gopnik, that the longer a child is allowed to maintain these complex and twisting "neural boulevards," the more creative and intelligent they will be as adults.

Because the brain is malleable (though less so as we age), it is possible to reopen passages that have been shut down. Thus, it is possible that an adult brain could reopen those "winding boulevards," recovering some of the divergent ways of seeing the world that may have been operative before. This insight returns us to the neurodiversity movement I discussed in the introduction—a movement that is gaining credence in both the humanities and in the sciences. In a 2004 article, *The New York Times* identified a "new kind of disabilities movement" in which "many of those who deviate from the shrinking subset of neurologically 'normal' want tolerance, not just of their diagnoses, but of their behavioral quirks. They say brain differences, like body differences, should be embraced, and argue for an acceptance of 'neurodiversity.'" The movement has gained medical support from such leading neurologists as Dr. Antonio Damasio, who told the *Times*, "What all of our efforts in neuroscience are demonstrating is that you have many peculiar ways of arranging a human brain and there are all sorts of varieties of creative, successful human beings. For a while it is going to be a rather relentless process as there are more and more discoveries of people that have something that could be called a defect and yet have immense talents in one way or another" (quoted in Harmon 2004).

One of the "defects" that Damasio and others are addressing is the commonly diagnosed childhood disorder known as attention deficit hyperactivity disorder, or ADHD. The number of ADHD diagnoses has skyrocketed 41 percent in the last decade, to the point that "one in nine children between the ages of 4 and 17 have now at some point in their lives received a diagnosis of ADHD" (Hinshaw and Ellison 2016, xv). Some critics say there is no real medical issue here but rather the construction of a condition by a network of controlling adults—parents, teachers, and others—who are impatient with rambunctious children and want to make their own jobs easier. There has also been substantial criticism of the involvement of the pharmaceutical industry, which has profited hugely from the medications prescribed to treat ADHD.

Two researchers who have studied ADHD, Stephen Hinshaw and Richard Scheffler, agree that ADHD has been overdiagnosed, and that many "normal" younger children exhibit signs of the nine symptoms that have been listed in the *Diagnostic and Statistical Manual of Mental Disorders*. The symptoms of inattention include "'often fails to give close attention to details or makes careless mistakes in schoolwork, at work, or other activities; often has difficulty organizing tasks and activities; is often easily distracted by extraneous stimuli.'" The symptoms of hyperactivity/impulsivity include "'is often on the go, acting as if 'driven by a motor'; often interrupts or intrudes on others; often talks excessively; often runs about or climbs excessively in situations in which it is inappropriate" (2014, 19). As Hinshaw and Scheffler say in critiquing these symptoms:

> one thing that pops out from a glance at these behaviors is that a lot of them indicate the behavior patterns of a very young child. In fact, if you have ever cared for a toddler or preschooler . . . you will have experienced many of these issues at annoyingly frequent rates. Why would the diagnosis of a psychiatric condition be based on the symptoms of acting too young: isn't this a clear instance of pathologizing normal-range behaviors? Don't all children have at least a bit of ADHD? (19)

Yes, probably, they answer themselves, arguing for a range of differences rather than a cut-and-dried diagnosis. However, they also argue that these differences cannot simply be subsumed within a mere recognition of diversity. Rather, they say that therapy and medication may be necessary to address the physiological needs of kids with ADHD; in other words, in some kids, there is a real, physical condition. These kids may have lower levels of dopamine and an underdeveloped frontal cortex, both of those leading to difficulty with executive functioning, making it harder for them to concentrate and regulate their impulses. Not helping these kids would be like dismissing people diagnosed with depression as having a "normal" degree of sadness.

To their credit, Hinshaw and Scheffler do not isolate the physiological but rather emphasize how intertwined it is with the social. They argue, for example, that the educational focus on testing and performance measures—which I discuss in chapter 4—are one reason for the increase in ADHD diagnoses. They say, "Today's classrooms may not be as factory-like as those of a hundred years ago, but students must still defer to the teacher and group-based teaching methods in most schools. Stringent classroom demands and the press for achievement and performance throw a harsh light on individuals with underlying problems in attention and self-regulation" (20). While it is impossible to say to what degree the heightened emphasis on academic success by conventional measures has contributed to the ubiquity of ADHD, Hinshaw and Scheffler are convinced there's a clear connection. In certain environments, the normative pressures to succeed will cause a child with a brain that is not geared toward that kind of concentration and thinking to react with frustration.

It makes sense. The frustrated child becomes the "unmanageable" child, prompted to force his or her brain to work in ways to which it is not given. Enter the social worker and/or the therapist, in the interest of helping the child understand what is making them feel frustrated and angry. What are you feeling? And we are back to the chart described at the beginning of this book. The child is compelled to point to an emotion that explains the frustration, and that kind of normalizing activity is meant to make the child feel better. It is also meant, however, to help the child conform to the environment that caused the frustration in the first place and to learn how to manage his or her body. This idea returns me to Massumi's theory of affect, which offers an alternative to this naming of emotions.

Affect and Media Studies

Central to the German study of the nine-year-olds with which I began this chapter is the question of the relationship between image and narrative. The conclusion seemed to be that there is no direct or causal relationship. Massumi argues that "the primacy of the affective is marked by a gap between content and effect: it would appear that the strength or duration of an image's effect is not logically connected to the content in any straightforward way" (84). In fact, in television studies of children, this gap has been the cause of some concern and critique: the idea that children can be mesmerized by an image to the degree that they do not actually follow the content of a show has been the focus of those who argue that television is not mentally stimulating and can actually harm children's intellectual development. In response, the television industry has over the past three decades expanded the realm of educational television, attempting to match programming content with children's developmental stages, precisely so that there is no gap between images and content (this is the focus of chapter 5).

To this end, academic scholar Daniel Anderson describes his work as a consultant for Nick Jr., the channel owned by the Nickelodeon Group aimed at kids under six. Anderson worked for the channel as they were developing the show *Blue's Clues*. He began with the premise that kids are active viewers; his study "showed that preschool children do not merely passively react to the changing images on television. Rather, they strategically pay attention when that attention is most likely to lead them to content that is most important for understanding" (2004, 248). In other words, kids pay attention to TV when it speaks directly to them at a level they can understand; this was the guiding principle in developing *Blue's Clues*, an interactive show that pulls viewers into the plot as the host, a 20-something man named Steve (in later years, Joe), asks children to help him solve the mystery of the day by following the clues that Blue the dog leaves for them. Anderson is trying to close the gap between the image and the content, defining this relationship much as Massumi does: "What is meant here by the content of the image is its indexing to conventional meanings in an intersubjective context, its socio-linguistic qualification" (84). This is exactly what Anderson wants to ensure: clarifying the relationship between image and content so that the combination—the overall show—makes sense to the child.

Yet what if something else, or something additional, happens when children watch television? What if they are not primarily interested in "making sense" of a show in the way that adults assume is most beneficial? This "something" is what Massumi calls "intensity," which may happen alongside the more conventional, assumed process of interpretation based on making sense of the signs and codes and storyline. Intensity, he says "is not semantically or semiotically ordered. It does not fix distinctions. Instead, it vaguely but insistently connects what is normally indexed as separate" (85). Intensity registers at the "surface of the body, at its interface with things," and is thus more of an observed as well as a felt reaction. Interpretation—what Anderson is trying to achieve for children—is a "depth reaction," which, says Massumi, "belong[s] more to the form/content (qualification) level," perhaps because interpretations "are associated with expectation, which depends on consciously positioning oneself in a line of narrative continuity" (85). Interpretation is what is solicited when a kid is asked, for example, "What do you think made the puppy sad?" Perhaps what the child is feeling, instead, is something like Ezra expresses in the quote at the beginning of this chapter: "When you feel scared, I feel brave. And now I'm hungry, I'm just hungry."

In contrast to interpretation, intensity is "outside expectation and adaptation, as disconnected from meaningful sequencing, from narration, as it is from vital function. It is narratively de-localized, spreading over the generalized body surface, like a lateral backwash from the function-meaning interloops traveling the vertical path between head and heart" (85). Intensity generates feelings that need not be expressed in a narrative; in fact, once thus expressed intensity becomes part of a meaningful experience, subject to interpretation, and hence no longer "intensity." Presumably, children watching television—or anyone, for that matter—will respond both at the level of intensity and of semiotic ordering. However, what gets discussed, and more importantly, valorized for children is the level of semiotic ordering, of making meaning. This emphasis elides and perhaps ignores entirely the sheer affective pleasure of kids' media consumption and production—pleasure that cannot be reduced to meaning and that might not "make sense" in the conventional use of that phrase.

Another common critique that relies on semiotic ordering is whether children can distinguish between fantasy and reality. As children's media scholar Máire Messenger Davies summarizes this body of work: "Many of these studies on children's fantasy/reality perception have been particularly concerned with teaching children to tell the difference as defined by adult experimenters, rather than investigating whether or not there is a difference, and whether, and how children see it. Such studies have proposed reality perception as a mediating variable to protect children against harmful effects" (2008, 122). Educators and other adults concerned about television viewing want to ensure, for example, that children know that physical violence in cartoons, like characters getting run over, squished, and repeatedly bopped on the head, is not "real," for fear that it will scare them or cause them to imitate such actions. Messenger Davies suggests both that children are usually quite capable of telling the difference between fantasy and reality and that the realm of fantasy should be valorized as one that allows children to explore different aspects of their real-world identities.

Yet even Messenger Davies's endorsement of fantasy seeks to interpret what meaning children make of texts in ways that make sense to adults—as revealed in her question: how do these fantasies help us deal with the real world? What about fantasy for the sake of fantasy? We can see fantasy as operating in the realm of affect, as producing sensations that are not meant to be translated into effects and meaning. Some degree of intensity is produced no matter the content; however, we could posit that television shows which are less concerned with narrative and the production of conventional meanings may be more likely to produce more powerful intensities. In other words, shows that resist meaning and semiotic ordering may more helpfully let children explore their feelings without managing them in an adult-guided fashion. Here is where Massumi's distinction between emotions and affect is especially helpful:

> An emotion is a subjective content, the socio-linguistic fixing of the quality of an experience which is from that point onward defined as personal. Emotion is qualified intensity, the conventional, consensual point of insertion of intensity into semantically and semiotically formed progressions, into narrativizable action-reaction circuits, into function and meaning. It is intensity owned and recognized. It is crucial to theorize the difference between affect and emotion. If some have the impression that it has waned, it is because affect is unqualified. As such, it is not ownable or recognizable, and is thus resistant to critique. (88)

Emotion and intensity are at one point indistinguishable; yet they diverge when emotion is "qualified" through its insertion into a narrative that seeks to make it mean something. This is also the moment when critique becomes operative, when the adult or critic or adult as critic assumes the position of interpreter of meaning. Intensity evades critique because it cannot be pinned down, or owned, or even recognized in the terms of critique.

To return to the snowman cartoon study, the confusion of the adult researchers may have been due to an overreliance on linguistic categories that did not fully register with the children, or did not fully correspond to their affective responses. When words were added to the images in the factual version, the intensity was "dampened," to use Massumi's phrase. Children were compelled to operate at the level of cognition; "this interfered with the images' effects." By contrast, the emotional version "enhanced the images' effects, as if they resonated with the level of intensity rather than interfering with it." Thus, language does not work in direct opposition to intensity; rather, "the relationship between levels of intensity and qualification is not one of conformity or correspondence but of resonation or interference, amplification or dampening" (85).

What dampens intensity for children? "A sense of futurity, expectation, an intimation of what comes next in a conventional progression," says Massumi (86). This, again, is exactly what Daniel Anderson was trying to achieve in his consulting work on *Blue's Clues*—helping children make transitions between elements of the story so that they would not get lost. Intensity, by contrast, "would seem to be associated with nonlinear processes: resonance and feedback which momentarily suspend the linear progress of the narrative present from past to future." Intensity is "filled with motion, vibratory motion, resonation" (86). This is an apt description of some kids' cultural production—nonlinear narratives, a rejection of forward progress, a series of images and events that to adults, simply do not "make sense." This nonlinearity is especially evident in internet productions—YouTube videos, memes, GIFs, fanart—as well as in gaming, as I discuss in the last section of the book.

Many times, children's television programming incorporates both affect and emotion. Initially, there occurs what in Massumi's terms could be considered a momentary suspension of "linear progress of the narrative present from past to future." This is the moment, or moments, before the naming of the emotion becomes part of the narrative. When something gets named as an emotion, it leaves the realm of affect and enters the realm of socialization—of, as I have been arguing, the management of emotion. As Massumi describes it: "Of course, the qualification of an emotion is quite often, in other contexts, itself a narrative element that moves the action ahead, taking its place in socially recognized lines of action and reaction. But to the extent that it is, it is not in resonance with intensity. It resonates to the exact degree to which it is in excess of any narrative or functional line" (86–87). In fact, this naming of emotion as part of a narrative element that "moves the action ahead" is precisely what characterizes the children's programming I discuss in chapter 5. It seeks, in a pedagogical way, to help children express their feelings; as part of the storyline, the lesson comes to seem less didactic and therefore (it is assumed) more likely to appeal to children.

By contrast, intensity "resonates" when it exceeds the narrative function; resonation requires no forward movement but neither is it exactly static. Its power lies in the moment, in its ability to generate an affective response that is simultaneously of mind and body, that, better put, does not function within that binary. The notion of excess is crucial in terms of seeking alternative cultural spaces for kids—spaces that allow kids to have feelings that need not be named but that for the purposes of my argument might be called exuberance, sensuality, nonsense. Media studies overall, and especially, in this context, those that focus on children, have largely ignored this realm of intensity, choosing instead to analyze what effects media have in children's lives. This focus on effects takes place most simplistically in the realm of conventional communications studies, psychology, and sociology, where the construction of the notion of "media violence" has relied on positing a direct cause-and-effect relationship—the belief that children imitate what they see on television, and, more recently, the internet, and possess no critical agency. "Effects," however, is also a focus in more complex studies by cultural studies scholars who emphasize the multifaceted practices of consumption; for these scholars, the question is often what do kids *do* with media texts, a question that remains reliant on meaning making.

The elision of affect occurs, in this vein, even by media critics who have treated children as perceptive consumers. Media scholars Sonia Livingstone and Kirsten Drotner describe the lessening influence of the "media harms" argument and the growing conviction that children have considerable control when it comes to media consumption: "Such discourses challenge established definitions of childhood as vulnerable, instead positioning children as the vanguard compared with 'their elders and betters.'" These discourses are often linked to the fact that children are empowered consumers, with consumption seen as a kind of agency that subverts adult authority: "These commercial discourses support a liberal, rights-based critique of traditional hierarchies of generational power in Western societies, recognizing that consumerism (and a pioneering approach to new technologies) is now a defining element of youthful leisure practices especially, supporting claims for further individualization of society" (2008, 3).

This approach is well illustrated in *Kids Rule!* (2007), Sarah Banet-Weiser's influential text on Nickelodeon. She illustrates how Nickelodeon through its programming and marketing insists on "kids as active consumers" (18), whereas "adults are dispensable" (32). Quickly, however, Banet-Weiser complicates this assertion of agency by focusing on the downside of agency as linked to consumerism—the citizen-consumer in kid form. Increasingly over the course of her chapters, which are mainly textual analyses of Nick's different programs, Banet-Weiser shows how this consumer impulse shapes programming, critiquing Nickelodeon for its superficial representation of gender and racial diversity. She says, for instance, that "popular discourses of race and images of non-whites become 'street cred' in the contemporary marketing world, so that, for instance, when Nickelodeon programs feature diverse characters and themes, the station is not only entitled to claim itself as the diversity station but also to connect this claim with its other claims: that the channel 'respects' kids and considers them citizens" (153). While a valid critique, it also reveals that Banet-Weiser is reading the programs as an adult, and as an academic, largely missing the different things kids might enjoy or look for in a show. Most young kids, for example, are not going to be looking for the ways in which "race is produced as a particular commodity and functions to deflect attention away from racist practices such as underfunded public schools and heavily policed immigration policies" (154). This is not to say kids are incapable of understanding immigration policies; rather, they likely consume media with a different set of criteria than those Banet-Weiser identifies.

In this dominant paradigm, ideology, identity, and interpretation are intertwined, with the goal of the textual reading being to reveal the manner in which texts shape children's consciousness in ways they may or may not understand; the critic, then, acting as teacher, reveals these ideological operations through their interpretation. In her chapter on girl power on Nickelodeon, for example, Banet-Weiser argues that the channel represents strong, independent female protagonists and works against "enforcing gender stereotypes about feminine appearance" (122). Yet, she adds, Nickelodeon's girl power is "ideologically complex" insofar as it is linked to "young girls and adolescents as an important consumer group that has more and more money to spend each year on 'girl power' products" (112). She further criticizes the channel's executives for shying away from endorsing an overt feminist position; the executives say instead that they "'care less about gender in our programs and more about kids'" (123). This, for Banet-Weiser, is proof that Nickelodeon is not sufficiently invested in empowering girls as girls—or perhaps only insofar as girls are consumers.

Banet-Weiser's critique assumes that children should be invested in the same kind of identity politics that have defined older generations. She fails to consider, for example, the possibility that perhaps gender and race as identities are experienced differently by children, and that perhaps this is not a politically retrograde or even innocent act. The kid fans of the show *Steven Universe* that I analyze in chapter 6 make it clear in their posts on the show that identity is malleable and many times not as important for them as the feelings generated by the show's refusal of clear-cut categories.

Affect, says Massumi, "is not about empathy or emotive identification, or any form of identification, for that matter" (102). So what is it about? Affect involves an experiential realm of feeling that is most visible through bodily responses yet which does not negate other forms of expression, such as laughing, crying, shouting, exclaiming, jumping, doing flips on the bed, flinging pillows. Exuberance, euphoria, sensations. What are the nonlinguistic ways in which children express themselves that might provide a better sense of what is going on than asking them which character they like or how they feel in response to a particular event within the narrative? Affect does not exist in a vacuum, yet it is distinct; Massumi calls it the "autonomy" of affect—it does not respond to containment, or it is created in resistance to containment, as an excess. This is the trick, the Catch-22 of affect—it is both what distinguishes children's "aliveness" and what threatens their ability to socialize. As Massumi says, affect is

> nothing less than the perception of one's own vitality, one's sense of aliveness (often signified as "freedom"). One's "sense of aliveness" is a

> continuous, nonconscious self-perception, its naming and making conscious, that allows affect to be effectively analyzed—as long as a vocabulary can be found for that which is imperceptible but whose escape from perception cannot but be perceived, as long as one is alive. (97)

This actually is a wonderful description of the energy of children, especially as we adults try to understand them: their "sense of aliveness" is palpable and visible, often musical and loud, sometimes maddening and distracting. They continually evade and sometimes entirely escape our attempts to control them. Yet even in ascribing to their aliveness this set of adjectives—in finding a vocabulary for the imperceptible—I have threatened that sense of aliveness. I have made it into my experience.

Since some degree of translation is inevitable, we can ask: how might adults allow children to experience their worlds with minimal intervention? More specifically, how might adults resist the urge to impose meanings that correspond with what we think kids need to know and feel? Adults who name a child's emotion may in fact be giving it the wrong name; giving them the language they need appears to be more in a child's interests than telling them to "be quiet," but in fact, it is another kind of discipline and management, channeling a child's intensity into forms that are acceptable to an adult notion of development. If, as Massumi says, "Intensity is the unassimilable" (88), then perhaps adults must acknowledge that not everything children do or say must be translated into prose that makes sense to adults. Perhaps they do not always need us to inform them, to mold them, or try to make them "feel better." The kid-produced texts I analyze throughout this book speak to this autonomy of expression.

One might legitimately question whether this valorization of the freedom of children is not an especially egregious form of adult appropriation—a nostalgic longing for our own, more innocent and more "primitive" childhood. As Massumi says, "Talk of intensity raises the objection that such a notion inevitably involves an appeal to a pre-reflexive, romantically raw domain of primitive experiential richness—the nature in our culture" (90). Although again Massumi is not referring to children here, they are more likely to be linked to nature than other subjects; as Jacqueline Rose describes it in her critique of adult appropriation of children's fiction, "childhood is set up as a primitive state where nature is still to be found if only one gets to it in time" (1984, 44).

However, affect is not instinct; the body, to put it another way, is not the same as pure nature or biology. If we attend to the manner in which children express themselves through their own cultural productions—productions that illuminate their "aliveness," we may get a sense of what is happening in their brains and of what they are feeling in their bodies. As Massumi argues,

> The body doesn't just absorb pulses or discrete stimulations; it infolds *contexts*, it infolds volitions and cognitions that are nothing if not situated. Intensity is asocial, but not presocial—it includes social elements, but mixes them with elements belonging to other levels of functioning, and combines them according to a different logic. How could this be so? Only if the traces of past actions including a trace of their contexts were conserved in the brain and in the flesh, but out of mind and out of body understood as qualifiable interiorities, active and passive respectively. (90–91)

In other words, over time, our bodies learn through repetition (as in Judith Butler's notion of performativity, for example), such that we no longer need to think about what we are doing. Elements of these learned behaviors become embodied. Think, for example, of the right-handed basketball player who has practiced the left-handed layup so many times, she no longer has to stop and think, when in the midst of a game, "Here is how I shoot a left-handed layup." There is still thought involved: a fake to the right, a drive to the left, but it happens quickly, amid the game's action, and because it has been practiced so many times, the thought resides in the body. Or the mother waking to her child's calls in the middle of the night: she has done this so many times that her body rises from the bed and walks into the child's bedroom. There is thought involved, but the thought resides in the body, and there is only a vague memory of this movement the next morning. Or the child, as I describe in the next chapter, who has seen a family member killed and whose body will always remember that event.

For children, whose brains are not so rigidly formed as an adult's, the thought that resides in the body will be less predictable, more malleable, and more open to a different mixture. A past action might be "autonomically reactivated but not accomplished; begun, but not completed," in

Massumi's words. "Intensity is incipience . . . *tendencies*, in other words, pastnesses opening onto a future, but with no present to speak of" (91). For children, an intensity is expressed as an opening into a future, an imagined world, for instance, that incorporates elements of the past—of experiences they've had, things they've learned—yet without having to worry about its usefulness in the present, since children have fewer immediate tasks to accomplish. The potential lies in maintaining the tendency *as a tendency*, without any pressure to act upon it. Rather, it is an exploratory state—what we call, for children, the realm of "play." As I discuss in chapter 4, early-child educators are calling for more play for younger children as part of a backlash against the push for standardized testing at earlier stages in elementary education.

The notion of children's ability to incorporate a "pastness" also acknowledges the importance of adults' supportive role in children's lives. It is far too easy to condemn adults for "managing children's emotional lives" while not dealing with the messy practicalities of everyday life. "Pastness" speaks to the importance of routine and structure; as anyone who works with children has likely learned, routines are crucial for creating the kind of environment in which children thrive. Structure creates stability and a set of expectations that does not need to be explained every day. The child's body becomes accustomed to the routine of getting up every morning, getting dressed, going out to the breakfast table. When the routine is embodied ("pastness" incorporated), no adult needs to remind the child to "do this, do that," and the child is freed to develop his or her own thoughts and ideas, to let his or her imagination wander into the future.

* * *

Ezra's routine is not defined by time in the sense that he watches the clock or even knows what time it is. Rather, he finds comfort in doing the same thing every morning—getting dressed, going to the bathroom, going to the breakfast counter, playing with his Legos, drinking chocolate milk, talking to the dog, going back to his room to play games on the computer, brushing his teeth, on with his socks and shoes. But does this routine lead to a recognition that now it is time to leave for school or we might be late? No, because for this six-year-old, routine is not about the fear of being late. It's about the repetition of the past in a way that provides a comforting place, a sense of security, for allowing him to play and relax and enjoy life. That's why it can be especially frightening when something interrupts the routine. The sight of *The New York Times* at the breakfast counter used to go unremarked by Ezra, for example. During the campaign leading up to the 2016 presidential election, he started glancing at the front page, and if there was a picture of Trump, he would usually exclaim in dismay. One morning, he shouted: "I hate Donald Trump! I am going to go his house and beat him up! Is he going to be president?" I doubt it, I said (this was in August, when a Trump victory seemed inconceivable, at least to me.) Ezra: "I could not sleep if he becomes president. He scares me." Me: How about you write him a letter? For a minute, this seems like a good idea. What would you say? Ezra: "I would tell him that I am scared if he is president, he will take over the internet and change all the pictures to pictures of himself." Me: I can see why you would say that. Can you write that down, or should I write it for you? People take you more seriously if you use your words. Ezra starts the letter, "Dear Mr. Trump, Why are you so mean?" but then he puts down the pencil. "If he gets this, will he come to my house and beat me up? I've heard he hates black people."

PART I

Political Subjects

In September 2016, a seven-year-old girl named Bana al-Abed started tweeting messages from her home in eastern Aleppo, providing daily updates about how it felt to be trapped in a war zone, her house bombed and her friends dying (see figure PI.1). Here is a sampling of her tweets, which were accompanied by vivid imagery, including the bodies of dead and injured children:

> Nov. 6: "Hi @hillaryclinton. My name is Bana I'm 7 years old girl in Aleppo, can you #StandWithAleppo children please.?"
> Nov. 27: "Tonight we have no house, it's bombed & I got in rubble. I saw deaths and I almost died. Bana"
> Nov. 27: "The army got in, this could be our last days sincerely talking. No Internet. Please please please pray for us."
> Nov. 29: "This is my reading place where I wanted to start reading Harry Potter but it's bombed. I will never forget.—Bana"
> Dec. 3: "This is our house, My beloved dolls died in the bombing of our house. I am very sad but happy to be alive. Bana"[1]

By December 2016, Bana had become an international celebrity, both admired and doubted. Her fans, including Harry Potter author J. K. Rowling, expressed admiration for Bana's courage, sympathy for what she was suffering, and horror at how children were innocent victims in a devastating war. Her detractors questioned whether the words were really Bana's. The primary contingent in this group said her mother, Fatemah, was running the account and using her daughter to publicize the devastation. More drastically, some critics claimed that Bana's Twitter account was completely false, a propaganda tool of anti-Assad forces, and that the tweets could have originated from anywhere and anyone. Syrian president Assad, in response to a question about whether he trusted Bana's account, said it was part of a "game of propaganda."[2]

Figure PI.1. Bana al-Abed's house after being bombed in 2016, https://twitter.com/AlabedBana.

News sources went from covering Bana's tweets to investigating whether she was real or not. *The New York Times*, *The Washington Post*, CNN, and other outlets ran stories reporting on the suspicions that the account was fraudulent because the tweets were too sophisticated for a seven-year-old girl whose native language was not English. In mid-December, the online investigative search network Bellingcat released a long report, summarized by *The Washington Post*, concluding that "'by far the most likely scenario is that @AlabedBana is an account run by Fatemah which tells the story of her daughter, a young child in East Aleppo.' While noting that there are obviously moments where the account has posted explicitly political and even rash messages, the attempts to discredit her 'verged into the ludicrous'" (Taylor 2016). The Bellingcat article, written by former British army soldier Nick Waters, relied on geolocation satellite that showed the tweets did come from eastern Aleppo, at times corresponding to documented bombings, including of Bana's home. Furthermore, the investigation ascertained that while Bana's mother manages the account and makes some of the posts, it is possible to distinguish between Fatemah's more sophisticated tweets and Bana's more direct messages. Furthermore, Waters said, Fatemah clearly signs and claims the tweets that are her own.

Bana's story, while arising from the circumstances in Syria, also speaks to the questions this book is raising. How does the technology of Twitter enable Bana to share her feelings with the world, albeit feelings that are mediated at least in part through her mother, in a way that provides people an almost immediate and vivid account of what's happening? Many of her tweets foreground her feelings—sadness, happiness, fear, loneliness—as she attempts to convey something of what it's like to be under siege. At the same time, these words seem inadequate—they are words describing emotions that her mother, the English teacher, taught her. What would Bana say in her own language, we wonder?

Yet this question is not much different from questions we would ask of any one speaking in a nonnative language, especially when speaking from such a difficult situation. Why, then, was there so much skepticism? Much of the doubt was focused on the elusiveness of Twitter, even though Twitter is used all the time (including by the president of the U.S.) without the "authenticity" of its sender being questioned. Seven-year-olds in the U.S. are adept at technology; even if they don't have Twitter accounts, they use iPads and smartphones, often times at younger ages than seven.

Here is the likely answer: Bana clearly defies the image of the innocent and vulnerable child, the victim waiting to be saved, that characterizes much media coverage of children in crisis.. As Wendy Hesford argues in her work on the spectacle of human rights discourse, suffering children are often used in human rights and other activist campaigns to "dramatize the righteousness of a cause" (2011, 151), usually with little attention to their complexity as "moral and political subjects who must negotiate the economic and social inequities of globalization at the local level" (155–56). Despite her suffering, Bana does not cast herself as a victim: she actively organizes campaigns such #StandWithAleppo, tweets politicians such as Hillary Clinton, posts graphic images of dead children, and expresses her emotions—including anger—in no uncertain terms.

Hesford urges attention to "children's *rhetorical* agency," which she defines as "children's ability to represent themselves" (153). One could argue that Bana has considerable rhetorical agency—with 353,000 followers—and that Twitter, with its 140-character messages, lends itself to an immediate, global reach. Although she appeals to adults around the world to take responsibility, she also reaches children, even young kids who don't have their own Twitter accounts but hear the news and feel compelled by her story. Two kids in Albuquerque, New Mexico, for example, learned about Bana on the news, and, with the help of their mother, Laura Rodriguez, set up a Twitter account and began messaging Bana. She responded, and the network then expanded to include Antonio Rodriguez's fifth-grade classmates, who made a poster board of encouragement and sent it along with a class photo to Bana via Twitter. "'It has inspired a lot of the kids in the classroom to be compassionate, and now they're truly concerned about what's going on in Syria,'" Valerie Coker, Antonio's teacher, told a local reporter (Atkins 2016). When Bana temporarily stopped tweeting in December 2016, the children feared for her safety. Antonio, however, said he would keep tweeting: "I feel like if I keep messaging her, more people will be messaging her if I tell them about it and more people will get involved and they'll keep helping, and will try and stop the war" (quoted in Atkins 2016).

Bana's tweets have a strong affective appeal for Antonio, who is moved to use Twitter to multiply and intensify Bana's message, contributing to an activist network that crosses generational and geographical boundaries. While Antonio likely understands something of the complex political situation in Syria, he is not an expert—nor is Bana. Yet the images and affective appeals form the basis of a powerful campaign, one that has had political effects.

Affect, however, is not what is normatively expected of political subjects, no matter their age. Rather, it is the language of rationality that is required of a political subject. In this section, I consider three sites of governance where kids are asked to speak in the language of rationality that is the basis of rights' discourse—the U.S. immigration system, the civil discourse of electoral politics, and the public-school system. Within each space, kids are allowed to express themselves, but in a manner akin to the naming of emotions that I discussed in the last chapter—the emotional intelligence that brings together rationality and emotions. This naming becomes a way that institutions manage the future of the children; does the naming of fear, for example, suffice for the granting of political asylum? Can the anger a child feels at Trump's election be sublimated within a polite letter? By contrast, kids responding to these institutional imperatives in their own, semi-autonomous spaces demonstrate a different kind of political response through their artwork, a response that defies categorization and speaks much more powerfully to the felt experience.

Policy and human rights activists have argued for the recognition of children's rights yet struggled with how to negotiate the sometimes contradictory needs of children for both support and autonomy. What does it mean to accord rights to subjects who are not yet able to fully express themselves in the language of rights? The landmark 1990 United Nations Convention on the Rights of the Child (CRC) binds all nations who sign it to act in the best interests of the child, as a matter of international law (the U.S. and Somalia are the only two nations not to sign the CRC). The treaty led to further advances; as Alison Brysk says, "The landmark 1990 UN Convention on the Rights of the Child has been matched by a proliferation of comprehensive norms, global agencies, and advocacy groups, new networks and coalitions, conferences, and campaigns" (2005, 37).

Yet just because these rights have been accorded does not mean they will be respected and enacted by different nation-states. In fact, argues Jacqueline Bhabha, an expert on children and migration, state treatment of child migrants is deeply ambivalent, with children perceived at times as vulnerable and at times as "threatening, unruly, and uncontrolled outsiders. Our neglect of child migrants' rights is therefore a strategic compromise that represents our unresolved ambivalence. It has enabled us to avoid the conceptual and political dilemmas raised by child migration and to sidestep the policy challenges it presents" (2014, 11). State attitudes to children, says Bhabha, can be both punitive and infantilizing— leading to ineffective policies, as reflected in these scenarios: "We legislate migrant children's rights to public education and health care irrespective of their legal status, but we erect practical obstacles to their access to these services; we accept an obligation to protect them from persecution, trafficking, and destitution, but we blame them for the risks they pose to our social fabric by finding ways to detain or remove them from our territories." Whatever solutions are arrived at, says Bhabha, "have to carefully calibrate the ongoing tension between the child's need for protection (the best interest principle enunciated in Article 3 of the Convention on the Rights of the Child) and the child's evolving ability to be autonomous (the right to voice and agency, expressed in Article 12 of the same Convention)" (14). Furthermore, says Bhabha, policy needs to acknowledge that children, especially teens, are complicated—they may choose, for example, to be smuggled, as a survival strategy, therefore disrupting the image of the purely victimized trafficked youth. "Their best interests," says Bhabha, "must involve an opportunity for both protection and exploration, dependence and independence" (14).

In her elaboration of ambivalence and the complexity of children, Bhabha hints at but does not develop the inadequacy of the language of rights, especially for younger children. How does a seven-year-old express both the dependency and the autonomy of childhood? At times, in fact, one does so clearly and directly. We can turn again to Bana al-Abed, and her tweet upon fleeing Syria and being welcomed by Turkish president Erdoğan, who had become her champion after reading her tweets from Aleppo. On December 25, 2016, she wrote, "I am a child with something to say. And that's let's help every child in war zone. – Bana."

2

The Production of Fear

Children at the U.S.-Mexico Border

At a U.S. Border Patrol station along the Mexico border in the summer of 2014, several agents interviewed a boy named Juan Felipe, whom they had recently arrested on suspicion that he had illegally crossed into the country. Addressing him in Spanish, a government agent told Juan Felipe, "I am an officer of the United States Department of Homeland Security." He informed Juan Felipe that "I want to take your sworn statement" and warned him that "this may be your only opportunity to present information to me and the Department of Homeland Security." "Do you understand what I've said to you?" The boy answered yes. "Do you have any questions?" The boy answered no. The agent then asked Juan Felipe, "Why did you leave your home country or country of last residence?" to which the boy responded, "To look for work."[1]

This interrogation was recorded on an official government form to be used if Juan Felipe later made a claim for political asylum. The testimony was written in a first-person, question-and-answer format, giving it the appearance of a verbatim transcription. The writings were sworn to by the government agent who administered the oath and countersigned by another agent who attested to having witnessed the entire interrogation.

But here's why it's hard to believe the transcript: Juan Felipe was three years old at the time he was interrogated. He was one of about 68,000 children from Central America who were arrested in 2014 along the U.S.-Mexico border, prompting the Obama administration to mandate expedited deportations and to reinstate a practice that has been thoroughly condemned internationally: detention of young children in locked facilities. Juan Felipe and his mother were transferred to a "family detention center" in the isolated town of Artesia, New Mexico. There, they were identified for representation by a pro bono attorney, Stephen Manning, who contested the transcript. In most cases, these documents go unquestioned by immigration judges when they are used by government lawyers seeking to deport people. If Manning had not intervened, Juan Felipe's statement would have been used as evidence to discredit any claim of having a credible fear of returning to his country—since poverty is not considered a valid reason for political asylum.

No one will ever know for certain what transpired: there is no reason to trust the officers, whether they were well intentioned or not, and Juan Felipe cannot explain, given his age and circumstances. As has been shown in other cases documented by the American Immigration Lawyers Association and Human Rights Watch, Customs and Border Patrol (CBP) is not following their own stated screening procedure, which requires them to ascertain if a person fears returning to their home country. If they do express a fear, they are allowed to continue in the asylum application process. In the case of children, the situation is egregiously flawed, with more situations such as Juan Felipe's reported in various human rights documents. Clara Long, an attorney for Human Rights Watch and author of a report on the problems with the screening process, found another case of a three-year-old who purportedly told CBP he came to the U.S. to look for work. Adults are also not being adequately screened, say Long and other attorneys; the upshot is that many people who express fear of returning to their countries are not referred to asylum officers.

It would seem to be a straightforward question: are you afraid to return to your home country? Yet to be able to name an emotion, to say it out loud to an official who may have just arrested you—that's not easy for anyone who has experienced trauma, especially a child. Yet U.S. immigration and border patrol policies do little to facilitate the naming and in some cases actively discourage expression. The stakes are high: when CBP does the speaking for the children, detention, deportation, and even death may ensue.

Children are not inherently fearful. Fear has to be produced, and CBP, as part of Immigration and Customs Enforcement (ICE), is adept at doing so. Perversely, rather than operating as a site of potential asylum that welcomes people fleeing dangerous situations, the agencies create conditions that make it difficult for children to express their well-founded fears of persecution in their home countries. During the arrest, the initial interview, and then the detention, ICE policies create a space of uncertainty in which fear flourishes. As Sara Ahmed describes the political production of fear, "It is the regulation of bodies in space through the uneven distribution of fear which allows spaces to become territories, claimed as rights by some bodies and not by others" (70). The Obama administration was not shy about making explicit its reason for reinstituting family detention in 2014: Vice President Joe Biden stated baldly, and without evidence, that none of the Central American women and children seeking asylum would qualify but rather be quickly deported. This, clearly, is a case in which authorities want children and their parents to be afraid, to inhabit their vulnerability, and to send the message of fear back to their home countries so that other people will not come to the United States. The Trump administration has been vicious in its treatment of immigrant children, beginning a practice in 2018 of separating them from the parents with whom they crossed the border in order to discourage other immigrants (Hennessy-Fiske 2018).

Children will feel the fear in their bodies as a form of vulnerability, exacerbated by their lack of material resources and dependence on adults that accompany them and adults that deter and detain them and who perceive their job to be the rejection of this vulnerability. As Ahmed puts it:

> Vulnerability involves a particular kind of bodily relation to the world, in which openness itself is read as a site of potential danger, and as demanding evasive action. Emotions may involve readings of such openness, as spaces where bodies and worlds meet and leak into each other. Fear involves reading such openings as dangerous, the openness of the body to the world involves a sense of danger, which is anticipated as future pain or injury. In fear, the world presses against the body; the body shrinks back from the world in the desire to avoid the object of fear. Fear involves shrinking the body; it restricts the body's mobility precisely insofar as it seems to prepare the body for flight. (69)

The U.S.-Mexico border is a space "where bodies and worlds meet and leak into each other." It *could* be a space of hope and possibility, where Juan Felipe and other children could feel safe expressing their fears. The conditions of arrest, however, as I show in this chapter, instead induce more fear, causing the kids to "shrink back from the world," often in situations of physical detainment.

Yet the naming of the emotion is, again, insufficient—in no small part because the legal process itself requires that a complex range of feelings be distilled into a set of objective questions and answers—initially, into a "yes and no" form. Understanding a child's reasons for migrating is more complex than understanding an adult's, since especially at young ages, they will not have the language to explain or the capacity to fully understand why they left their homes. What if Juan Felipe in fact heard his mother talking about coming to the U.S. to look for work, and repeated some version of that to the officials? Should that preclude his application? Does the feeling of hunger not coincide with fear? What are the range of things Juan Felipe was feeling at that moment, and how are these feelings precluded by the need to distill them into one emotion?

Feelings are about movement, says Ahmed, noting that the word "emotion" comes from the Latin *emovere*, referring to "move, move out."[2] Yet feelings are also about attachments—she says: "what moves us, makes us feel, is also that which holds us in place, or gives us a dwelling place" (11). Movement does not necessarily cut us off but can connect us to other bodies, and the places where that happens can become temporary homes, an alternative to the alienating site of the detention center, where refugees are asked to speak in a language that is not their own, in order to remain in a country that appears not to want them.

Recognizing this connection between attachment and feelings, activists in south Texas organized a space for children recently released from detention to make their own art. The activists set up two art stations in McAllen—one at a church and the other at a bus station, both to give the children something to do while they awaited their buses and to give them a way to express something about the experiences of leaving their homes, crossing Mexico and the border, traveling for 30 days or more, then being apprehended and detained in harsh conditions. One of the activists, Rev. Gregory Cuellar, gathered the art into an exhibit that he called *Arte de Lagrimas* (Art of tears). The children's art, I argue, shows the limitations of distilling all of one's feelings into a singular emotion under the rubric of "fear." The pictures illustrate a range of feelings that we can only guess at—sadness at leaving one's home, exhaustion from the journey, longing for one's family and friends, hope for a new life, relief at having made it across the border. The pictures compel us to ask how the immigration system causes more trauma by denying children the space and resources they need to process their experiences. *Arte de Lagrimas* functions as an "archive of feelings" that, as it circulates, may help create the conditions for the public recognition of children as political subjects.

Who Is a Child?

U.S. border control and immigration officials are woefully unprepared and in some respects appear frankly unwilling to grapple with the particular needs and capabilities of children. These failures became painfully obvious in the summer of 2014 when the numbers of Central American children entering the U.S., both with and without family members, skyrocketed in response to extreme levels of violence in their home countries. The number of unaccompanied Central American children apprehended by CBP rose 77 percent, to 68,541 from 38,759 in fiscal year 2013; the number of family units apprehended during the same time period rose 361 percent, to 68,445 from 14,855.[3] The Obama administration struggled to respond in both a "border enforcing" and "humanitarian" fashion. The children have paid the price. In every stage of their journey to and through the United States, the children are mistreated, misunderstood, judged, and evaluated by adults who often have very little awareness of or interest in their particular lives and who rely on a problematic binary construction of inarticulate child versus potentially dangerous/future criminal. The consequences are devastating, as the majority of these children will be sent back to life-threatening situations without ever having had the chance to express their claims for legal protection in the United States. In fact, the United Nations High Commission on Refugees (UNHCR) interviewed 404 children who had recently crossed the border on their own and concluded that 58 percent of them "were forcibly displaced because they suffered or faced harms that indicated a potential or actual need for international protection" (UNHCR 2014, 6). If, by some rare combination of events, a child does reach the stage of making an asylum claim before an immigration judge, he or she will have to contend with the fact that U.S. asylum court for children is unusual insofar as it does not employ a "best interests of the child" standard as do other legal proceedings that involve children in the United States.

The crisis is not just of the moment but one with deep roots in the violent histories of Central America—violence produced in part by U.S. intervention, including assistance to right-wing governments and death squads throughout much of the 20th century. The countries of El Salvador, Guatemala, and Honduras have not recovered; they continue to struggle with poverty and social injustice in addition to new forms of transnational violence in which gangs and other criminal elements target children, and states are unable to protect them, forcing many children to make the difficult decision to migrate. The children traveling without adult caretakers—so-called "unaccompanied minors" in the U.S. system and my focus in the rest of this chapter—introduce another complexity: at least temporarily existing outside the usual defining parameters of a biological family, these children are seemingly more vulnerable than children migrating within the protective ambit of a family unit yet also more autonomous, less defined by their parent(s).

What happens when a child is not perceived to be a child? This contradictory response was seen in the United States in the summer of 2014, when the growing numbers of Central American unaccompanied minors attracted considerable media attention and protests in numerous communities across the country where the children were being sent for temporary shelter. While some communities called the situation a humanitarian crisis and welcomed the children, others rejected them as outsiders and future criminals. As Jessica O'Connell Davidson puts it, "to speak of child migrants is to bring together two very different cultural categories"—the category of the innocent, passive child and the category of the "illegal immigrant," who is "generally attributed with agency and cunning." She adds,

> "Immigrants" supposedly constitute a threat to that which we hold dear, whereas children are one of the things that we hold dear—they are our future, they are precious and loveable. The social value of children (as a general group) is assumed, taken for granted, unquestioned. The value of "immigrants," by contrast, is constantly questioned and almost completely unacknowledged in popular discourse. The "child migrant" is thus almost a contradiction in terms, and certainly disturbs the victim–agent binary that is so important to the way we make sense of the world, especially to the way we think about injustice, suffering and victimhood.

> We (adult nationals) have a duty to protect children as real or potential victims, but we supposedly need to be protected from immigrants who really or potentially make us victims. (2011, 462–63)

The reality, as O'Connell Davidson argues, is much more complicated, with all children who migrate facing dangerous situations and difficult decisions. "Children" is never a static category. The current chair of the UN Committee on the Rights of the Child, Jean Zermatten, recognized this complexity in an essay in which he says that a child is "a developing being in need of different degrees and levels of guidance, protection, and participation at different stages of her life." Zermatten says that pursuant to Article 5 of the CRC, "direction and guidance should be given to the child to compensate for her/his lack of knowledge, experience and understanding and be restricted according to the evolving capacities of that child" (quoted in Schoenholtz 2013, 1001). In other words, the CRC attends to the difficult act of figuring out how autonomous a child is—given the fact that "growing up" is a highly contingent act, dependent on cultures, life experiences, and so on. As legal scholar Andrew Schoenholtz argues, this contingency is exactly what the best interests of the child standard seeks to ensure, such "that the voice of the child is heard, the child as a thoughtful and emotional being is understood, and particular developmental and survival needs are addressed. The CRC requires governments to apply the best interests of the child in a manner that honors this unique evolving nature" (1001).

The U.S. government is not following this standard when it comes to the Central American children crossing the border because, simply put, children are not treated as "thoughtful and emotional" subjects with "particular developmental and survival needs." While some progress has been made at the final stage—the asylum hearing—many children never reach this stage because, up until then, their specific needs and agencies are not respected, nor their emotional lives considered worthy of serious consideration.

The Best Interests of the Child?

The U.S.-Mexico border space has become—or rather, it has been for quite some time—a militarized and violent space, with CBP deploying aerial surveillance and other military equipment, especially at points they have identified as frequent crossing spaces. Because of this, many people have sought to cross in more dangerous and isolated places, such as areas of rough terrain and deserts. Others cross at the official ports of entry, presenting themselves to officials. Unaccompanied children apprehended by CBP officers are placed in cars or vans to be taken to a border patrol facility for questioning, sometimes in handcuffs (although handcuffing children is against CBP policy). Some minors who were interviewed by the UNHCR reported being hit, kicked, manhandled, or roughly handcuffed during their initial apprehension, or insulted and cursed at by CBP officers (UNHCR 2014, 33). Yet it is these very officers who do the initial interviews, raising considerable doubt about whether children will tell them anything at all.

The children are then held for up to 72 hours in detention spaces where they are supposed to be screened to see if they have valid claims for international protection. Few of these spaces are designed for children. A 2011 investigation by the immigrant rights groups Appleseed describes these spaces as more like prisons. They are well guarded by uniformed agents. The holding cells are bare, usually with only a bench and an unenclosed toilet and kept so cold that the children call them "ice boxes." Generally, no beds, pillows, fresh clothes, or even blankets are provided. Children are segregated from the adults, but often the holding cells of adults and children are in sight of each other. Medical treatment is very limited, and the food often consists of packaged cold sandwiches and snacks. The interviews are conducted at a metal desk, in open sight and earshot of the adults. As the Appleseed reports summarizes: "In all cases, nothing in the physical environment is designed to provide a sense of warmth or comfort for the child. Everything about this experience tells these unaccompanied children that they are in a detention center run by a powerful U.S. law enforcement agency and that the alternative to repatriation is to be 'locked up' in the U.S." Under these conditions, children are not likely to divulge sensitive information to the officer. Even one CBP agent interviewed by Appleseed called it a "'police station' environment and said he didn't expect the minors to trust him or his colleagues" (Appleseed 2011, 35).

Furthermore, agents have had little or no training in how to talk to children, especially younger children who, as I argued in the last chapter, often have different ways of relating a story than adults due to their varying physiologies. The United Nations team recognized this specificity: "Children cannot be expected to provide adult-like accounts of situations they have faced and may have difficulty articulating their fears. They may be too young or immature to be able to evaluate what information is important or to interpret and convey what they have witnessed or experienced in a manner that is easily understandable to an adult. . . . They may wish to avoid talking about difficult subjects, or they may not directly connect hardships or other experiences or fears with the questions they are being asked" (UNHCR 2014, 20). Accordingly, when the UNHCR interviewed the kids, they were sensitive to different modes of expression. Rather than insisting on a linear account, the interviewers built into the interview the opportunity for repetition because "children's responses to questions, such as why they left home, are often layered, with easier responses shared first" (21). Children need to be allowed this kind of flexibility and nonlinearity in telling their stories, and adults need to avoid a kind of translation that sees such repetition as a form of deception or subterfuge.

When agents do not attend to these different modes of expression, kids may well not express their fears in a manner that improves their chances of gaining some kind of stay of deportation and eventual legal status. What this failure suggests is that even when progressive immigration laws are passed, they may not have much effect. For example, until December 2008, unaccompanied Mexican children were upon apprehension returned across the border, due to a law that allows the United States to immediately deport anyone from a contiguous country. Then Congress passed the Trafficking Victims Protection and Reauthorization Act of 2008 (TVPRA), which required the Department of Homeland Security (DHS) to interview every unaccompanied Mexican minor to "make the determination that the child is (i) not a potential victim of trafficking, (ii) has no possible claim to asylum, and (iii) can (and does) voluntarily agree to go back home" (Appleseed 2011, 1). However, two years after the law was passed, Appleseed investigated whether it was actually being followed; they interviewed 130 children and found that "no meaningful screening is being conducted" (31). The investigation concluded that "the unaccompanied Mexican minors who are apprehended at the border are, for all practical purposes, just as vulnerable to trafficking and other forms of exploitation after the passage of TVPRA as they were before" (49). In its visits to nine holding centers in Texas, California, and Arizona, Appleseed encountered only 13 Mexican children, which indicates that the remaining thousands of children who had been apprehended had been immediately deported. At their meeting with the Mexican consulate in Nogales, Appleseed was told that of the 5,507 Mexican minors detained in that region alone through November 30, 2009, there was not a single case in which CBP had transferred control of a child to the Department of Health and Human Services (HHS).

The failure is due in part to the fact that interviews are conducted by CBP officers, who have no expertise in child welfare and have not been trained since TVPRA was passed. Says Appleseed, "Minors are not being informed of their rights, have little or no comprehension regarding their options, and are encouraged to believe that they have no real choice other than to return to Mexico, regardless of their circumstances" (31). Mexican officials are consulted in order to provide information on the children and act as their advocates; however, Appleseed uncovered another problem here. In most cases, the Mexican officials assume family reunification is best and do not consider the possibility of domestic abuse or gang activity in children's hometowns—the situations that prompted them to leave in the first place. Says Appleseed: "Our visits revealed that, in almost all cases, DIF facilities opt for swift family reunification in lieu of an in-depth evaluation of a child's motives for crossing the border or an evaluation of the child's home environment" (56).

To determine if the children have a credible fear of returning, CBP agents are supposed to help them fill out two forms. The first, called form 93, has just three questions: "why did you leave your country, do you have a fear or concern of being returned to your country, and would you be harmed if you were returned" (Appleseed 2011, 39). Although the interviewer is instructed to follow up with "age appropriate" questions if any of the indicators are present, there is no guidance on how to craft such questions. Even more egregiously, Appleseed found that CBP officers do not often even use this form: "roughly half of the children we interviewed who had been, or were about to be, repatriated were not asked the three formulaic questions, nor were they asked any questions about trafficking" (40).

The second form—I-770—is designed to determine if the child is able to make an "independent decision" about whether to return to Mexico. It also informs them of "their right to call a family member or adult friend, to be represented by a lawyer, and the right to a hearing before a judge in order to determine" whether they may stay in the United States. The children must read the form and sign it, or, if they cannot read it, have it read to them. Yet Appleseed found that three-quarters of the children interviewed had not been informed about any of the above: "Many children stated that they were never asked whether they wanted voluntary departure; they were simply told they would be returning to Mexico" (Appleseed 2011, 40). More than half were told to sign a form written in English, even though the form is available in both English and Spanish. Furthermore, the children are not informed that if they express a fear of repatriation, they will be sent to a shelter facility—not kept in the detention center—and that they will have access there to social services and possibly legal representation. Thus, many of the children believe that their two choices are to remain in the prisonlike detention center or return to their home country, and thus "choose" the latter.

An important question emerges: how do the CBP officers determine whether the minor is capable of making an "independent decision" to return voluntarily? There is no agencywide policy on this issue; the Nogales and Tucson regions, for example, have determined that no child under 14 is capable of making such a decision. In other regions, the decision seems to be made on a case-by-case basis, but, again, by agents who have no expertise in evaluating children.

We see here the governmental failure to recognize children as subjects with particular experiences and capabilities; in other words, the "best interests of the child" standard is in no way being employed in the screening process. On the one hand, the children are treated as if they were adults—arrested, held in detention, and given no special care, either in terms of physical needs or assistance in understanding their legal rights. The position seems to be: they acted like adults in making the journey and crossing the border illegally, so they are going to be treated as adults. On the other hand, the children are treated as incapable of making their own decisions—when they are automatically returned to their families in Mexico and when it is assumed that they do not have valid reasons for leaving.

What would it mean to create the conditions in which children feel safe expressing their fears? Of course, the first step would be not holding them in jail-like conditions but rather putting them immediately in the children's shelters that they are required to be transferred to after 72 hours. Furthermore, it would require immigration officials to respect children; yes, they are at risk and in need of protection, but they are also capable of making their own decisions if provided the information they need to do so. Appleseed suggests steps for determining whether the right conditions exist for a child to make such a decision, including ascertaining that the child understands "in whose custody he or she would be placed" if returned to Mexico, the kind of shelters available if he or she decides to stay in the U.S., "the removal proceedings the child will face, the child's rights in those proceedings and the consequences of being ordered removed," and the potential length of time it will take for the case to be determined (46). These criteria address the specific needs of a child and respect his or her ability to make a decision if these needs are fulfilled.

If these conditions are not created, then the risk to the child increases exponentially, most starkly in the form of deportation, to a situation of possible death. This was the finding of a comprehensive study on childhood migration from Central America published in 2015 by the Center for Gender & Refugee Studies at the University of California Hastings College of the Law and the Migration and Asylum Program of the National University of Lanús, Argentina. The study concluded: "The United States has returned some children back to persecution or death, and returns children to the very circumstances that compelled them to leave. Following repatriation, the United States provides no support for children's reintegration, despite the great need for medical, mental health, educational, and job training support, as well as the need for basic safety" (Musalo, Frydman, and Cernadas 2015). Repatriated children are marked—more obvious to gangs, more at risk than before they left.

In the Courtroom

We come, then, to a critical juncture in these children's journeys: if they are not immediately repatriated at the border and if they satisfy the initial requirements for showing they have a fear of returning to their home countries, they must be transferred to the Office of Refugee Resettlement (ORR), a unit within HHS, within 72 hours of being apprehended.[4] They are then transferred to one of four kinds of facilities, ranging from foster homes, with the least amount of restrictions, to group homes, minimum-security shelters, and high-security shelters (essentially jails) for those deemed flight or security risks. While the majority of children are placed in foster care or released to family members if they come forward, those children who are sent to the more secure shelters are not receiving the care they need but rather being treated more like criminals than refugees. This has increasingly become the case for a greater percentage of the children due to growing numbers and the ORR's inability to place everyone in foster care or shelters—such that even children who should be in foster care are placed in secure facilities.

It can take months or even years for their cases to be heard, especially given the growing backlog of cases: according to the Transactional Records Clearinghouse (TRAC), the total number of immigration cases in the backlog was 496,704 as of July 2016; nearly a third of those cases involve minors (69,278) and family units (74,502) waiting for their court date.[5] Furthermore, there is no guaranteed right to an attorney the way there is in other court systems in the United States, such as the juvenile justice system. The Center for Gender & Refugee Studies report says that this "lack of counsel renders many of children's rights under U.S. immigration law meaningless, as children and adolescents lack the skill, knowledge, and maturity to secure these rights on their own" (Musalo, Frydman, and Cernadas 2015). Having an attorney greatly improves the child's chances of being allowed to stay in the United States; a 2014 study showed that 48 percent of children were represented in immigration proceedings in the prior six months, and those children had a one-in-two chance of being allowed to stay, compared to one in ten for those lacking representation (Musalo, Frydman, and Cernadas 2015). The situation has been greatly exacerbated by then President Obama's call in mid-2014 for expedited removal proceedings for unaccompanied children—to which the Executive Office of Immigration Review (EOIR) quickly concurred. The result is that children have even less time than before to find attorneys, meaning they are being deported much more quickly than in previous years. At some courts, up to 45 children at a time appear before a judge; advocates have critically termed the hearings "rocket dockets" (Musalo, Frydman, and Cernadas 2015) and say it has become increasingly difficult for children to win their claims, even if they have strong cases, because their attorneys do not have time to prepare. Time is especially crucial because children often need longer than adults to disclose sensitive information and feel comfortable with new people.

Even with an attorney, it is very difficult for anyone to win an asylum claim in the United States—and even more difficult for a child. Claimants confront a complex set of requirements needed to prove their well-founded fear of future persecution on one of five grounds (race, religion, nationality, membership in a particular social group, and political opinion). They must also prove that their home government is unable to protect them. Furthermore, while U.S. asylum law is derived from the 1951 United Nations Convention Relating to the Status of Refugees and its 1967 protocol, the U.S. interpretation of who qualifies is actually much narrower than the international approach. Most importantly for my purposes, the United States "does not require adjudicators to employ a child-sensitive analysis of the elements of the refugee definition that acknowledges the differences between children and adults" (Musalo, Frydman, and Cernadas 2015). While the UNHCR has produced guidelines for a child-sensitive approach, and the United States encourages its adjudicators to apply them, they are not binding. Thus, many minors "experience great difficulty in establishing their eligibility for asylum," as an immigration judge will be unlikely to acknowledge that children experience harm differently than adults do—that "an act that might not be persecution when inflicted on an adult could certainly be so when inflicted on a child, especially if it has long-lasting emotional and psychological effects" (Musalo, Frydman, and Cernadas 2015).

It is also particularly complicated for a child to prove membership in a "social group," the category most often deployed in attempts to establish the basis of persecution. A social group is defined as a "group of individuals" who share a common characteristic that they are unable to change"; in addition, many courts require the claimant to prove that this group is perceived as a particular, visible group by society, and that the persecution was directly linked to membership in this group. Yet asylum adjudicators have been reluctant to define children as a particular social group; in claims based on persecution by gangs, for example, adjudicators have said that the group "children" is too broad to explain the situation and have refused to acknowledge that some children are targeted precisely because of their status as children.

Most judges seem to be making little effort to see the situation from the child's point of view. Another requirement for asylum is proving that one's government cannot provide protection from harm; such proof might take the form of reporting threats to authorities. Yet children might well find it difficult to go to authorities, for many reasons, ranging from lack of transportation to lack of knowledge about where exactly to go. Nevertheless, "adjudicators often hold children to the standard of adults and will refuse to find the government was unable or unwilling to protect if the child did not report persecution to the authorities" (Musalo, Frydman, and Cernadas 2015).[6]

The courtroom is an intimidating space, dominated by the judge and a government attorney who works for the DHS, with proceedings conducted in English, with a translator if necessary. The Executive Office of Immigration Review has issued guidelines for making the proceedings more child-friendly—such as judges appearing in normal attire rather than robes—but the guidelines are not binding. Advocates express considerable concern about insensitive questioning on the part of both judges and DHS attorneys. One such example will illustrate. In this case, a government attorney questioned a 13-year-old about attacks on his family that had taken place some years earlier:

Q: Do you know why [your family's attacker] didn't like your grandmother?
A: No.
Q: Do you know why he said Communist?
A: I don't know what that word means.
Q: Okay. And did you hear it yourself or did someone tell you that's what he said?
A: He stated Communists.
Q: And you don't know what he meant by that?
A: No. (quoted in Musalo, Frydman, and Cernadas 2015)

Based on this line of questioning, the DHS attorney argued that the child could not establish a direct connection to persecution based on his family's political beliefs; the immigration judge agreed and denied the child's asylum petition.[7] This child is held to a standard completely inappropriate for his age; indeed, many adults could have a difficult time explaining the history of how the term "communist" has been used in Central America as a justification for persecution.

An Archive of Feelings

Being detained is a traumatic experience for anyone, but especially for a child. A detention center is a site of dispossession, where it is impossible for children, even when detained with their mothers, to have a sense of belonging, defined by the routines and everyday activities that make life meaningful, enjoyable, and safe. The families do not know when—or if—they will be able to leave to join family or friends while they await hearings. Child psychologist Luis Zayas evaluated 20 children in the Karnes City, Texas, family detention center in 2014 and found the following: children suffering from ongoing stress, despair, and uncertainty, manifested in the form of nightmares, dissociative reactions, aggression toward other children, fatigue, loss of interest in playing, weight loss, and even, in two of the teenagers, suicidal ideation. The long-term effects could be serious, he wrote in an affidavit: children for whom emotional attachments are interrupted or cut off often suffer in the future—they have difficulty making friends and are more likely to get into trouble at school and elsewhere.[8]

The volunteers in south Texas who organized the spaces for recently released children to create their art recognized the need for a clear alternative to detention; as the *Arte de Lagrimas* brochure says: "offering love and hospitality, we invited many refugee children into a creative and sacred space of art making." In this safe space, many of the children expressed their longing for home. Several of the older children drew pictures of their Central American homes—neat, orderly rows of houses, the trees neatly circling the mountain. For example, 15-year-old Laura, from El Salvador, entitled her picture "Mi Comunidad," and drew seven neat, symmetrical houses—little rectangles with triangle roofs, all brightly colored, with paths leading between them, all connected, with trees and grass interspersed. In the background is a row of mountains, blue sky, and sun. Strikingly, though, there are no people in the picture;

a sense of emptiness pervades the drawing. It could be that everyone is inside, hiding from the gangs and other sources of violence that make people afraid to leave their homes—yet ultimately, like Laura, drive them to make the dangerous journey north.

Similarly, 16-year-old Javier, from San Miguel, El Salvador, drew a picture of his hometown that was calm and peaceful, with a church at the center. It is less realistic than Laura's, with a volcano also in the center that is about the same size as the church, and several other images that could seem out of place—what appears to be a ladybug that is roughly the same size as the church, a small truck driving up the road to the church, and a small person to the side of the bug, waving and smiling. Like Laura's, there is a row of mountains in the background, and a smiling sun peeking up over the mountains. One note of contrast is an airplane flying overhead, perhaps indicating Javier's desire to leave San Miguel. Like Laura's, the drawing encompasses a range of feelings, at which we can only guess, but that seem connected to a longing for stability and order that their homes at one point in time provided. The drawings do not negate the possibility of fear but also do not demonize their homes or portray the U.S. as an inherently better place.

While Javier's person is smiling, his diminutive size, a feature of other drawings as well, indicates the children's sense of their own lack of control over their environments. This disempowerment becomes more intense in the drawings depicting crossings of rivers. While the kids may or may not have been aware of the significance of national borders, they are clearly aware that the dangers of the journey intensify at these key places. The self is small, as we see in a picture by seven-year-old Dayana of her crossing the Rio Grande on a raft with her mother, in which she makes herself tiny.

In his picture entitled "El Barco," five-year-old Fredy from Guatemala draws the boat he and his mother used to cross the Usumacinta River dividing Guatemala and Mexico (see figure 2.1). The jagged red lines traversing a more subdued, mottled brown and blue indicate his intense feeling. We could name it fear and recall Sara Ahmed's description of what happens to the body: "Fear projects us from the present into a future. But the feeling of fear presses us into a future as an intense bodily experience in the present. One sweats, one's heart races, one's whole body becomes a space of unpleasant intensity" (65). The feeling of fear is

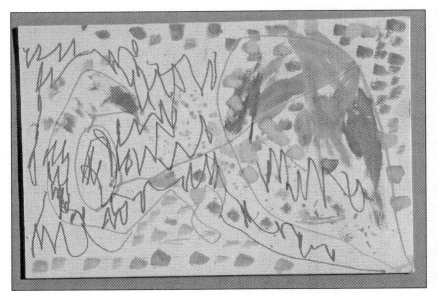

Figure 2.1. "El Barco," by Fredy, *Arte de Lagrimas* exhibit, Austin, TX.

both connected to the sense of immediate bodily vulnerability and to the threat of the unknown; for a child, both of these may be more intense than for an adult—a sense of physical vulnerability due to smallness, for example, and to a greater fear of the unknown because the future is so uncertain. We name this conflagration of feelings "fear," but for Fredy, it is likely much more complicated than that, perhaps too intense to name but all the more felt because of the intensity. As Massumi describes it, "The body doesn't just absorb pulses or discrete stimulations; it infolds *contexts*, it infolds volitions and cognitions that are nothing if not situated" (90).

One can sense this uncertainty and complexity as well in other drawings, such as Maybeline's "La Culebra in Desierto." In four-year-old Maybeline's drawing, the cobra she saw in the desert on her 14-day journey from El Salvador is rendered with red jagged lines not unlike Fredy's boat. It appears coiled, ready to strike, with an angry eye above a harsh mouth (see figure 2.2). Fear can be connected to another feeling—anxiety—insofar as there is a convergence around the fear of loss, especially the loss of a loved one. "Anxiety," says Ahmed, "comes in part from love, for the (m)other, as a love that can be taken away, as the taking away of that which secures the subject's relation to the world" (67). The kids likely have left loved ones behind in Guatemala. Furthermore, they may experience the loss of another loved one during the journey, or at the border crossing—this is seen in four-year-old Ashley Gabriela's depiction of her father not being able to cross into the U.S. with her and her mother. Their bodies are floating, as if there is no foundation or grounding, indicating a sense of instability and insecurity. As described in the exhibit brochure, Ashley Gabriela told a volunteer while she was drawing that "this is my dad—he has strong hands." Because she associates her father with strength and caring, his loss likely causes a heightened anxiety about the present and the future—insofar as she may fear losing her other parent (see figure 2.3).

The act of drawing can help the artist process a difficult experience; the goal is not to name and categorize it but rather just to express it, in any form. The process is just as if not more important than the final product. The very act of creation may allow difficult feelings to emerge in nonverbal form, and adults can help in this process, without saying much at all. For example, seven-year-old Dayana began drawing what

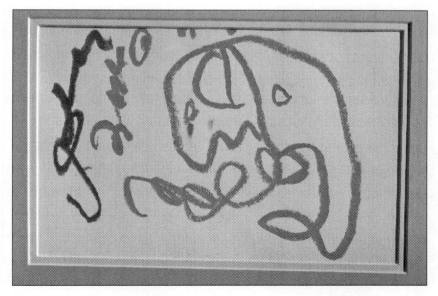

Figure 2.2. "La Culebra in Desierto," by Maybeline, *Arte de Lagrimas* exhibit, Austin, TX.

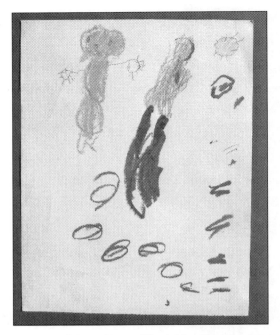

Figure 2.3. "Manos Fuertos," by Ashley Gabriela, *Arte de Lagrimas* exhibit, Austin, TX.

happened on her and her mother's journey from Guatemala—she made a long, black road on the left side of the paper to illustrate the first stages of the journey, by car and bus, both of which are drawn at the top of the road. It seems the bus brought them to the U.S.-Mexico border, where they had to cross in a raft—represented on the right side of the paper as a circle with two small people on top, afloat in a river. Gregory Cuellar asked as Dayana drew: "Did anyone say good-bye to you?" At this point, Dayana drew a picture of her aunt on the riverbank, waving good-bye. Then this exchange transpired: "'Was there anyone else?' asked Gregory. Not saying anything, she removed the rosary from around her neck and traced the crucifix over the Rio Grande. She then began to sing a hymn, "En la Cruz" (On the cross): "En la Cruz, en la Cruz, yo primero vi la luz, y las manchas de mi alma yo lavé, fue allí por fe yo vi a Jesús, y siempre feliz con El seré." A key moment in Cuellar's rendering of the encounter is the sentence "Not saying anything, she removed the rosary. . . .'"

We can hypothesize that Dayana does not feel like answering Gregory's question with words but rather with a symbol that for her holds powerful meaning and memories, and then with a song that communicates the faith in Jesus that helped them cross the river on a raft. Here, "fear" does not encompass or capture Dayana's experience; something more spiritual and abstract emerges from the material practice of drawing. Dayana seems to feel confident that Gregory will understand.

A similar pattern is seen in the description of Maybeline's encounter with the volunteer Nohemi. When Nohemi asks her what she saw on her trip, the four-year-old does not answer but proceeds to draw. Only while drawing does she respond, "I saw a cobra"; we can assume that the act of drawing enables the description of the experience. Similarly, it is while she is drawing that Ashley says how she feels about her father not being able to cross the border with her—"he has strong hands." His hands stand out because they are drawn in pencil and not colors like the bodies of herself and her father. The pencil-sketched hands embody Ashley's feelings about her father—they are what she remembers, and

Figure 2.4. "Amor," by Lesli, *Arte de Lagrimas* exhibit, Austin, TX.

what she misses, and what she longs for, even as, sketched in pencil, they are fading.

The creative act produces expressions that seem more important to the children than the product itself. For example, five-year-old Lesli drew a picture of three hearts and called it "Amor" (see figure 2.4). We learn from the brief synopsis that "before she boarded her bus, she ran to volunteer Nohemi and gave her a hug and a kiss. She also gave her this picture, saying, "'es amor.'" For Lesli, it seems, the feelings generated by making the drawing compel her to share it rather than claim it as her own. The meaning is partially produced by the very ephemerality of the art.

The paradox noted by Cvetkovich is that while is it crucial to document and archive the cultural productions of marginalized subjects, doing so risks a form of institutionalization that threatens to reify the art. The drawings that hang on the walls of whatever institutions house the exhibit are inevitably divorced from the children's lives, as well as from their moment of production. This moment is the one that holds the most meaning for the artist; the value is not in possession of the product but, as Lesli demonstrates, in the act of drawing and then giving. What matters to Lesli is not the piece of paper but rather the feeling that the drawing exudes and that it can convey when given to someone.

The paradox intensifies: if the Rev. Cuellar had not gathered the drawings and put together the exhibit, no one else would be affected by them. They might have been thrown away, or carried around by the child or a parent or friend for a short while until too crumpled to keep. Importantly, the archive also gathers the drawings, such that they become documents of a group's affective lives—not just the random expression of a single child. Only when concretized to some degree can the artwork circulate, affecting viewers in other locations, perhaps eventually having some kind of influence on wider perceptions of refugee children (their struggles are specific, but they are kids not unlike "our own"). It is only adults, in this situation, who have the power and access to disseminate the art, and thus the kids are reliant on them to circulate their expressions, to create an "archive of feelings."

3

"I Hate You, Dunel Trump"

Anger or Civility?

On the morning of November 8, 2016, I shared an unenviable task with millions of other U.S. parents: telling my child that Donald Trump had defeated Hillary Clinton to become the nation's 45th president.

My eight-year-old son's reaction was immediate and visceral: "I want to push him off a cliff!"

"Well...," I said, then hesitated, understanding the reaction but not sure whether to encourage such an angry response. I settled for something like "I can see why you're angry. I am too." Ezra then expressed a range of other feelings, from fear ("Is he going to kill all black people?") to uncertainty ("Is he going to visit my school?") to sorrow ("I feel sorry for Hillary").

I checked my email shortly after this conversation and found a message from Ezra's school principal directing concerned parents to a *Huffington Post* column by Ali Michael entitled "What Do We Tell Our Children?" It contained specific, practical advice. "Tell them, first, that we will protect them," she said. "Tell them, second, that you will honor the outcome of the election, but that you will fight bigotry." And third: "Teach them how to be responsible members of a civic society. Teach them how to engage in discussion—not for the sake of winning, but for the sake of understanding and being understood."

I rebelled. I didn't want to honor the outcome; neither did I believe, nor had I for a long time, that we live in a "civic society," or that teaching our children to "engage in discussion" would actually lead to social justice, not only for biracial children like Ezra but for any child outside the mainstream. I am far from certain that I will be able to protect him from the virulently racist, misogynistic, homophobic, sexist policies of the Trump administration.

Michael's article is typical of the many news articles that described and responded to children's responses to the 2016 election and continue to the current moment—voicing concern but wanting to reassure them that they are safe, that the democratic process is still in place, and to correct misinformation that might have been disseminated by the president himself. Due to widespread exposure to different kinds of media and Trump's Twitter-driven presidency, young children are likely regularly exposed to news emanating from and around the Trump regime.

The news is confusing to many people, and kids between the ages of five and nine likely need help from adults in processing the information and their feelings. Yet too often, this assistance comes in the form of a kind of reassurance intended to teach kids the rules of "civility" that ostensibly undergird the democratic process. Implicitly, this approach argues that reason will triumph over emotions, that Trump's excesses can be explained as just that—an anomaly within an otherwise rational process. In the first part of this chapter, I analyze the discourse of civility—which goes under the name of "niceness" in elementary schools—as it appears in kids' letters to Trump about the election. Teachers and parents advocating letter writing do so as an exercise to help kids process and name their emotions in a manner that makes them feel like they can do something within the system. This approach amounts to another version of the "emotional intelligence" paradigm I described in the introduction, in which kids learn that it is fine to feel strongly about things as long as you learn how to properly express (and control) those feelings. In the second part of this chapter, I turn to three locations in which teachers gave kids the opportunity to say and especially draw whatever they want; in these cultural productions, I find a much greater affective range, illustrating feelings of anger, fear, and hatred in a manner that does not adhere to the discourse of niceness.

This chapter also speaks to the ambiguous position younger children occupy when it comes to political situations. I argued in the last chapter that refugee children are paradoxically treated by immigration officials as too immature to have political opinions and yet also as risks to national security. In a similarly contradictory fashion, young children responding to the Trump victory are treated as too young to understand the situation fully and yet in need of political education, as they represent the "future of the nation." Teachers and parents surveyed after the election by various media and civil rights groups expressed a quandary about how to both protect and educate elementary school children expressing anxieties about what would happen under the Trump administration.

Child psychologists use a developmental model to explain why young children are not ready to process political information. *Newsweek*, for example, ran a column by Barbara Milrod (2017), identified as a "child and adolescent psychiatrist and psychoanalyst with expertise in anxiety disorders," who drew on Jean Piaget's model to argue that before "third or fourth grade," children are not yet capable of understanding "cause and effect" relations, and thus "magical (nonrational) explanations predominate." Without the ability to process information and events rationally, says Milrod, children's fears and anxieties can grow, causing physical reactions such as stomachaches and sleep disorders. Her main example is a six-year-old named Lucy, who while standing at a bus stop with her babysitter heard a man shouting at others, "Watch out, you're all going to be deported," and who then missed three days of school with a stomachache.

It is curious that Milrod would choose this example, since Lucy's fears are not irrational nor her bodily reaction exaggerated. Many people have been deported since Trump took office, some while waiting at bus stops. In this chapter, I show how kids' artwork, especially regarding immigration issues, indicates that kids understand what might and can happen under Trump. Their drawings illustrate the "structure of feeling" that animates childhood in the U.S. under Trump—especially childhood for immigrant and Muslim children, as well as children who might appear to be immigrants or Muslims and are similarly at risk of racial profiling.

Kids' responses to Trump do not occur in a vacuum; they are shaped and mediated by well-meaning adults who want to help them through a difficult time. There are varying degrees and kinds of mediation, from those that are heavily shaped by a belief in civic discourse to those that are more open-ended. The former, not surprisingly, are more invested in helping children manage their emotions, both for the sake of the kids themselves and for the "team"—the classroom, or the nation. Those adults providing more open-ended prompts are more willing to let children express anything they feel; though their goal may still be a kind of management of feelings that derives from a cathartic outpouring, the kids' responses are more likely to reveal their insights into the political situation—insights that demonstrate children are far savvier about Trump than some adults want to acknowledge.

YouTube and the Home

A stock feature of the classic television show *Candid Camera*, which first aired in 1948 and continued for almost 30 years, were the everyday antics of kids. Host Alan Funt would narrate as a hidden camera captured a child doing something cute or sneaky—like offering "outrageous" explanations for certain events or trying to explain why they took a cookie from the plate left out for Santa and his reindeer.

No doubt, YouTube has given kids more control over their self-representation, especially older kids, who can make and post their own videos on YouTube and other platforms. Yet the issue of self-representation remains problematic for younger children who are subject to their parents' preoccupation with documenting everyday life and who have little or no say about which images are posted. As Patricia Lange describes it, "YouTube can feel like a giant, networked family album. It is filled with images of young children in daily life" (2014, 126). In her ethnography of kids using and being represented on YouTube, Lange found that "in some cases, adults felt very comfortable distributing an array of highly personal images, whereas several kids were more circumspect about how their images should be shared online" (157). Growing up in these "heavily mediated environments," says Lange, means that kids are becoming media literate from a very young age. Yet it also raises a number of ethical questions about the space of the home, privacy, and children's rights. For one, YouTube may decide on its own to advertise on a parent's channel, meaning their kids' images are being used for advertising purposes without their knowledge. For another, parents post images of their kids online for millions of people to view without the kids' permission and perhaps without considering the short- or long-term implications. Lange recounts numerous such examples, such as the situation of a mother and daughter who together posted a video of the 16-year-old dancing that was then reposted, without their permission, to a pornographic website. Lange points to the complex and often understudied relationship between production, distribution, and reception: "In the initial playful moments of mediated recording, certain behavior was coded as acceptable. In contrast, during specific mediated moments of viewership and image-appropriation, media makers reconsidered their behavior. But not all participants have the knowledge, world experience, or agency to reflect on how their image is being used online" (164).

Among these participants are younger children, Lange notes, whose private moments, such as watching television in their underwear, are recorded for their "cuteness," then circulated to thousands of viewers. While parents may defend their postings as authentic moments of family life, Lange asks, "What are one's obligations to one's children, whose human images are represented in a media that may exist in perpetuity online?" (176). Perhaps the ethics of posting kids' images online is not even considered because kids themselves will not be in a position to protest in a way that adults will be compelled to listen to (even though many kids do protest having their pictures taken). Adults know best, in other words; or "they're just kids." In its most egregious form, condescending attitudes toward kids take the form of good-natured ridicule, as in "kids say the darnedest things." This form of comedy occurs even within serious political situations, such as Donald Trump's electoral victory.

One such example occurred on the Jimmy Kimmel talk show two days after the 2016 presidential election.[1] Kimmel began the segment of his late-night show on a respectful note, saying, "We've heard from a lot of people about this election so far—we've heard from pundits and surrogates and experts and anchors. But we haven't yet heard from kids." So, he explains, that afternoon they went outside their studio and asked kids on the streets what were their feelings about the election results. The first kid, a boy of about ten, says he feels "iffy" about Trump because "he's really rude." The second kid, another boy of about the same age, says he feels "not really comfortable, but the world keeps moving on." So far, so good. The third child, however, is a younger boy, of perhaps seven or eight, and the interviewer gets more specific, asking him, "What was the face you made?" upon hearing Trump had won. The boy responds, "I made an angry face," and the interviewer says, "Let me see." The boy pinches together his eyebrows and glares, upon which the audience breaks out into laughter. The process then becomes more facetious when the interviewer approaches a young girl and her baby sister in a two-seater stroller and says, "Do you like Donald Trump?" at which point the baby begins to cry, again prompting audience laughter.

Other kids reveal they know a fair amount about Trump, but still their responses meet with laughter. When two brothers are asked, "What do you think Donald Trump should do?" the younger one, perhaps eight, says, "He should clean up the whole earth," and the older one, ten or 11, says, "He should be a plumber because he gets dirty, and he has to clean the toilets." This boy puts Trump in the position of the people who work in his hotels. When asked to do an impression of Trump, a boy of about 12 says in a husky tone, "I'm Donald Trump, and I'm the best person in the world, and Hillary Clinton sucks."

In the last interview, a boy of about 11 or 12 (wearing a *Minecraft* T-shirt) is asked if he would want Donald Trump to be his dad, and he responds, "Of course not." The interviewer asks, "Why not?" And the boy responds, "He might murder my mom." The boy speaks without smiling, clearly not intending to be funny, but the audience laughs. Of course, much of the blame lies not with the audience but with the *Jimmy Kimmel Live* producers and their decision to frame kids' responses in a comedic fashion. In another context, a child saying he was afraid that the president could murder his mother would not be considered funny.

Yet this is exactly the point: why are children's responses to political situations considered fodder for comedy? On the surface, it would seem that the very idea that children can assess political candidates is ludicrous enough to generate a laugh. In this case, we also could posit—since the overall tone of the Kimmel show is critical of Trump—that the audience is dealing with its own anxieties about Trump's sexism and crudeness by laughing, all the while inwardly squirming. This reading, however, still views the children's feelings through adults' emotions, suggesting that the latter are more important and that the former can be sacrificed in the interest of the adult production. In short, the children do not laugh. Why does the audience?

This uncomfortable gap is widened when one considers the YouTube video compilations responding to Kimmel's original on-the-street interviews. One YouTuber, a man named Noah Fish, posted a "Hey Jimmy Kimmel! I Told My Kids the 2016 Election Results" video that showed kids' intense reactions to the news that Trump had won—ranging from extreme crying to anger to disbelief.[2] Many of the kids are quite distraught, and many are also quite young—two- and three-year-olds cry and scream. A boy of about five, looking very scared, kneels on the floor and appears to be on the verge of tears: "I'm just trying to calm down," he says.

Here, the humor apparently derives from kids' overreactions—they fall onto the floor or rush at the camera, clearly intending to hit the parent. The audience laughs at each example, and the posted comments range from "LOL. Even the kids hate Trump" to "Kids opinions don't really matter." The video received 1.4 million views and 18,000 "likes." What is revealed as well in the comments is that this video is a fake—it was originally aired as kids' responses to parents eating their Halloween candy—and Fish has just substituted a new voiceover. The idea is that kids overreact, whether that be to the presidential election or to parents eating their Halloween candy. In other words, the situation is no longer political when kids are involved, and the manipulation of the video is not considered an ethical breach or a violation of privacy but rather a source of humor.

The Downside of Civics

Other media accounts reported more matter-of-factly on children's fears, though still with the assumption that these fears are exaggerated because kids don't fully understand, along the lines I described above in relation to the psychologist Milrod. For example, three journalists writing for *The Atlantic* interviewed forty public-school teachers and counselors after the election and concluded that "rhetoric from the election had transformed in the children's minds into doomsday scenarios." The use of the term "doomsday" suggests the kids are overreacting, which is elaborated by the magazine's choice of quotes:

> "Are we going to be sent back to the places we were born tomorrow?" one 8-year-old reportedly asked Angela B., a music teacher at a school in southwest Philadelphia. Angela is white, but virtually all of her students are children of color, and many fear Trump's election means instant deportation or worse. "I'm going to die today," a first-grader at his school said as he got out of his family's car Wednesday morning. He'd heard that as president, Trump would push a button and send a bomb that would

blow everyone up. Aly A., who teaches science at a high-poverty and predominantly black middle school in Miami, said two students on separate occasions asked her whether the new presidential administration would reinstate slavery. "Can you keep me safe?" a fifth-grade black girl asked. (Deruy, Wong, and Glatter 2016)

The Philadelphia teacher, Angela Bower, explained that the kids "see the speeches and they hear the sound bites and they don't necessarily have a ton of context for how the political process works. So to a kid, if someone says 'I'm going to deport people' and then they win the presidency, they don't necessarily understand what sort of steps would have to be taken to do that" (quoted in Deruy, Wong, and Glatter 2016).

This was a common theme in educators' suggestions for how to reassure children: explain to them the political process. It's unclear, however, why explaining the process would be reassuring since the process itself is what had led to Trump's election. What is missing from many of these accounts is the possibility that children could be critical of and angered by the fact that, in some situations, Trump would be able to act to hurt people. In fact, Trump *had* acted immediately to step up deportations. As much of the art produced by Latino children reveals (see below), their understanding of the political situation was quite accurate and deserves to be immediately and openly addressed rather than deferred or skirted, which, it seems, could create more confusion and anxiety.

Adults may think younger children are not ready to understand such situations. However, the problem with a developmental approach is that it assumes, as does Milford, universal, generalized stages of development. If compelled to process information and deal with certain situations, kids may well be able to do so: it's not that brain and body don't factor in, but rather that the brain is malleable, subject to different rates of development given different situations, as I argued in the introduction and chapter 1. The kids' artwork I discuss here indicates that kids in some neighborhoods are being forced to deal with the threat of deportation; one child whose picture is on display at a Houston museum, for example, included in their mixed-media piece black-and-white copies of instructions for what to do if ICE comes to your door ("Do not open the door; remain silent; do not sign anything; report and record").[3] This picture illustrates how Raymond Williams's structure of feeling works;

as I said in the introduction, the weight and force of institutions is felt through the embodied, affective experiences of everyday life. In this picture, one cannot disarticulate the artist's thoughts about ICE and America from their feelings about possible deportation.

By contrast, the dominant assumptions are the following: that young children are unable to keep their emotions in check and thus likely to exaggerate situations rather than seeing them realistically (read rationally). Then, when children are considered old enough to be taught to manage their emotions, they are also considered old enough to prove their ability to rationally understand (rather than letting their understanding be impeded by emotions). This set of assumptions governs not only the above examples of "exaggerated fears" but also the emphasis on teaching kids the discourse of civility, which is based on rationality. This discourse has formed a substantial component of the pedagogical response to Trump—to show children that even in the face of such bombast, they should not stoop to such a level but rather maintain civility—or, for younger children, "niceness." This response is part of an attempt to reassure children that the democratic process is still in place, even if Trump does not represent it. Herein lies one of the ways in which teachers and parents fail to directly address children's fears in a way that might, in the long run, produce more systemic change. In fact, Trump's victory indicates a problem with the democratic procedure: how can someone so blatantly hateful, so antithetical to notions of equality, still get elected? This is neither a rational nor an emotional question but rather a matter of feeling in thought and thought in feeling.

Democracy's emphasis on civility gets translated into niceness for young children. To be nice is to be "collegial, egalitarian, nonhierarchical, and able to work well with others," argues Adeline Koh in her essay on community building (2014, 95). She elaborates:

> This concept of civility has its origins in Western conceptualizations of liberal democracy. Mentions of "civility" immediately evoke associations with the historical emergence of "civil society" in Europe, which implies a domain of private citizens with a certain degree of autonomy from the state. In major narratives of the European and American revolutions of the seventeenth and eighteenth centuries, the empowerment of civil society and the emergence of critical reason have been linked to the historical

development of modern democracy. In the majority of these accounts of the genealogy of the concept, civility is considered an integral element of a well-functioning democracy, as a robust civil society creates a well-informed citizenry who make better voting choices, participate more in politics, and hold government more accountable. (97)

This series of associations is what Michael, Bowers, and other teachers invoke as the answer to Trump—teach students to be critical readers of the media, to reject his inflated rhetoric, to work within the system, and to counter his bombast with a more reasoned discourse.

However, the dark underside of these invocations, observes Koh, is the violence imposed in the name of civilization: "While civility has been held up as a model component for modern democracies, the term has also been used in service of the extremely violent histories of slavery and imperialism, begging the question as to whether the imposition of civility is actually civil by its own definition." She notes the work of postcolonial and race theorists who "have documented the ways that race demarcates the boundaries of fragmented forms of citizenship for those who are deemed categorically uncivil through skin color and culture" (97) as well as feminists who have shown how the social contract functions as a sexual contract, keeping women in their place. Similarly, when teachers insist that democracy is still functioning in the U.S., they cover up the fact that ongoing histories of racism and sexism are what enabled Trump to win. His victory is not an anomaly but rather a sign of unaddressed inequalities.

"Niceness" is not exactly an emotion but rather a mode of behavior, a way to manage one's emotions; being nice is a way of proving that you are better than the person who has made you feel bad because you can govern your emotions and demonstrate your rationality by keeping your body under control. If everyone in the classroom can act nicely, then it will function better, and this becomes the model for citizenship. It intersects with the more general management of emotions that I discuss in the next chapter that has assumed greater importance through the valorization of emotional intelligence. Niceness is a way to cultivate rational discourse, in which everyone follows the rules and respects each other. This model, then, helps people feel happy—the good emotions flourish, and the bad emotions are weeded out. As Sara Ahmed puts it: "The hierarchy between emotion and thought/reason gets displaced, of course, into a hierarchy between emotions: some emotions are 'elevated' as signs of cultivation, whilst others remain 'lower' as signs of weakness.... If good emotions are cultivated, then they remain defined against uncultivated or unruly emotions, which frustrate the formation of the competent self. Those who are 'other' to me or us, or those that threaten to make us other, remain the source of bad feeling in this model of emotional intelligence" (3–4). Ironically, Trump became the "source of bad feeling" over the course of the campaign and in the aftermath of the election, which presented teachers with an unsettling dilemma: how to teach children that the president himself was impeding the development of the "competent self"? Teachers and parents struggled to help children identify his flaws while still being civil, or, in elementary school parlance, "nice."

In pursuit of civility, Molly Spence Sahebjami, mother of a five-year-old son, set up a Facebook page called "Dear President Trump: Letters from Kids about Kindness." Her plan, she told *The Huffington Post*, was to "invite parents to join her Facebook group and have their kids write positive, non-partisan letters to the president-elect, explaining the importance of being kind to others." Sahebjami added, "It's a patriotic thing, and such an American thing, for kids to write letters to their president, expressing their hopes for the nation. These are our future voters" (quoted in Herreria 2016). Within days, thousands of people joined the private group, posting photos of their children's letters and sharing them on social media with the hashtag #KidsLettersToTrump.[4]

Given Sahebjami's invitation, it's not surprising that the majority of these letters fit Koh's definition of civil discourse, focusing on manners, kindness, not calling names, and so forth. Very few raise issues of race, gender, or sexuality, though a number reference immigration. Many appear to be mediated in some manner by adults, as they begin with carefully penned salutations and end with polite closings. For example, five-year-old Brynne writes: "Be nice, Donald Trump. Be kind. Take care of our earth. Don't take our toys. And please don't call people stupid or other mean names. Thank you. Sincerely, Brynne." Only the child's name is in her handwriting, with scrawled letters topped by a rainbow; the body of the letter is neatly printed. One child drew a rainbow and underneath wrote the words, "Dear Mr. Trump. Be kind. Please." Six-year-old

Figure 3.1. Avery, age six, *Huffington Post*, February 27, 2017.

Avery writes, "Dear President elect Trump, Please be kind and let the love shine through. Love, Avery." Avery's letter is adorned with a heart, a rainbow, two trees, and a place setting (see figure 3.1).

Some of the kids whose parents posted their letters on the Facebook page were more direct, telling Trump bluntly that they were scared or sad and occasionally mentioning race or gender, though they still professed hope for the nation. Nine-year-old Ada writes: "I love my country so please don't tear it apart. I would like it if you treat everyone with kindness, love, respect, and equality. Please make everyone hold hands not frown at each other. I have friends who are African American and I don't want anything to happen to them. Can you make things more affordable? I hope this letters helps you." Three flowers decorate the bottom of Ada's letter.

The letters remain within the terms of respectful letter writing, holding out hope that Trump will listen to them while cautiously expressing their fears. Abby, age six, writes: "Kids in my class are very scared. Please don't kick them out. In my school, we get sent to the wall when we're in trouble. My friends did not do anything wrong. Don't send them to the wall. Love, Abby Fones. Age 6." She adds a face with scared-looking eyes, and an open mouth with a balloon that says "Please." Another child writes, "Dear Donald Trump, Can you please be nicer to the poor and the Mexican people? Help people with brown skin." Another writes, "Don't you trust in women?" and is signed, "Sincerely, Alex Vanek, Chicago." Eight-year-old Charlotte writes, "Dear President Elect Trump, The morning that I herd you became present I cryed because I thought that you won't be fair to women. But please please prove me wrong. Hopeful Charlotte 8."

The intersection of niceness, civility, and the management of emotions further plays out in the public-school system in its emphasis on objectivity and nonpartisanship. Teachers either truly believe it is their obligation to provide information about the U.S. government without taking sides, or they fear the consequences of taking a position, even if they realize it's very difficult if not impossible to be objective. These tensions are illustrated in many news accounts of the campaign and the postelection fallout, in which teachers are interviewed about how they are helping their students process the results. In an article in *The Atlantic*, for example, published the July before the election, writer Emily Richmond (2016) reports on an anti-Trump petition started by two third graders, Micah and Alexis, in Newton, Massachusetts. She puts the petition in this context:

> But national civics experts, educators, and researchers say the actions of Micah and Alexis are indicative of a wider trend—and some significant issues—for public schools. A recent survey of teachers found many are struggling to reassure students, particularly those from immigrant and Muslim families, who are frightened about what a Trump victory in November might mean for them. . . . At the same time, educators report they are afraid to violate school district policies that prohibit political advocacy in the classroom. They also worry about alienating families that might hold divergent viewpoints. On the upside, there's a chance this could spur great civic engagement by young people—but at what price?

While even young students like Micah and Alexis are becoming politically active, says Richmond, that activist optimism seems to pale in comparison to the anxiety and fear many students are feeling, and the threats they are experiencing from other students. Richmond describes a preelection survey conducted by the Southern Poverty Law Center of 2,000 teachers that found the following:[5]

> More than two-thirds of the teachers reported that students—mainly immigrants, children of immigrants and Muslims—have expressed concerns or fears about what might happen to them or their families after the election.
> More than half have seen an increase in uncivil political discourse.
> More than one-third have observed an increase in anti-Muslim or anti-immigrant sentiment.
> More than 40 percent are hesitant to teach about the election.

The SPLC found, for example, the following situation: "In Tennessee, a kindergarten teacher says a Latino child—told by classmates that he will be deported and trapped behind a wall—asks every day, 'Is the wall here yet?'" African-American children asked if they would be "deported back to Africa." Muslim children worried that if Trump was elected, they would have microchips implanted under their skin. By contrast, some students have been "emboldened" by the so-called Trump effect: "some are using the word Trump as a taunt or as a chant as they gang up on others. Muslim children are being called *terrorist* or *ISIS* or *bomber*."

The situation became more dire, not surprisingly, after the election. In a follow-up postelection survey, the SPLC found the following:[6]

> Nine out of 10 educators who responded have seen a negative impact on students' mood and behavior following the election; most of them worry about the continuing impact for the remainder of the school year.
> Eight in 10 report heightened anxiety on the part of marginalized students, including immigrants, Muslims, African Americans and LGBT students.
> Four in 10 have heard derogatory language directed at students of color, Muslims, immigrants and people based on gender or sexual orientation.

Half said that students were targeting each other based on which candidate they'd supported.

Although two-thirds report that administrators have been "responsive," four out of 10 don't think their schools have action plans to respond to incidents of hate and bias.

Over 2,500 educators described specific incidents of bigotry and harassment that can be directly traced to election rhetoric. These incidents include graffiti (including swastikas), assaults on students and teachers, property damage, fights and threats of violence.

Because of the heightened emotion, half are hesitant to discuss the election in class. Some principals have told teachers to refrain from discussing or addressing the election in any way.

How do teachers address these volatile conditions when they are supposed to remain politically neutral? Both Richmond in her interviews and the SPLC survey's authors found that many teachers are deeply conflicted. Here's how the preelection SPLC report put it: "Two responses from teachers illustrate their dilemma. A teacher in Arlington, Virginia, says, 'I try to not bring it up since it is so stressful for my students.' Another, in Indianapolis, says, 'I am at a point where I'm going to take a stand even if it costs me my position.'" The report comments that "the avoidance often arises from a desire to maintain civility and keep kids safe and calm." One high school teacher in Utah told the SPLC that "I try to be more careful—rather than stoke the fires." The SPLC urges teachers to use "instances of incivility as teaching moments, and to support the children who are hurt, confused and frightened by what they're hearing from the candidates."

The question remains, though, as to whether the public-school system, in most places, will facilitate a less than civil critique of the government—a critique that embraces rather than undermines children's skepticism about the president. The real teaching moment might come not just in pointing out Trump's rudeness but also in encouraging students not to grant the president's office an inherent respect or assume its holder is usually honest and ethical. The "uncivil" truth is that there is hierarchy and injustice within democracy and that all presidents, at one time or another, abuse their power. Many letters suggest that children are being taught to still respect the office if not its current holder. First grader Nicole, for example, writes, "Dear Mr. Trump, Please be onist and kind. I hope you wile not cause any fights. Beetwen people that or not borin in owir own country. I think if you do ol these rooles you wile be a wandirfl presidet. Love Nicole."[7] And Szaba writes, "Dear Mr. President, Be nice to things. Do not say mean things. This helps me calm down: meditation, reading, and resting. Good luck with your new job! Let me know if I can help."

In expressing their hope that Trump will listen to them, the kids demonstrate that they are learning to be good citizens; their teachers are therefore succeeding in imparting the civics lesson of belief in the system. In addition, adults might encourage students to question the system that allowed Trump to win, and to ask: what has been done in the name of "civilization"? It might be that kids are already asking that question, in different terms, due to what is happening in their lives.

Deconstructing the Wall

Throughout the campaign and in the aftermath of the election, Ezra frequently asked me: "Why does he want to build a wall?" It was an image that was concrete, disturbing, and inexplicable. It was a "structure of feeling," insofar as it represented "the specificity of present being, the inalienably physical, within which we may indeed discern and acknowledge institutions, formations, positions, but not always as fixed products, defining products" (Williams 1977, 128). A wall is an imposing physical structure, familiar to kids as something that keeps them out of places they are not supposed to go as well as keeping them within places that are ostensibly safe. Yet it can also be a site of punishment, as emphasized by the six-year-old who wrote to Trump: "In my school, we get sent to the wall when we're in trouble. My friends did not do anything wrong. Don't send them to the wall." The very notion of the wall elicits a strong sense of injustice and unfairness.

In this section, I focus on three examples of kids' affective resistance to Trump: a set of pictures collected by an elementary school teacher in Austin, Texas, that was subsequently published by *The Huffington Post*;[8] a set of drawings submitted to a Houston art museum, also from an elementary school in Texas, after the museum issued a request for art related to Trump; and a set of artwork from a Philadelphia program that sponsored a workshop in which kids were encouraged to express their feelings about Trump through art.[9] Cumulatively, these collections function as an "archive of feelings" that represents and also transcends the individual child; they bring a certain materiality to the often fleeting and forgotten feelings that children express. In the Houston exhibit, all the drawings have the word "anonymous" on them, powerfully creating an archive of feelings based on a collective rather than individual consciousness.

In contrast to the adult mediation in the Facebook examples, it appears that these drawings were encouraged through much more open-ended prompts. In the Austin situation, for example, the teacher invited her students to "write or draw what they were feeling" after an immigration raid in the city shortly after Trump took office (quoted in Carro and Planas 2017). In the case of the Houston exhibit, curators Randall Kallinen and John Paul Hartman told *The Houston Chronicle* that they put out a request for "work relating to Donald Trump"; to their surprise, they "received a whole bunch of art from elementary school children on the topic of immigration policy." Kallinen said "the art came from various parts of Texas and was hand-delivered to him by someone whose identity he chose not reveal" (quoted in Ramirez 2017).

At the workshop run by the Mighty Writers in Philadelphia, the organization's director, Tim Whitaker, said he and his staff noticed that in the weeks leading up to the election, the Mexican American kids were getting "increasingly anxious," and that anxiety grew exponentially after Trump won, as the kids attended community meetings where their families were being advised what to do if the parents got detained by Immigration and Customs Enforcement (ICE). So the Mighty Writers hired Nora Litz, a Mexican American artist, to help the kids develop stories and pictures that described how their families came to be in the U.S. and how they were feeling about the election. Whitaker says the kids were relieved to be expressing their feelings rather than hiding "in the shadows." He describes them as being "more angry about it than sorrowful" (quoted in Palan 2017). Whitaker's wording suggests he himself considered anger to be a valid response to the election; this stands in contrast to an emphasis on niceness.

These three collections also stand in partial contrast to the letters because they center on the image; while most also have some words, the

Figure 3.2. Osvaldo, age seven, Mighty Writers' Workshop, Philadelphia. *Philly.com*, June 12, 2017.

focus is on the art itself. This allows the kids to circumvent some of the codes of rationality that require a certain kind of language (such as the polite salutation and the closing). The question at hand is not what kind of language is necessary to show a proper understanding of how to communicate disagreement with the president but rather how does one feel, in this time and place. To quote Williams again, "not feeling against thought, but thought as felt and feeling as thought." For example, Zara, age eight, drew a picture of a family in front in front of their house, with a dark foreboding sky in the background. One child in the picture is saying: "We feel that our families will be separated." And another says: "My sister and I feel pressure when we watch the news." Zara is expressing her thoughts about her feelings, and vice versa, in a manner that makes the question of exaggeration superfluous. The same can be surmised from these four drawings:

Osvaldo, age seven, Philadelphia: "Don't eat me Donald Trump." Osvaldo may or may not think Trump could eat him, but that's not the point. The image conveys Osvaldo's feelings of being overwhelmed and threatened, in a visceral way, by someone who has the power to make him disappear (see figure 3.2).

From Houston: "I wish Donald Trump was in prison for 76 years." A large red circular figure smiles broadly at a stick figure of Trump behind bars. The picture is signed, "Anonymous (seriously)" (see figure 3.3).

From Houston: "We want America to be full of immigrants from every country so we can be a great natin," says a child who calls himself "nobody." The child adds: "In your face, Donald Trump." This last expression would not be allowed in a "proper" letter to the president, yet for this child, there is no contradiction between expressing a patriotic sentiment and then dismissing the president's authority.

Jonathan, age six, Philadelphia: an ICE agent saying, "Te voy a llevar a la carcel" ("I'm taking you to jail") and a person marked "Mexico"

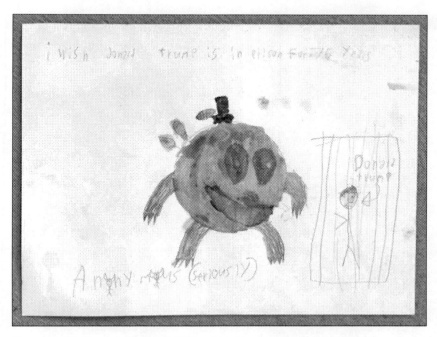

Figure 3.3. "Anonymous (seriously)," Houston. *Houston Chronicle*, May 23, 2017.

Figure 3.4. Jonathan, age six, Mighty Writers' Workshop, Philadelphia. *Philly.com*, June 12, 2017.

saying, "No quiero ir!" ("I don't want to go!") (see figure 3.4). This picture indicates that Jonathan understands quite well that Trump has the power—which he has deployed—to increase the number of arrests and deportations. Furthermore, the labelling of the person as "Mexico" suggests that Jonathan understands the racism and xenophobia of the campaign—that it will affect all people of Mexican descent, since it is carried out with indiscriminate sweeps and racial profiling. Understanding the situation does not detract from Jonathan's feelings of resistance and rebellion. In fact, many of the kids' drawings, like Jonathan's and the preceding two, show kids' resistance.

Five pictures from the Austin classroom emphasize the physical intensity of the situation:

A sad face, with tears running down the cheeks.
Similarly, one child writes, "I am so scard," and draws hearts, one with a sad face.
Outright hatred, based on fear: "Yo tengo miedo que se llevan a mi mama y mi papa [I am afraid that they are going to take away my mommy and daddy]. I hate you dunel trump." Face with a frown (see figure 3.5).
"I am angry and sad because I thinck I am going to Mexico. I don't speak Spanish. I know English. I am frum Austin."
"He dunt have to mak fun of peoples skin because we are still people."

Almost all the artwork given to the Houston gallery critiques Trump's vision for "America." Some of the pictures echo themes of the letters

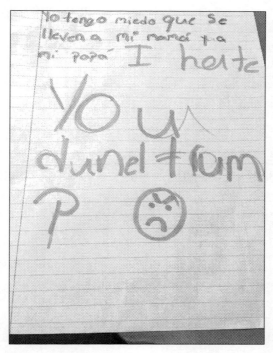

Figure 3.5. Anonymous, Austin. *Huffington Post*, March 1, 2017.

I analyzed above—a belief in equality, for example, and the idea that Trump has violated a basic premise of democracy. They are more critical, however, insofar as none of the 26 drawings invokes "niceness" as an alternative to Trump's vision. In calling for a more inclusive rhetoric, they don't mince words or strive for politeness:

"All hands in, no matter what. Stay if you want," says one picture, with hands of all different colors interspersed with the words.

"Respect immigrants like we respect you."

"We want America to be fair to everyone and immigrants to. I want to destroy the border. Donald Trump is bad." The letters are colored in the different hues of the rainbow, and there's a rainbow in the corner. The sentence "Donald Trump is bad" is in pencil at the bottom.

"America shall be fair. . . . Let's fight for our rights." In this drawing, the words "ICE," "War," "Immigration," and "Unfairness" are all written, encircled, then crossed out.

"Immigrants must stay because if kids stay away from their parents they will be sad every time they see a family thogeter. Sow treat people the same. Be happy." These words are above a drawing of a family, smiling, in a park.

"Make American Great Again! Immigrants we are all friends and families. Fight for what's right."

Finally, some of the kids make fun of Trump. Nine-year-old Sophia from Philadelphia demonstrates her irreverence: in one, Donald Trump (made most obvious through his orange hair) says, "The Wall!" in four different picture boxes; in two of them, he appears to be about to walk off a wall. In the fifth box, he bends over awkwardly, trying to pick up his orange hair, which is made out of a mass of orange yarn. "Ooops!" he says. Then: "The end." The same orange-yarn-haired Trump appears in another of Sophie's pictures, where he is smiling rather stupidly and saying, "Blah. Blah. Blah. Blah. You're fired" (see figures 3.6 and 3.7).

In the Houston exhibit, one drawing has the words "I want America to be loved." Ten different stick figures adorn the drawing, including a floating blobby person who is farting; a "Fat Albert" look alike who is saying, "Hey, hey, hey"; a girl with a bow in her hair who is saying, "Ah my hair!"; and seven other figures, all of whom are smiling, and all of

Figures 3.6 and 3.7. Sophie, age nine, Mighty Writers' Workshop, Philadelphia. *Philly.com*, June 12, 2017.

Figure 3.8. Anonymous, Houston. *Houston Chronicle*, May 12, 2017.

whom have strikingly different hairstyles. Ingeniously, this artist represents difference while evading the terms of diversity and inclusion that usually dominate the debate. The artist does not say, "We love America," but rather asks America to act in a way that makes people want to love *it* (see figure 3.8).

4

"Criss-Cross Applesauce"

Keeping Control in the Classroom

"Boys and girls, it's rug time!"
 The 20 children slowly stop their coloring, put away their crayons and paper, and move to their assigned spots, sitting "criss-cross applesauce." Miss M. calls out, "I like how Rachel[1] is sitting. I like how Aiden is sitting," until eventually, all but a few stragglers are obediently and quietly sitting, awaiting the morning announcements. For those two or three who don't make it on time, there are numerous looks and admonishments from Miss M. and Miss R., one of the teacher's aides. Finally, they are cajoled and shamed over: "Brandon, do you want the class to lose story time?" Brandon finally plops down and rests his chin in his hands. Miss M. starts the morning announcements, and a few kids start to wiggle. As soon as anyone rises or moves too far into the space of another child, an adult voice calls out: "Jaden, sit down!"
 While some of the kids seem able to completely tune out these voices, others become more agitated. After three warnings, Jaden simply gets up and walks to a corner of the room, saying nothing and wearing no expression. I admire his integrity. He is not going to play this game. There is a price to pay, however. The teachers seem to have given up on him. They let him go, and he wonders off, disinterested, sitting at a table in the far corner of the room by himself. Later in the week, when I am visiting for lunch, he falls off the end of the bench in the cafeteria, and the teacher's aide merely glances at him, shakes her head and walks by, not even asking if he is OK. Later, he leaves the lunch table and is flinging his necklace against the wall, occasionally bumping his body up against the wall as well. No one does anything, and although I call out to him to come and sit by us, he ignores me. When Miss M. arrives at the end of lunch, the aide says to her, "Jaden was throwing himself against the wall again," as if this was expected behavior with which she no longer wanted to engage.

107

Next, back in the classroom, Miss M. leads the students through a review of what they learned yesterday about the differences between frogs and toads. The kids have good memories, rehearsing many of the key facts. Then she gets up and stands at the board, pointing to the letter sound of the week—"oo." There is already a list on the board of perhaps 20 words with the "oo" sound, and she asks them if they can think of any more. "Kaboom," calls out Michael. Great word, I think to myself. But Miss M. is sort of scrunching up her face. "Kaboom," she repeats, "like when something crashes and makes a loud sound. That's good, but that's not really a word. I'm not going to write that down." "Awwhhhh," says Michael, looking a bit crushed. Ezra is wildly raising his hand. At first she ignores him, as if he is too eager. Then (could it be because I am there?), she says "Ezra?" and he says, "Oooh, like when something is yucky." Not bad, I think. But I see that face scrunch. "That *is* the oo sound," she says, "but that's not really a word either." It almost goes without saying that when another child calls out, "Poop!" Miss M. says sternly, "We said we weren't going to say that word in school." I force myself to avoid eye contact with Ezra because I know if we look at each other, we will both start giggling.

This scenario, from my younger son's kindergarten experience in a public school in Ithaca, New York, sets up my discussion in this chapter: how does the school as an institutional space discipline and regulate the bodies of children in a manner that makes it difficult for them to express themselves outside normative modes? How does this educational space intersect with kids' television (next chapter)? What is the link between emotional regulation and bodily control? How is this regulation connected to the demand in the U.S. for implementation of national curriculum standards and higher test scores? Miss M's insistence on certain words that illustrate the "oo" sound was no doubt connected to the assessment she was constantly required to do. As I observed during my volunteer time, she frequently carried around a notepad with students' names and required skills, and at times, I helped with the assessment—mainly monitoring to make sure, as Miss M. said, that students did not help each other complete the task at hand (that would be "cheating").

Yet Miss M. was also very concerned that the children be happy; she may well have agreed with critics of the Common Core who have argued that these standards are problematic for many reasons, across age groups, and are especially inappropriate for younger children. The standards ignore the ways in which most five- and six-year-old children learn—through play rather than through drilling, memorization, and testing. The standards are another example of the gap between adults and kids, as adults in policy-making positions make decisions for children—which are purportedly in their best interests—without considering their perspectives or positions, or even the perspectives of early childhood educators and teachers who work most closely with children. In her critique of the Common Core, educational policy expert Diane Ravitch noted that "early childhood educators are nearly unanimous in saying that no one who wrote the standards had any expertise in the education of very young children. More than 500 early childhood educators signed a joint statement complaining that the standards were developmentally inappropriate for children in the early grades. The standards, they said, emphasize academic skills and leave inadequate time for imaginative play" (quoted in Strauss 2014).

Public-school teachers like Miss M. thus find themselves in a complicated position: how to respond to the pressure for higher test scores while still allowing the flexibility and diversity that younger (or perhaps all) learners need. How to manage the energetic bodies of five-year-olds so that they can learn their numbers and letters? How to integrate emotional intelligence within a routinized, managed classroom space?

From the kindergartener's point of view, the classroom becomes a site of contradiction and possible confusion. On the one hand, you are surrounded by other kids your age, perhaps for the first time in your life. Opportunities for friendship abound. Yet at the same time, you are discouraged from expressing yourself in your own way, taught that some of your words are inappropriate, and directed to look to the teacher as the mediator for all interactions. While you are invited to express some feelings, these feelings have to go through a number of stages of validation, gradually becoming less "your feelings." Spontaneous interactions between kids are limited to times such as recess—and even these are mediated by adults—or designated as interruptions to the "real" work of the classroom.

Learning to be "Prosocial"

Learning can be fun. Actually, learning *should* be fun. That is the message of multiple media commercials and learning-related sites. Take, for example, a recent commercial by the for-profit online early learning center ABCmouse.com in which more than 100 school-age children dance and rap to a version of the Jackson 5's "ABC." The children display their exuberance for school for the benefit of a young girl who has just gotten off the bus and is looking around nervously; she is clearly a new student. The commercial is described by this October 8, 2015, headline in *The Los Angeles Times*: "Watch How Hip-Hop Choreography Can Get Kids to Behave." The article opens with these two sentences: "Getting dozens of hyper kids to behave is usually the job of a teacher. Recently, though, two leading hip-hop choreographers who go by the name of Nappytabs took an unlikely stab at the daunting task."

The suggestion is that making learning fun can actually stave off behavior problems; kids won't even think of misbehaving if they're allowed to move, dance, and express themselves. The choreographers quoted in the article emphasize the young girl and her anxieties, not the issue of behavior. Says Tabitha Dumo: "'It was this little girl, and she gets off the bus, and she's a little nervous and a little frightened. Everything feels overwhelming and there's all these new people—but then you begin to see this world in a different way. Everything becomes a rhythm. The bus, the zippers on the backpacks. Then we use these sounds to create the sort of soundtrack that's in her mind." Gradually over the course of the commercial, the girl begins to smile and relax, eventually joining in the dance routines.

Ultimately, though, the commercial is implicitly about behavior, as all the children end up in their seats, having expended their energy, and now appear eager to learn. The experience of shooting the video became another testimony to the power of fun and movement in learning, as shown by how the other choreographer, Napoleon Dumo, complimented the student performers: "'They were super professional, listened all the time—and they just wanted to dance. They just want someone not to say 'Sit still!' And that's how we feel that kids learn better."

This commercial illustrates a number of tenets explored in this chapter: preparing young children to enter successfully into the realm of institutional education requires educators to be aware of their need to move around, within certain structures. Given this freedom of movement, children can learn how to manage their bodies on their own, rather than being told to constantly "sit still." This comportment coincides with the management of feelings; if children can understand why their bodies are feeling happy, sad, anxious, and so forth, they can name their emotions and bring their bodies under control. Then, they will decide "on their own" to sit down and learn. This is the self-management illustrated in the video—children dance, sing, rap, and move with intense energy, yet the movement is also highly choreographed and structured, ending with a close up shot of the previously nervous young girl, sitting in her desk with her hands clasped, looking ahead at the teacher with an eager grin. And then the ABCmouse.com slogan comes in: "Discover how fun learning can be."

This emphasis on recruiting children to believe learning is fun occurs within a backlash against Bush's No Child Left Behind and even to Obama's Common Core curriculum, which, while more popular than No Child Left Behind, still had many detractors.[2] The reasoning goes something like this: if children *want* to be in school, they will be more motivated, more emotionally stable, and more successful. As I mention in the introduction, studies show that "emotional competence" is crucial to school success; a July 2003 report by the Clearinghouse on Elementary and Early Childhood Education concludes, taking issue with an emphasis on pure academic achievement: "Research, however, indicates that young children's emotional adjustment matters—children who are emotionally well adjusted have a significantly greater chance of early school success, while children who experience serious emotional difficulty face grave risks of early school difficulty." The report adds: "Specifically, emerging research on early schooling suggests that the relationships that children build with peers and teachers are based on children's ability to regulate emotions in prosocial versus antisocial ways and that those relationships then serve as a 'source of provisions' that either help or hurt children's chances of doing well academically (Raver 2003, 2).

How do such programs propose to "regulate emotions in prosocial ways"? Where does one draw the line between "prosocial" and conformist? I argue that the goal of emotional intelligence is to gradually decrease the power and frequency of affective responses; the paradigm that assumes emotions and rationality can work together to produce well-adjusted, intelligent children relies heavily on the power of language to name a set of acceptable behaviors. While necessary and even admirable in some regards, the risk is that the pursuit of emotional intelligence emphasizes a narrow range of appropriate reactions and thus contributes to normative views of childhood development. This normativity is not imposed; rather, the institutional imperative is to teach children how to operate autonomously—to learn how to solve problems so that they don't always need to rely on adults. This independence is part of the "fun" of learning—the noncoercive element. Problem solving becomes the order of the day. However, for children who do not get on board—or who cannot, for whatever reason—there is a high price to pay.

Schooling for National Success

George Bush's No Child Left Behind program was signed into law in January 2002; according to Ravitch—a one-time supporter and then eventual critic of the law—it "changed the nature of public schooling across the nation by making standardized test scores the primary measure of school quality" (2010, 15). As Bush described NCLB, it would ensure that "every child is educated" and "no child will be left behind—not one single child" (quoted in Ravitch 2010, 94).

The bill received broad bipartisan support, which Ravitch attributes to post 9/11 patriotism: "after the terrorist attacks of September 11, 2001, Congress wanted to demonstrate unity, and the education legislation sailed through" (94). Democratic senator Edward Kennedy "called the legislation 'a defining issue about the future of our nation and about the future of democracy, the future of liberty, and the future of the United States in leading the free world'" (95). After years of different proposals for school reform from a variety of political positions, NCLB was hailed as the answer, one that came with a promise to measure improvement: "Everyone, it seemed, wanted 'accountability.' By accountability, elected officials meant that they wanted the schools to measure whether students were learning, and they wanted rewards or punishments for those responsible" (95).

Toward that end, all states were "required to establish timelines showing how 100 percent of their students would reach proficiency in reading and math by 2013–14" (Ravitch 97). Every child in grades three through eight would be tested every year on reading and math, using state tests; low-performing schools would receive help to improve; schools that did not improve would face penalties; and their students would have the choice of attending a different school (94).

It was up to each state to decide what curriculum would work best, but the effect, says Ravitch, was to ignore any area outside of math and reading, the two areas that would be tested—so history, civics, literature, science, the arts, and geography all suffered in the push toward "excellence." Public education became a numbers game: "In this new era, school reform was characterized as accountability, high-stakes testing, data-driven decision making, choice, charter schools, privatization, deregulation, merit pay, and competition among schools. Whatever could not be measured did not count" (21). It was a largely corporate maneuver, one that was hugely profitable for some: "Adult interests were well served by NCLB. The law generated huge revenues for tutoring and testing services, which became a sizable industry. Companies that offered tutoring, tests, and test-prep materials were raking in billions of dollars annually from federal, state, and local governments, but the advantages to the nation's students were not obvious" (Ravitch 101).

By contrast, children's interests were not well served, in part because they were grouped together under the category "children" and assumed to be one homogenous mass that, if pushed, should be able to reach the national standard of success. No acknowledgement was made of the fact that children learn differently. Says Ravitch,

> The most toxic flaw in NCLB was its legislative command that all students in every school must be proficient in reading and math by 2014. By that magical date, every single student must achieve proficiency, including students with special needs, students whose native language is not English, students who are homeless and lacking in any societal advantage, and students who have every societal advantage but are not interested in their schoolwork. All will be proficient by 2014, or so the law mandates. And if they are not, then their schools and teachers will suffer the consequences. (102)

Yet the goal of total proficiency is completely unrealistic, says Ravitch: "such a goal has never been reached by any state or nation" (103).

As schools struggled to meet the requirements, "test scores became an obsession . . . test-taking skills and strategies took precedence over knowledge.... In urban schools, where there are many low-performing students, drill and practice became a significant part of the daily routine" (107). Yet, as Ravitch notes, "Ironically test prep is not always the best preparation for taking tests. Children expand their vocabulary and improve their reading skills when they learn history, science, and literature, just as they may sharpen their mathematics skills while learning science and geography. And the arts may motivate students to love learning" (108). Not surprisingly, then, "NCLB did not even bring about rapidly improving test scores" (109).

In February 2009, President Barack Obama's Race to the Top program was signed into law, inviting states to compete for $4.35 billion in extra funding based on the strength of their student test scores. While both Race to the Top and NCLB focus on standardized testing, they differ insofar as the latter was mandatory while Race to the Top was a competitive grant program that gave states monetary incentives to reform their educational systems; the program incorporated new curricular standards, known as the Common Core. Testing opponents have decried both initiatives for their continued reliance on test scores, a complaint Obama himself seemed to echo on March 28, 2011, when he said: "Too often what we have been doing is using these tests to punish students or to, in some cases, punish schools" (quoted in Werner 2011).

Under the pressure of the Common Core, "development" takes on a new intensity, as teachers are pressured to make all children conform to a certain model of academic advancement, a pressure that has negative effects on children—especially the youngest ones—and in the long run does not produce greater achievement. This was the conclusion of a report by early child educators that focused on the Common Core's insistence that all kindergarteners should be able to "read emergent-reader texts with purpose and understanding." The Alliance for Childhood's Defending the Early Years (DEY) team says that, beginning in the 1980s, there was a "shift in kindergarten education from play-based experiential approaches to more academic approaches, from hands-on exploration to worksheets and teacher-led instruction." Likening this movement to a "snowball growing in volume and speed," the educators say that it gained momentum with No Child Left Behind and then, under the Common Core State Standards (CCSS), "the snowball has escalated into an avalanche which threatens to destroy appropriate and effective approaches to early education" (Carlsson-Paige, McLaughlin, and Almon 2015, 2). In place of a pedagogy that attends to individual differences, the CCSS impose one model of childhood development, with harmful effects:

> Many children are not developmentally ready to read in kindergarten. In addition, the pressure of implementing the standards leads many kindergarten teachers to resort to inappropriate didactic methods combined with frequent testing. Teacher-led instruction in kindergartens has almost entirely replaced the active, play-based, experiential learning that we know children need from decades of research in cognitive and developmental psychology and neuroscience. (Carlsson-Paige, McLaughlin, and Almon 2015, 2)

In fact, noted the DEY team, the Common Core authors cited no scholarly evidence about children's development and—perhaps most tellingly—there was not a single early childhood educator or teacher on the CCCS team.

Many teachers have actively criticized the Common Core standards yet often feel forced to comply, out of fear for their jobs. This uncomfortable position was indicated in a survey done by DEY, which found that "of about 200 early childhood teachers (preschool to grade three) across 38 states, 85% of the public-school teachers reported that they are required to teach activities that are not developmentally appropriate for their students" (Carlsson-Paige, McLaughlin, and Almon 2015, 3). A New York public-school kindergarten teacher with 15 years' experience told the DEY team: "Kindergarten students are being forced to write words, sentences, and paragraphs before having a grasp of oral language.... We are assessing them WEEKLY on how many sight words, letter sounds, and letter names they can identify." The report cites experts who have done studies proving that that there is "no solid evidence showing long-term gains for children who are taught to read in kindergarten. In fact, by fourth grade and beyond, these children read at the same level as those who were taught to read in the first grade" (3). Children can suffer setbacks in their education because other activities such as play and socialization skills that actually contribute to their learning are sacrificed.

Another Common Core standard requires kindergarteners to "recognize and name all upper- and lowercase letters of the alphabet" (6). However, the report's authors say that most kindergarteners and first graders write in all uppercase letters, and that, again, there is nothing to be gained by forcing them to learn upper- and lowercase before they are ready. The worksheets and drills that require them to memorize these letters without fully processing the information can lead to anxiety and insecurities for those children who get frustrated and perhaps are then identified as slow learners, sometimes even being pulled out of the classroom. Children who succeed are rewarded for learning the proper mode of expression earlier than their peers, thus dividing kids into "advanced," "on task," and "developmentally delayed."

The pedagogical goal is that children come to govern themselves, initially to learn the rewards of proper behavior and eventually to internalize those behaviors, such that the school becomes a place of order and routine, of preparation for one's place in civil society, to recall a theme from my last chapter. As Elizabeth A. Gagen argues: "Indeed the goal of self-government is entirely compatible with, and indeed presupposed by, neoliberal democracies. With regard to childhood, the goal of harmonizing the desires of the subject with the desires of the state remains the business of governmentality; and young bodies are persistently normalized, tutored in self-regulation" (2010, 180). In other words, the educational system is actually *not* formulated around the assumption of children's silence or passivity; there is general agreement that children need to be taught to be self-reliant, self-actualizing citizens. Thus, children become active participants in their own socialization, a much more effective process than one in which they are "forced" to conform.

As long as one learns to behave properly, one remains part of the group. When a child misbehaves, however, he or she is spatially set apart. In Ezra's classroom, for example, there was a "thinking chair," where misbehaving children were sent to "think about" why their behavior was wrong. Ezra was bemused by this notion; as he said, "the chair doesn't think." He was also often confused as to why he was made to sit there and at times couldn't remember why he was being punished. "What were you doing?" I asked him one day, trying to understand. "I just couldn't stop singing a new song I learned at recess," he said. "Missed me, missed me, now you gotta kiss me." I observed during my frequent volunteering sessions that children were sent to the thinking chair because they were disrupting the classroom space in a wide range of ways. For example, everyone had to line up and wash their hands after recess and before lunch; one child was a very methodical hand washer and would hold his hands under the faucet for several minutes, leading to much restlessness behind him. He was assigned the thinking chair, as was the child who, several people back in line, finally lost patience and started jumping up and down and jostling his classmates. While walking down the corridor to lunch, too much talking or not staying in a straight line could lead to the thinking chair. My job as volunteer was to bring up the end of the line and make sure that the kids walked quietly and directly to the cafeteria, a difficult task for many, who were hungry and excited to be liberated from the order of the classroom.

There is a direct link here to the management of emotions. Young children may be especially vulnerable to the experience of being punished or shamed or ostracized, since they are still relatively new to institutional spaces—sometimes, completely new, if they haven't been in preschool or institutional daycare. Children may be missing their parents and their home spaces and may see their teachers as substitutes for parents. Thus, winning their approval and love are crucial components of making the transition from home to school without too much anxiety. In this situation, proper behavior and emotional expression becomes a powerful tool for gaining these feelings of acceptance; maintaining belonging in the group means that one is likely to get the approval of the teacher. Somewhat paradoxically, acting out physically or verbally becomes another way of getting the teacher's attention, even if it's negative attention—still it is a form of recognition. Thus, the classroom space is set up hierarchically around the teacher's approval, with students situated to concur or risk marginalization. Again, the modes of communication kids have with each other are minimized because the teacher becomes the focus.

These are the power dynamics Louise Holt describes in her research into disabled children's education in the UK, particularly the integration of disabled children into mainstream education. Drawing on Judith Butler's theories of subjection and recognition, Holt explores "how discourses that situate bodies hierarchically become embodied, via the subconscious, intertwined with corporeal bodies, and reproduced as seemingly 'natural.'" This naturalization occurs in part because "individuals have an emotional need to be 'recognised' within acceptable frames of reference for personhood. Thus, subjection, which enables an individual to become a subject/agent who can act, simultaneously constrains the possibilities of personhood" (2010, 206). In kindergarten, for example, children's needs to be recognized occur within discourses that establish "acceptable frames of reference for personhood"—in this case, acceptable bodily behavior. This recognition requires students to act, to subject themselves to the frames of reference, and this process, repeatedly performed, shapes the successful—and well-liked—student. This process coincides with the discourse of niceness I analyzed in this last chapter; individual behavior is linked to the overall functioning of the classroom.

Kindergarten under the pressures of state and national standards is a space of order, where children must sit still for long periods of time. In Ezra's kindergarten day, children received only one 20-minute recess over the course of the six-hour day. Most of the day is structured learning, with little time for free play. For many children, this restriction represents a significant departure from home life. As Patricia Holland writes, "to achieve an orderly regime, childish spontaneity, which is so highly valued in the family imagery, must take on negative connotations. The restlessness of childhood, its random and purposeless movement, indicates precisely those qualities that school is designed to modify. Spontaneity may be pictured as naughtiness, inattention or downright disobedience" (2004, 79). One of the most common ways of squashing spontaneity is to designate certain areas as spaces of play, with every other space assumed to be one of bodily control. As Holland says, "Above all, on entering school, children find their right to undirected play limited to a designated space, the playground, and time, playtime. The playground image itself may be seen as a threat, infested by bullies and children running wild. Play itself is linked to uncontrollability and the fear that children may move beyond the reach of the school's disciplinary regime" (79–80).

One of my volunteer tasks at the kindergarten was to supervise at recess; Ezra's teacher sent an email to parents asking for volunteers to come and organize games for the kids to play. During my first recess, I stood in the middle of the playground wondering how that might happen, as five-year-olds from all three kindergarten classrooms came streaming out onto the playground and started racing off in all directions. They'll calm down in a few minutes, I thought to myself, and then I'll try to organize them into a game of kickball. But they didn't. While a few kids played on the slide, monkey bars, and swings, the majority were literally running in circles, sometimes cutting through the middle of the playground, sometimes chasing each other, but most often just running randomly, nonstop. When I approached a few of them to ask if they wanted to play a game, they looked at me as if I were some kind of alien. This happened even after I volunteered on several occasions and many of them knew that I was "Ezra's mom." I came to understand that the last thing they wanted in their 20 minutes of unstructured playtime was an adult trying to organize them into some kind of game with rules in a demarcated space.

Opportunities for creative and perhaps spontaneous expression may occur in art and music classes; however, these classes have been cut in many public schools across the country in response to the pressure for better test scores in math and reading. In Ezra's school, this has significant spatial repercussions: there is no designated room for music class but rather a traveling, part-time teacher who visits each class once a week in their regular classroom. One day, when I'm volunteering, the music teacher arrives, and I settle in for what I think will be a good time for the kids, including Ezra, since he loves music. I couldn't have been more mistaken. Twenty kids crowd into a space roughly 12 by 15 feet. The teacher shows them exactly how to move to a song. It's a catchy tune. Ezra follows the movements to begin with, but then clearly wants to do his own thing. He moves off to the side, which the teacher allows. But then he becomes a DJ, pretending to spin records on the table, and the teacher says, no, he can't do this, because not every student has a table. Ezra gets up his courage, raises his hand, and asks politely if he can do the turntable. "That's a good idea, but no, we can't do it," says the teacher, "because not everyone has a table in front of them."

A dismissal of student expression is more likely to occur when the teacher feels pressure to follow a demanding curriculum, which has happened under both the Bush and Obama administration's programs for school reform. In a strong yet diplomatic critique of the Common Core standards, the report issued by a group of progressive scholars in educational policy research says that students will not feel motivated to learn if their desires are not taken into account, and those desires are often ignored in the push for measurable success:

> Obsessed with measuring adequate yearly progress, we sometimes forget the importance of cultivating the immeasurables—such as a love for learning, a passion for inquiry, and a zeal for creative expression. Furthermore, the contemporary national dialogue about how to reform our schools is often guided by assumptions that are out of sync with what we know about how students learn and why they choose to do so. Consequently, we write out of a deep concern that the movement to raise standards may fail if teachers are not supported to understand the connections among motivation, engagement, and student voice. (Toshalis and Nakkula 2012, 2)

The authors advocate a "student centered" approach premised on what "makes sense" to students "in their world." This notion of "what makes sense" requires one to examine the everyday, practical lives of children (things such as income level, for example) in combination with the affective realm—what the report compellingly calls "the power of desire," which, they say, "is often lost or buried in the jargon of mainstream academic discourse. One of our goals is to excavate desire from the layers of jargon heaped upon it" (2). Doing so, they predict, will be a much more effective method to enhancing learning than imposing a standardized-test driven notion of success.

What would it mean to "excavate desire" among the youngest students? One has only to observe five-year-olds at play in a park or other open space to know that desire abounds in myriad forms—as bodies cavort, contort, and careen. It is hard to imagine how such forms of desire can be "measured," yet that is exactly what standardized testing requires. Teachers such as Miss M. find themselves in a difficult position—wanting to celebrate the play of young children while simultaneously preparing them for the next step of their education in public schooling. Picking Ezra up from school one day, I ask her how his day went, and she makes a "so-so" motion with her hands. "I just want him to like coming to school," she says plaintively.

We return, thus, to the point I made above regarding young children's need for recognition from teachers and other authority figures within the school. Because most children are eager to meet expectations, to feel accepted and valued within this new institutional space, they are particularly vulnerable to demands that—try as they might—they are unable to meet. At the same time, they will not likely be able to articulate the reasons for their frustration, since they are unaware of the politics of standardized testing and even that they are being tested. Yet despite being unaware of these institutional pressures, they will be perfectly aware of their own feelings—of frustration, of not belonging, of being set outside the circle, separated from the peers with whom they are best able to communicate. As the DEY report puts it, "They feel less in charge of, and invested in, the learning process—and their internal motivation is thwarted. They begin to feel that learning, and its deep satisfactions, do not belong to them. Many early childhood experts agree that the current pushdown of teaching of reading skills to 4-, 5- and 6-year-olds that used to be associated with older children is demoralizing young learners" (Carlsson-Paige, McLaughlin, and Almon 2015, 9).

Motivating children requires some knowledge of the individual child, of the ways in which different children learn differently. One effective strategy for letting these differences play out within a structured environment is to provide materials at various stations for children to play with as they move through a space. The kindergarten report says that children learn through playing with materials, gradually building a physical foundation that will serve as the basis for understanding the symbolic and abstract. For example, when children pretend that a banana is a telephone, the accompanying conversation helps them to connect a symbol with a series of words. Such games also demonstrate how talking and listening provide the basis for reading: "As children engage in active learning experiences and play, they are talking and listening all the time. They attach words to their actions, talk with peers and teachers, learn new vocabulary and use more complex grammar. As they build, make paintings, and engage in imaginative play, they deepen their understanding of word meanings. As they listen to and create stories, hear rich language texts, sing songs, poems and chants, their foundation for reading grows strong" (Carlsson-Paige, McLaughlin, and Almon 2015, 5).

In other words, directed playing is often the best way that most children learn because it is the "language" children speak. The kindergarten report urges classrooms with activity centers, "typically filled with open-ended materials that spark investigation, imagination, and problem solving: wooden unit blocks, sand and water, play dough, objects from the natural world, and a wide range of building, collage and art supplies. With open-ended materials children can work on concepts at their own level as they develop and invent their own ideas" (7).

A classroom oriented toward difference and independence is less likely to rely on the generalized notion of "the child" that undergirds many pedagogical policy and practices. The very notion of "standards" and benchmarks that define where children should be at if they are learning what they should indicates that the individual child is subsumed within the category of "children" and placed in a deferential relationship to the adult authority figure who assumes that he or she is acting in the best interests of the group of children. As Allison James says, "Children's individual identities are transformed and homogenized through their categorization as children, with their individuality, their Selfhood, often made secondary to their status as children" (1994, 31).

The homogenized category of childhood is also part of the developmental discourse theorized by the child psychologist Jean Piaget, who defined the stages through which a "normal" child proceeds, as I summarized in the introduction. According to Piaget, children in the two-to-seven age range should progress from the sensory-motor stage—where learning takes place through the infant's senses and concrete actions—to representative thought, although initially they ostensibly have difficulty understanding causal relationships and anything from another person's point of view. As Chris Jenks has argued, if a child does not proceed through these stages, they are seen as immature or abnormal:

> These stages are chronologically ordered but also hierarchically arranged along a continuum from low status, infantile, "figurative" thought to high status, adult, "operative" intelligence. This sets a narrative in the discourse of cognitive growth that is by now global and overwhelming. The "figurative" thought that emits directly from our state of childhood is instanced by particularistic activity, a concentration on the here and now and a consequent inability to transfer experience or training from one situation to another. The child, for Piaget, is preoccupied with the repetitive

and highly concrete replication of object states . . . Beyond this, figurative thought knows no distance or consideration; it is organized through affective responses in specific settings. Clearly we have here a recipe for "childishness." (2005, 22)

The "normal" child demonstrates an "achievement ethic" when he or she proceeds from figurative to operative thought; the latter "exemplifies logical process and freedom from domination by immediate experience" (22). This devaluation of the realms of affect and immediate experience and the privileging of rational thought is what, says Jenks, signals the process "by and through which the child is wrenched from the possibility of difference" (23).

In this model, says Liselott Mariett Olsson, "what the teacher is looking for is the lack of proper development; she/he is functioning as a detector of lack, an observer of error" so that she/he can step in and "fill in" the gaps. This model makes sense to most people, notes Olsson: "to help the child develop seems unquestionably right" (2009, 35). The teacher has total authority to determine which children are "lacking" and thus in need of intervention. However, Olsson also notes that some researchers in critical pedagogy studies believe that the field is moving away from the Piagetian model into a somewhat different view of the child, one based less on "lack" and more on skills of competence, autonomy, and problem solving: "This child is presumed to have a desire and capability to learn and is encouraged to ask questions, resolve problems and seek answers. This image of the child could be seen as a challenge to the individual, natural and developing child, since the ambition is no longer to map the child with the help of developmental psychology" (36). Ultimately, however, this model is no less normative, says Olsson, even though it ostensibly is more respectful of the child's independence: "It concerns an ambition to get children to want to learn and willingly adapt to the new logic of continuous learning through autonomous and flexible problem solving." Each child "is supposed to have its own competencies to bring forward" (36), and these competencies are then measured against a predetermined standard—such as the standardized testing undergirding the Common Core curriculum. Emotional competence, as I argued in the introduction, is perceived to be one of the "skills" children need to learn in order to be successful.

Gauging Emotional Intelligence

The scenario is familiar to any caregiver. The park on a sunny day, or the play area in the children's museum, or any fun place where kids are having a good time. The alert: "Five minutes and we need to go." The child pretends not to hear, or perhaps doesn't hear. "Three minutes! We have to get groceries for dinner." That was a mistake—no kid wants to leave the park for the grocery store. "Time to go!" Just one more thing, he or she calls out. "All right, but then we absolutely have to go—we're going to be late. . . . OK, time to go. Now!" The child keeps playing—running away, refusing to comply. A kind of civil disobedience. The adult gets frustrated. "We have to go! Why don't you listen?" And the power struggle is in full force; both adult and child may get angry. If one does, it will be easily visible and palpable: rising adrenaline can cause blurry vision; dry mouth; a quickened heart rate; fast, shallow breathing; sweating and blushing; tension in shoulders, back, and neck; queasy stomach; shaky body due to the release of lactic acid when extra energy is produced. Clenched fists, red face, thin lips, furrowed brows. These reactions can lead to a further physical response, like kicking, hitting, shouting. The person is physically incapable of listening or reasoning.

Child psychologists explain emotional responses as comprised of three elements: cognitive-experiential, behavioral-expressive, and physiological-biochemical. Two of the psychologists responsible for helping defining emotional intelligence, Brenner and Salovey, explain the differences between these three elements: "The cognitive-experiential component comprises one's thoughts and awareness of emotional states (i.e., what most people refer to as 'feelings.') The behavioral-expressive component comprises such domains as speech, body movement, facial expression, posture, and gesture (i.e., the visible signs of emotion). The physiological-biochemical component comprises physical states and is reflected in such measures as brain activity, heart rate, skin response, and hormone levels" (1997, 170). The psychologists are concerned with how children can develop coping strategies in the domains of cognitive-experiential and behavioral-expressive that help them regulate their physiological-biological responses. The implication, thus, is that the former two realms can help control the latter—and if that doesn't happen, then a "maladaptive" form of aggression might ensue. They also argue that children's ability to self-regulate increases with age, as they are better able to name, process, and master their emotions as they develop.

While their analysis illustrates some of the generalizing tendencies of developmental psychology, it also illustrates the importance of attending to children's mental and physical capacities. Since children's brains are still developing—especially the parts that control rational decision making, they are not simply "small adults." They in fact do need to learn how to express their feelings and understand why they are having the physical reactions that they are having. Compelling them to do things before they are physically ready will increase frustration and emotional outbursts, leading to further frustration and low self-esteem, ultimately counterproductive to goals of learning and social interaction.

What Brenner and Salovey do not account for, however, are the differences in power between adults and children that might legitimate the child's feelings of anger and call for a redress in power rather than a sublimation of feelings. In my hypothetical example, for instance, "emotional intelligence" calls for the child to learn how to control the physiological demonstration of anger and understand why it is time to leave. The child might disagree and/or express some unhappiness, and the psychologists would say it's fine to express one's feelings, but children must learn to do so in a reasonable manner. However, if one considers the power differential in this situation, perhaps a physiological reaction does not seem out of place. Why should the adult get to say what happens next just because he is bigger and has the car keys? Why can't they just have whatever is in the fridge for dinner? What if another adult came along and told the parent to leave before he or she was ready? How much of kids' anger is due to their inability to control how and when and where their bodies move and are moved? How does one mark the transition from the baby who of course has to be carried, to the toddler who increasingly moves on his or her own, to the three-, four-, and five-year old who doesn't want to be picked up, who wants to walk, run, jump, and do flips on the bed that has just been made? As children in this age group acquire the ability to express their own desires to go where they want and do what they want, they will invariably clash with their caregivers, who have their own busy schedules and need their children to cooperate, to be on time, to understand the very notion of a schedule.

The conflict for kids involves coming into their own as individual subjects without possessing the agency to be able to control their movement into and out of various places. From their point of view, frustration and even anger seems understandable. Yet for adults, the goal is to teach them that such frustration needs to be managed, and, ideally, headed off before it even begins, by teaching them the skills of routines, rules, schedules, and other forms of orderly behavior. This all takes the form of a gradual process, with greater leeway granted to younger children and less leeway as they grow and are expected to assume more understanding of how to control their feelings. At what point do emotions considered "normal"—like those belonging to the stereotypical phase of "the terrible twos"—become problematic? Identifying that moment is key to identifying "intervention" strategies. For example, acts of aggression are considered to be normal, appropriate responses by frustrated two-year-olds who are actively trying to figure something out but cannot. Gradually, aggression is expected to decrease over the preschool years as children learn to identify their feelings and learn strategies for conflict resolution that do not involve physical acts. Similarly, defiance is considered a normal sign of emerging independence for a two-year-old, and then gradually transforms into what is called "positive self-assertion" with the development of language skills that allow for verbal negotiation. While this process is made to sound both natural and necessary, it relies on the gradual subsumption of affect within a language defined by adults as normative; it does not allow for the kinds of language and movements I described at the beginning of this chapter.

In the next chapter, I will show how television programming helps to define what is normal and expected behavior in order to help children manage their emotions. This is, to put it reductively, socialization—becoming part of a family, a classroom, a community, a nation. Children are made to feel that acceptance and belonging rest on learning these rules, yet perhaps without fully understanding why they are better and without the language to articulate their questions. In Massumi's terms, learning "how to behave" necessitates linking emotion to a problem-solving narrative. This requires the child to learn how to suppress desires and ideas that don't fit the space and/or time of the classroom; they must grasp the notion of "what's appropriate." If emotional and bodily control cannot be mastered, the child becomes the problem child, the outsider, the one in need of intervention. Yet some children in fact will not be able to put into words the way they are feeling because, for a variety of reasons, their feelings are not easily translatable, and the adult who is helping them manage their feelings might get it wrong. What is happening may not be an intentional act but rather an inability to match words with body. Frustration builds up in the body—the screaming, thrashing "temper tantrum" may be a fully embodied expression of what's going on inside a child's head and body that they simply cannot find the words to express. Or they may find the words but be rejected by adults who are trying to teach them the rules. Hence the conundrum: how to teach children that anger can be a natural and even positive response to certain situations, triggered, for example, by fear or danger or humiliation, all of which are likely based on a lack of power. Anger can also be remarkably productive—think of all the "angry people" who have sparked social movements. Yet anger can also be destructive and damaging, to both the child who expresses it and to others.

For the educators and psychologists who have joined forces to push for the teaching of "emotional intelligence," the beginning school years mark a crucial developmental period. As psychologists Greenberg and Snell have argued, children between the ages of five and seven "undergo a major developmental transformation that generally includes increases in cognitive processing skills, a growth spurt, and changes in brain size and function," all of which allow them to assume greater independence and responsibility (1997, 106). The logic is this: the areas of the brain responsible for controlling rational and emotional components are intertwined but still distinct. The area of emotions (the limbic) develops prior to that of reasoning and management (the prefrontal cortex). Around the age of five, the prefrontal cortex starts to catch up with the limbic area, allowing the child to gain greater control over his or her emotions. This growth is contingent on certain problem-solving skills, namely the ability to recognize emotions and name them, in both oneself and others, and to begin to self-regulate one's response in order to fit the situation. There is a certain flexibility and fluidity built into this chronology: children do develop at different rates (that's fine), and they should be allowed to continue to express their emotions (that's good), but there should still be a gradual subsumption of the emotional and the physiological to the rational.

Educational psychologist Carolyn Saarni (1997) describes how she teaches emotional intelligence in a systematic, orderly fashion to all children—not just to children who have problems or at moments of crisis. Her stages proceed from "awareness of one's emotional state, including the possibility that one is experiencing multiple emotions" (47), "to the ability to discern others' emotions, based on situational and expressive cues that have some degree of cultural consensus as to their emotional meaning" (49). Then, children begin to "use the vocabulary of emotion and expression terms commonly available in one's (sub)culture and at more mature levels to acquire cultural scripts that link emotion with social roles." With this step comes the "capacity for empathic and sympathetic involvement in others' emotional experiences" (49).

Saarni's next two steps are interesting insofar as they stress the need for management and regulation and introduce the possibility, or perhaps inevitability, of a gap between how one feels and how one responds: the "ability to recognize that an inner emotional state need not correspond to outer expression, both in oneself and in others" (50), followed by "the capacity for adaptive coping with aversive or distressing emotions by using self-regulatory strategies that ameliorate the intensity or temporal duration of such emotional states." In other words, kids at this age should be able to learn when *not* to express themselves or at least lessen the intensity of their expressions. Ideally, the culmination of the stages, in the world of emotional intelligence pedagogy, is "emotional self-efficacy—the individual views her or himself as feeling, overall, the way he or she wants to feel" (Saarni 58). This last step speaks, again, to self-management; the child comes to believe in his or her own powers by proceeding through the steps laid out for them.

Similarly, for Greenberg and Snell, the "developmental transformation" occurring between ages five and seven assumes a linear progression, from the physiological to the emotional to the cognitive. By this age, they say, most children will have "internalized much of what could previously be accomplished only with conscious effort"—but this happens "only if the child has accurately processed the emotional context of a particular situation." By contrast, "if children misidentify their own feelings or those of others, they are likely to generate maladaptive solutions to the problem, regardless of their intellectual capacities. Thus, the relationships between affective understanding, cognition, and behavior are of crucial importance" (106). Despite the wording here—that the three areas are intertwined—there is a linear order established, from affective experience to cognition to behavior. They do not return to the affective; such a return would presumably constitute a "maladaptive" response.

All of these theories rely on unarticulated assumptions about what it means to "accurately process the emotional context of a situation." What is a "maladaptive solution"? While there is some acknowledgement about the need to see situations from multiple points of view, there is no attention to the differences in power that make such exercises, in many situations, futile, for a child who—even if he or she can understand a teacher's or parent's point of view—must accommodate herself to the rules. One can easily think of any one of a number of rules that are in place for the sake of order that might not make sense to a child. Why should farting be a manner of politeness, for example? Most of the time, it is an involuntary and natural bodily response, yet one is expected to say "pardon me" or "excuse me" and be embarrassed or even ashamed.

The thinking chair illustrates perfectly the problems with an emotional intelligence paradigm that assumes kids can be taught, through cognition, to control their bodies in a manner that helps them understand and thus control their emotions. The kids I observed sitting in the chair were either fidgeting and squirming around, or so ashamed that they tried to shrink their bodies into the chair. They weren't thinking—they were feeling bad. Yet at the end of their time in the chair, the teacher would ask them what they had learned. What they learned was to give her the answer that would get them out of the chair. For Ezra, that lesson was not to sing during class.

How does a teacher embrace the affective even as she or he is teaching kids how to manage their emotions? How can difference be valorized while recognizing that there are some things all kids need to learn? As one approach to these issues, I close this chapter with a brief description of two classrooms of three- to six-year-olds at the Elizabeth Ann Clune (EAC) Montessori School in Ithaca. The kids' activities comprise a kind of archive of feelings, a way of expressing what they feel through their bodily movements. Needless to say, there is no thinking chair here.

Movement Matters

The classroom is a quiet buzz of activity. Two girls sit at a table, one doing a puzzle and the other pouring water from a glass beaker into four small metal cups. Two boys sit on a rug together, building a structure out of wooden blocks. Two girls are at another table, cutting out heart-shaped pieces of paper and coloring them, talking in an animated fashion. I overhear the word "chocolate" several times. Soon, two more girls join them and participate in the conversation. Across the room, in a corner, three boys sit on the floor, gathered around a table where they are lining up blue and red rods, measuring them against each other and writing down their calculations. One girl skips across the room, back and forth between a shelf with colored pencils and a table with paper in front of a wooden abacus.

At first glance, one may not see a teacher; then, a voice calls out. "Good morning, George. You still have some number writing to do," says Donyan, who is sitting on the floor with another child. George goes over to a bookshelf and pulls down a tray with beads, papers, and pencils, and sits down in a corner with his work. The other teacher, Virginia, can be spotted sitting at a table with five children seated around her; she is painting in circles with various colors as the kids count in Spanish. When she's done with the lesson, she asks one girl to return the papers to a shelf, instructing the others to watch where she goes, so that "next time, you can choose it yourself and you'll know where it's at."

Despite the frequent movement of children between stations and the constant chatter, none of the children seem distracted. Some of them stay focused on one activity for 30 minutes; some change more frequently. The girl who began the morning pouring water from the beaker finishes that activity, places everything back on the tray, puts the tray on a nearby shelf, and gets a new project—a plate with two different-sized glasses on it and a small container of beads—then returns to her original seat and table. She measures beads into the glasses and observes the level of beads; she then puts everything back in place and returns to the shelf. When she finishes this activity, she returns it all to the shelf, picks up a basket with large plastic baubles that can be joined together, and returns to her chair. She then strings them together to make a necklace, taking it apart and putting it back together several times, talking to herself as she does so: "Let's have two yellows, then a green, then two yellows, then a green. It's a pattern." Sitting quietly next to her is a girl doing a puzzle. They occasionally interact but mainly work quietly and independently for the greater part of 45 minutes.

No one tells the children to sit still or be quiet. In fact, the teachers never have to admonish any of the children, in part because they are not expected to sit still or be quiet. Occasionally they ask someone what they have been doing, and they move among the children giving "lessons," or brief demonstrations of various "works." The idea is to create an environment in which children learn to make their own choices, become independent learners, and cooperate with each other as they construct their own spaces and environments. They are as likely to be talking to each other as they are to a teacher.

While a visitor to the class might assume that all of this happens seamlessly, the classroom and philosophy have been carefully constructed according to the philosophy of Maria Montessori: teachers structure the classroom so that children can move throughout it at their own pace and initiative. Children are often encouraged to "make a choice." Or make the right choice—as when a child at Virginia's Spanish-numbers table interrupts and Virginia tells him to make a choice as to whether he is going to stay at the table and hear the lesson or go someplace else. He sits back down; "That's a great choice," she says. In an adjoining classroom, also for three- to six-year-olds, teacher Meridith says to a child, "You have to choose your own work." The child appears about to protest but then looks around the room and goes to join a child working on the moveable alphabet, a set of large wooden letters.

Thus, unlike the public-school classroom I described above where children are constantly being told where to go and what to do, the Montessori classroom—while not devoid of such instructions—is much more heavily premised on children's independence. The result is that many children make decisions about which work to do, for how long, and with whom. In Meridith and Leah's classroom, for example, a boy who has just turned four gets a short lesson from Leah. She helps him take apart a puzzle of a flower; each piece is a part of the flower whose name she gives him as she takes it apart: stamen, petal, leaf, stem. "Would you like to do this on your own?" Leah asks. He nods, she says, "Great," and leaves him on the small white rug that marks the space. He goes to work.

It is not an easy puzzle; the pieces are cut in unusual shapes. He twists and turns some of the pieces multiple times before he finds the right fit, putting one down and picking up another. He looks up and around a few times but doesn't ask for help and never gives up. After almost 15 minutes, he finishes. He looks at the puzzle with a satisfied grin, then picks it up and puts it on the shelf next to another puzzle. He then looks around, walks across the room to another shelf, gets a small basket, returns to the rug, puts the basket down, and starts pulling out animals from the rain forest. Also in the basket are small pieces of laminated paper with the names of the animals: the red-eyed tree frog, tamarin, sloth, caiman, macaw. Slowly, he takes out each animal and puts each one on the paper with the correct name. This exercise takes him about 20 minutes; again, he never wavers or asks for help. He maintains his concentration even though children are walking around him, pulling out a chair a foot from his head, talking in quiet voices, laughing occasionally.

If this boy were to look up and out the window, he would see another class at recess, climbing a rock wall. Across the room, a girl and a boy are sitting at the snack table, helping themselves to some cheese sticks. In the hallway, two students from an adjacent classroom take turns pushing each other in a large plastic tub down a straight line. In the room, children's bodies are in various stages of movement and repose—sprawled out on the rug, sitting in chairs, standing up, skipping. The Montessori approach represents, in many ways, a direct rebuttal of the confinement of many public schools—not that it should be read in opposition to that approach, because it has its own integrity and is not espoused in opposition to anything. However, the contrast is stark since, as I have been arguing, the classroom for many children, especially younger ones, links learning to sitting still while the Montessori classroom integrates movement into learning. The approach is explained in a book for teachers written by an EAC teacher, Melani Fuchs, and her colleague, Diane Craft, who explain that "movement is integral to the way our brains and bodies learn. We take information into our bodies through all our senses. The information we receive from the senses is integrated within the brain and guides our movements. From these never-ending cycles of sensory input and motor output, we create ourselves" (2012, 5).[3]

A student who is observed to be wiggling and fidgety will not be told to "sit still" but rather to move, as this example from the book illustrates:

a child building words using the moveable alphabet gets distracted and fidgety. The teacher offers the child a "locomotor movement box," from which he or she can pick a card—walk, jump, gallop, skip. The child is then invited to put a rug across the room from the rug where the moveable alphabet is located, choose a card, and perform that physical activity while holding the letters. Upon reaching the other rug, the child builds a word using the large letters. The child can choose more than one movement card—jumping, walking, galloping, sliding across the rug—returning to get more letters, until words are built. In this manner, movement is integrated into the learning process, and a child actively uses his or her body rather than being told to quiet it.

Because learning is overtly linked to movement, teachers can partially gauge a student's progress through observation of their movements; thus, pedagogy is less interpretive—less about getting inside the child's head, which will likely involve a high degree of bias on the evaluator's part, and more about objective observation of what the child is doing. How is he or she moving between stations? Which station is being ignored? Which one is he or she most attracted to? How is he or she holding his or her body—with confidence or not? Maria Montessori based her philosophy on her observations of children with the idea that they should lead the way; unlike the No Child Left Behind or Common Core standards, her methods of instruction were based on what she saw children doing and what they needed. As Fuchs and Craft put it: "observing the way a child works with materials and internalizes information conveys to teachers in what way the child accesses academic concepts. The way a child moves—the coordination and the control of the physical body—gives teachers information that speaks to motor development and integration" (11).

This observation of movement partially circumvents the question of language, of, for instance, what happens when adults ask children a question that to the latter doesn't make sense. The situation is compounded when the child's answer doesn't register with the adult, who then translates it into something that the child didn't mean at all. This is particularly an issue for younger children, who may well have a different way of expressing things than adults demand. So, for example, when I asked Ezra in kindergarten why he was made to sit in the thinking chair, his answer that he didn't know was not insincere. He really didn't understand the teacher's explanation; it made no sense to him that singing a song was not a proper classroom activity. Or, in a different vein, I might ask Ezra why he seems sad or angry, and he will say, "I don't know." If I then offer a series of possibilities, he may say yes or no just to get me to stop talking; I may impose an answer that really has little to do with what he is feeling.

Furthermore, the Montessori curriculum is much less reliant on the developmental model that I have critiqued. Rather, it acknowledges that each child learns at a different pace, and it does not penalize or stigmatize children who learn more slowly in one area or another. Students are considered as individuals who differ in the ways they learn—there is no attachment to a norm or a national standard, though there are benchmarks. In the classroom, thus, students often move autonomously between work stations. "A child with control over self has the ability to move at liberty throughout the classroom, working independently and with concentration. When children develop the ability to choose for self, find calm in a sense of order, have the inner discipline to concentrate freely for long periods of time, and have sufficient coordination to access the rich environment at their fingertips, the mind/body connection emerges" (Fuchs and Craft 2012, 9). As Fuchs and Craft put it, "Montessori said, 'Follow the child.' She did not say, 'Follow the typical child.' . . . All classrooms have children with varying degrees of abilities and disabilities. We are all differently able" (12).

The Montessori approach, thus, actively works against a normative developmental pattern to which all children should adhere, at the risk of being identified as a "slow learner." So, for example, explains Fuchs, say there is a student in the class whom the teacher knows has a sensory processing issue, or difficulty connecting mind and body, such that he or she often feels overwhelmed by loud noises, strange tastes, or new physical sensations of any kind. The teacher could introduce a work to the class with a squishy object, designed especially to give children with sensory processing issues a chance to feel, squeeze, and experiment with a new object. However, because the work is introduced to the whole class, then put at its own work station for each child to access individually, there is no stigma attached to it. The child with the sensory issue can go as many times as he or she likes to the shelf; other kids can also benefit from squeezing the squishy object.

In its emphasis on the "differently able," the Montessori philosophy encompasses the notion of neurodiversity that I described in the introduction—it embraces differences in each child without trying to correct them or compel them into a more acceptable way of learning. Furthermore, it does not subsume the affective within the cognitive or try to manage emotions for the sake of classroom control. When the child is followed rather than expected to follow, the question of control becomes moot, as does the ruse of self-management. If the management emerges from the child's experiences, it is not a strategy for conformity but rather an exercise in autonomy and creativity.

PART II

Kids' Television, from Problem Solving to Sideways Growth

It's such a good feeling, to know you're alive. It's such a happy feeling, you're growing inside. And when you wake up ready to say, I think I'll make a snappy new day, it's such a good feeling. A very good feeling.
—Fred Rogers, host of *Mister Rogers' Neighborhood* on PBS

For more than 30 years, Fred Rogers befriended children in his viewing audience by addressing them directly as kids whose feelings mattered greatly to him. Dressed in his trademark cardigan and tie and sporting his casual sneakers, Mr. Rogers was a gentle, reassuring presence, a kind of community activist who made kids feel like part of his neighborhood and whose main message was acceptance of every child. His long-running show—from 1968 to 2001—was not trying to manage kids' emotions or help them match a single name to a feeling but rather creating multiple outlets for feelings, often in the form of bodily movement. In the episode "Mad Feelings," for example, the puppets in the "neighborhood of make believe" have had an argument, and Lady Elaine "turned the castle upside down" in a fit of rage. She realizes what she has done is wrong and apologizes to her friend: "I'm sorry, my mad got the worst of me." Returning to the "real world," we find Mr. Rogers, who says:

> Lady Elaine says she'll try to do healthier things next time she's angry. It's so important to know there are things you can do when you're angry that don't hurt you or anybody else. (He starts singing.) What do you do? Do you punch a bag, do you pound some clay or some dough? Do you round up friends for a game of tag and see how fast you go? (He stops singing.) The more of those things you find, the more grown up you're getting to be. You know, as you do that, I hope you'll remember how very proud I am of you and how glad I am to be your neighbor.

In suggesting the physical activities, Mr. Rogers acknowledges the possibility that kids won't be able to—or won't want to—"name their feelings" in the way I have described "emotional intelligence" in previous chapters. Notably, he doesn't try to give them the words they need or tell them how they're feeling. Still, there are concrete outlets for anger that will help them feel good, and if they can find those outlets, that's a sign that they're growing up. He thus counters the developmental model that valorizes a linear movement from feeling to naming and control of one's body.

Mr. Roger relies on the old-fashioned kind of interactivity—simply breaking the fourth wall and welcoming kids into his house. By contrast, most kids' programming today, including *Daniel Tiger's Neighborhood*, the PBS spin-off of *Mister Rogers*, connects the television show to multiple online platforms, making interactivity more technological. In the app "Sing-Along with Daniel," for example, "children can choose from 18 of their favorite Daniel Tiger's Neighborhood songs, each one fully animated and expressing a different feeling." With the "Feelings Photo Booth," children can "take pictures of themselves making their sad or mad or happy faces. See how Daniel looks when he feels that way too!" Using the language of emotional intelligence, PBS elaborates: "Daniel Tiger's Grr-ific Feelings is based on the PBS KIDS series Daniel Tiger's Neighborhood, produced by the Fred Rogers Company. Targeting kids ages 2–5, the app is designed to extend the series' social-emotional curriculum, helping kids identify and express their feelings."

At a time when kids are using smart devices at ever younger ages, the "social-emotional" education component allows media companies to address parental concerns about the long-term effects of too much screen time. In January 2018, for example, two of the largest investors in Apple wrote an open letter to the company urging them to take steps to counter children's "addiction" to iPhone usage. They wrote: "Apple can play a defining role in signalling to the industry that paying special attention to the health and development of the next generation is both good business and the right thing to do" ("Apple Investors" 2018). This phrase—"good business and the right thing to do"—intersects with the "good for the team, good for the nation" message of emotional intelligence as it plays out in schools, as I argued in the last chapter. Businesses are urged to look out for the "health and development" of children, linking them with schools and government, all of whom are interested in cultivating technologically savvy citizens, beginning in preschool. As media scholar Amy Shore says: "The new media landscape for pre-schoolers is a world that fosters the development of 'convergence citizens' capable of navigating across media platforms by understanding how the various platforms seamlessly construct 'their' world. Convergence citizenship becomes the ultimate destination. . . . Emphasis is placed on a new ideal of participatory culture that Henry Jenkins describes as shifting the notion of media literacy away from one of individual expression to community involvement" (2009, 29).

Yet how participatory is this convergence culture? While some kids do range across platforms, actively seeking games and characters they like, the language of social-emotional development gets reinforced through the constant repetition of the "naming of feelings" discourse—ironically, quite in contrast to Mr. Roger's open-ended questions. At this age, few kids are interacting with other kids online in a manner that allows them to construct their own language and communities. Interactivity functions as self-management, as kids navigate spaces that have already been constructed for them, "choosing" from options that have been predetermined.

The hook is the narrative—a story that begins on television and continues across screens, often in more fragmented ways, in the form of games and video clips. In the next chapter, I analyze these televisual narratives, returning to Massumi's critique of the manner in which emotions are embedded in storylines so as to qualify affective intensity. These storylines are based on the idea produced by the industry and grounded in focus-group research that television can benefit kids if special care is taken to match programming complexity with their cognitive and emotional development. If kids stay tuned in, then they can actually learn from television, countering the still prevalent belief that younger children are just attracted to the images: "In contrast to some populist claims that young viewers are 'hooked' on or 'hypnotized' by television, research has found that preschool viewers clearly demonstrate very frequent changes in orientation, moving back and forth between the screen and the surrounding environment. Attention continues to grow as a function of the child's development, personality, program content, and environment. The ability to sustain interest in the television program for longer stretches of time and to manipulate one's own attention to television, as well as to competing activities, is gradually strengthened and modified" (Lemish 2008, 155–56). In fact, several long-term studies found that children who watch a greater amount of age-appropriate programming—such as *Sesame Street*, *Blue's Clues*, and *Dora the Explorer*—did better in school than their counterparts who watched less of these shows. Their performance improved in skills related to numbers and letters, in the understanding of diversity, and in dealing with emotions (Lemish 160). In addition, "watching programs that use attractive storytelling formats was found to be associated with positive language development" (Lemish 159).

Who could object to television watching for kids, even young ones, if it makes them smarter, more well-adjusted? Connections to other screens could enhance this development, especially because interactivity seems to mitigate passive consumption. Yet as David Buckingham argues in his work on kids' media, "'activity' should not in itself be equated with agency, or with social power" (227). Insofar as interactivity coincides with the discourse of emotional intelligence, it helps produce the normative view of the well-adjusted child that I have been critiquing throughout this book. Television and its convergence with other media are powerful sites for how the very category of "children" gets constructed in the U.S. Thus, while I am not making an argument in this chapter about how any one child interprets or takes up these programs, I am arguing that they shape the way kids manage their emotions—both directly and through their larger role in the social construction of "the child."

The degree to which kids take up the subject positions constructed for them will be, as Buckingham says, a question of negotiation and struggle: "Texts position readers, but readers make meanings from texts. . . . [M]edia producers imagine and target audiences; but audiences are elusive, and the changing behavior of audiences in turn produces changes in the practices of media institutions" (228). I offer evidence for the "elusiveness" of audiences in chapter 6 on the program *Steven Universe*, where I analyze fan comments about the show and fan-art on Tumblr. Not only does this research demonstrate that kids don't always take up the position constructed for them (by, for example, adult critics), it also shows the ways kids start talking to each other about the texts. These conversations decenter the text and compel us to consider the context, such as Tumblr, where these conversations take place. As Buckingham puts it, "rather than regarding what children say at face value, as some kind of self-evident reflection of what they 'really' think or believe, . . . talk should itself be seen as a form of social action or performance" (226).

Finally, I wish to emphasize that "children's television" cannot be homogenized. As I describe in the next chapter, there is a whole genre of what I call "sideways growth" television for kids that encourages them to defy proper behavior, to revel in their bodies, and to occupy spaces of intensely affective pleasure. Furthermore, these programs, mainly on Cartoon Network, do not negate the need for problem solving; they just define problem solving in much more creative fashion. *Steven Universe* extends this genre by providing subject positions for kids who don't fit, or don't want to fit, into any easily defined categories. The show provides a space of affective pleasure—of pure experience, as the character Garnet suggests.

5

TV's Narratives for Emotional Management

Karen Chau's web site of animated characters inspired by her Chinese American childhood attracted the attention of a Nickelodeon producer in 2003; it was an opportune moment for the freelance artist to develop her Hello Kitty–inspired characters into a series because they spoke to two goals of the network. One, Nickelodeon was looking to expand its repertoire of shows with diverse characters, and two, the network loved the fact that Chau's story ideas focused on emotions. Initially, the network planned to call it *Downward Doghouse,* playing on the protagonist's "mind-body" connection and use of yoga as a coping mechanism. Then, however, the network picked up another show, *Lazy Town,* that emphasized fitness and nutrition and opted to "'pull back on the yoga and focus on emotional intelligence'" (quoted in Hayes 2008, 26). They called the show *Ni Hao, Kai-Lan* (Hello, Kai-Lan).

The series as it developed into a popular Nick Jr. program illustrates the appeal of both emotional intelligence and diversity—two discourses that coincide around the management of difference. Six-year-old Kai-Lan speaks frequently in Mandarin, translating for her audience, and with her grandfather Ye-Ye embraces Chinese cultural traditions. She also frequently negotiates disputes between her friends—Rintoo the tiger, Tolee the koala, and Hoho the monkey; at the successful resolution of the conflict at the end of each episode, Kai-Lan says, "You make my heart feel super happy!" Similarly, Nick Jr., Disney Jr., and PBS all feature shows with a wide range of racially and culturally diverse characters, from the Latina/o protagonists of Nick Jr.'s *Dora the Explorer* and *Go, Diego, Go* to the African American stars of Disney's *Doc McStuffins* and *Jake and the Neverland Pirates* to the diverse casts of almost all PBS shows. Managing cultural differences is linked to managing emotional differences, leading to the multiculturally integrated classroom and, eventually, the tolerant nation.

The goal of all this management is to help kids become adept and independent problem solvers, as I argued in chapter 4. The "problem" is the emotional outburst—and the "solution" is the management of the emotion. Television programming embeds these solutions in a narrative geared especially for kids between the ages of three and six, the period during which their cognitive skills are presumably developing such that they can follow a story with a cause-and-effect trajectory. In this normative view, their skills include the "understanding of storylines and narratives, including the ability to reconstruct events, understand sequence, distinguish between central and incidental information, connect causes to consequences; the understanding of characters such that they are able to describe characters not only by exterior appearance, but also by personality traits, motivations, feelings, personal history, and social orientation, as well as the contexts in which they interrelate with others" (Lemish 2008, 157).

This combination—the ability to follow a story and identify with a character—leads us back to Massumi's description of the way in which emotion enters into narratives. Recall his point (as explained in chapter 1) that "the qualification of an emotion is quite often, in other contexts, itself a narrative element that moves the action ahead, taking its place in socially recognized lines of action and reaction" (86). Emotions become the vehicle for advancing a story whose ultimate goal is to help kids successfully enter into the institution of the school, to learn how to manage both their bodies and their emotions, and to respect the emotions of others. This successful socialization is best achieved when parents are actively involved in their children's television consumption, such that they can "encourage them to internalize messages selectively and critically, to intervene immediately when children are exposed to objectionable content in their opinion, to handle emotional reactions of the children and the like" (Lemish 2008, 162–63). Television thus serves as the bridge between home and school, as parents and teachers are linked in the common goal of helping kids become good team players. However, kids are also encouraged to process these lessons on their own—to self-manage—through the various kinds of interactivity I described in the preface to this section.

Not all programming aimed at younger kids valorizes this kind of management, however. The focus on diversity often extends to an embrace of physical differences—all kinds of bodies of different shapes, sizes, and colors appear on these shows, with no attempt to hierarchize or categorize. This embrace becomes more obvious in the shows I analyze from Cartoon Network; while these shows may still endorse a kind of linguistic management of feelings, the affective realm often triumphs through the sheer force of bodily energy. These shows revel in farts, boogers, vomit, twerking buttocks, and a wide variety of other malleable body parts. Together, they exceed all forms of management and provide kids a space to begin to develop cultural expressions emanating from and returning to the body.

Where to Go after *Sesame Street*

Daniel Anderson is the first to admit that as an assistant professor lecturing on child development and behavior in the 1970s, he subscribed to the commonplace idea that young children did not actively engage with television. He relates how, when asked by a student why children seemed to engage with *Sesame Street*, he replied "glibly, and with the aplomb of a person who is deeply ignorant," that "the child's sustained attention was illusory" and that "TV was just a distractor" (242). Troubled, however, by his own glibness, Anderson decided to look further into research on children's television viewing; finding very little, he decided to pursue it himself and discovered through his focus group studies that even young children can learn from television, if the programming is designed to meet their cognitive levels of development. Eventually, in 1993, he was asked by Nickelodeon to assist in the production of a new program, what was to become *Blue's Clues*, as part of the network's efforts to design kids' programming that was both educational and entertaining.

As Sarah Banet-Weiser (2007) describes it, Nickelodeon started in 1977 as the first cable channel for kids, marketing itself as an alternative to both PBS and the broadcast channels' programming. Like PBS, it was initially commercial free, responding to widespread concerns about the commercialization of children's programming. Initially known as Pinwheel, it was part of Time Warner's QUBE cable network, and "was designed to offer children's programming that was prosocial, nonstereotypical, and commercial free" (52). Much like PBS, it received corporate underwriting; also like PBS, parents liked it, but most kids found it boring. Then in 1983, Geraldine Laybourne took over; "she immediately sought to make Nickelodeon the MTV equivalent for younger children, a hip, fun home base" (53). Nick Jr., aimed at children under six, began as a programming block in 1993 and was launched as its own channel in 2009 (while also continuing as a block on Nick).[1]

What did Nickelodeon have to offer to distinguish itself from the long-running and reputable *Sesame Street*? Launched in 1969, the show has been lauded for increasing kids' school-age readiness in counting and reading as well as for advocating "multiculturalism through the presentation of diverse communities interacting in an idealized neighborhood where antagonisms are channeled into dialogue and 'teachable moments'" (Shore 2009, 29). As "teachable moments" suggests, the show offered a magazine-style format, not a narratively oriented show.[2] By contrast, Anderson set out to prove that young children can actually concentrate on a sustained narrative—if it is pitched at the right level, incorporating repetition and clear transitions, with an interactive narrator. Anderson found that many television producers had no background in child development theory and did not understand that children do not intrinsically have short attention spans; rather, they will stay actively and mentally engaged with a program when it is premised on their developmental capabilities.

This commitment to narrative opens the door as well to the integrated appeal required of emotional intelligence; whereas *Sesame Street* has not overtly distanced itself from emotional expression, its focus has been on academics and diversity, as Shore notes. The research into *Blue's Clues*, by contrast, was more amenable to the discourse of emotional intelligence I have described: "Understanding the cognitive, emotional, and social capabilities of preschoolers is helpful in every aspect of design" (Anderson 2004, 256). The 30-minute time slot allows for a narrative development that incorporates these elements into a story designed to maintain kids' attention. If frustration can be avoided, then kids are more likely to follow the narrative, to help solve the problem, and to feel good about themselves. *Blue's Clues* was premised on the idea that not only can television make kids smarter but also that intelligence increases when kids' feelings are affirmed. "As children learned to solve the problems," Anderson notes about his focus groups, "they would shout out the answers" and "jump with excitement" (263). Similarly, in Nick Jr.'s popular *Dora the Explorer*, the seven-year-old Latina invites the audience to help her negotiate a quest that involves following her trusty map.

She pulls the audience in through various interactive devices, including moments when a virtual viewer clicks on a mouse to direct Dora on different paths. Each episode culminates in success, of course, with Dora and her sidekick, Boots the monkey, breaking into song: "We did it! Lo hicimos!"

Not to be outdone by its primary competition, Disney implemented its preschool programming as a block on its regular Disney channel in 2011, then a year later as its own separate channel. By 2013, *The New York Times* reported, Disney Jr. had overtaken Nick Jr. in the Nielsen ratings, with hits *Sofia the First*, about a princess who attends a prep school run by fairies, and *Doc McStuffins*, about a young girl who runs a clinic for stuffed animals who come to life. One reason Disney seems to have taken the lead, suggests the *Times*' reporters, is its recognition that academic success is no longer the only or even primary parental concern: "What matters more now, Disney said, is emotion-based storytelling that captures attention long enough to teach social values and good behavior" (Barnes and Chozick 2013). Disney's insight, as I noted in the introduction, captures perfectly the ingredients of an emotional intelligence that aims to help children become better team players.

The Benefits of Teamwork

The problem-solving approach defines the central narrative of many young children's shows, including PBS's *Peg Plus Cat* (2012–); Nick Jr.'s *Team Umizoomi* (2010–2014), *Dora the Explorer* (2000–2014), *Blue's Clues* (1996–), and *Wonder Pets!* (2006–); and Disney Jr.'s *Jake and the Neverland Pirates* (2012–2016) and *Max and Ruby* (2002–). In many of these shows, one of the main characters turns to the viewers and welcomes them into the story world, often asking them to join in a chant or other trademark opener. Then, the problem of the day is introduced; this problem almost always involves the need to help someone express some kind of emotion such as anger, sadness, boredom, or fear. At times, this emotion is explicitly named (as in "Sam is feeling sad. Can you help us make him feel better?") At other times, the problem is more physical and/or practical, such as something is lost or someone is in trouble. The crew/team then have to put their heads together—again, frequently involving the audience—to figure out how to solve the problem for their friend. The journey then begins, replete with numerous obstacles that require the team to come up with solutions, often involving word or number games. There are definite moments of failure and frustration, but always a "can do" spirit that prevails until the puzzle is solved or the quest completed. The narrative ends with a return to the person or animal in need, now happy and safe.

Each of these programs engages children in a kind of guided creative exploration in which along the way they encounter various challenges, either emotional or cognitive. In a classic example of Althusserian interpellation, viewers are hailed, as the host often looks directly into the camera and asks them questions, then pauses, waits for the answers, and assumes, of course, that the answers will be the ones that allow them to move forward with the quest. Viewers are never alone because they are sutured into the narrative and often times help provide the character with the answers.

Viewers are further guided to recognize their place in this world, to look around them and see what characters are feeling and experiencing. What names do we give these feelings, and how are we contributing to them? For example, in the "Brand New Game" episode of *Blue's Clues*, the adult (but boyish) host Joe skips up to Sidetable (literally a side table), who is looking happy, and says to him, "Hi, Sidetable, we're here for our notebook." Sidetable's face immediately becomes sad, and he says, "Joe, you didn't say please. That makes me sad." And Joe breaks into a song, "I'm sorry! I did that. I made Sidetable feel sad. May we *please* have our notebook?" Sidetable grins and says, "That makes me happy. Yes, you may!" Joe dances and jumps around, then says it's time to look for clues. "Will you help me?" he says to the audience and pauses. "You will? Thanks. Let's go!" He starts running and singing, "We are looking for Blue's Clues, wonder where they are." And then a child's voice calls out, "A clue!" Joe pretends not to understand: "A shoe? A shoe?" Then the child says again, "A clue!" Joe finds the clue and sings, "You did that!" and writes it down in his "handy-dandy notebook." Children learn that saying "please" makes people happy and facilitates the social interaction entailed in learning, much as I described the focus on "niceness" in chapter 3. The lesson requires them to participate and move along a path toward a goal.

In another episode, "Body Language," children are invited to learn the concept of "body language" by guessing the emotions Joe and Blue (the dog) are expressing through their expressions and body postures. "Hi!" says Joe. "Blue and I are playing the feelings game. You'll play with us, right? [pause] You will? Great! Come on!" He jogs along happily, calling out for Blue. "Here's how we play: first you look at me and figure out how I feel, OK? What feeling is this?" He smiles broadly and Blue jumps around, and a child's voice calls out, "Happy!" Joe runs up to the camera and says, "You look happy! You're really good at this game." He then acts out "sad," and tells the audience to act out, in succession, sad, sleepy, scared, and angry (with scrunched-up eyebrows). "You are so good at using—and reading—body language. Thanks for your help!" The episode is geared toward children who are just learning to articulate their feelings; it illustrates that words aren't always the best way to figure out how someone is feeling.

The naming of a discrete emotion early in the episode works to preclude other reactions—though of course some children will respond differently. What if the child were to decline Joe's invitation, for example? One can imagine an affective response to Blue, a very cute puppy who could inspire the viewer to run and jump and exclaim. Yet doing so outside the terms of the narrative would mean that the child is excluded from the quest. By contrast, if the child accepts Joe's invitation, and, in this example, plays the feelings game, he or she feels included and learns that naming one's emotions leads to belonging and success. The child still gets to move along with Joe—no need to sit still—but the movement is along a guided and structured path, with stops along the way for further naming of emotions.

This emphasis on agreeing to the terms of the narrative does not require that children immediately agree. In fact, the very notion of problem solving is intended to put the child in the position to figure out the answer. These narratives allow children to resist, to say no, to question the authority figure—but then, gradually, to agree to be guided into the appropriate response. In the language of diagnosis, child psychologists call this "healthy" disagreement a form of "assertive noncompliance," which is considered normal behavior for young children, as opposed to "problematic noncompliance": "Normative noncompliance is characterized by affectively regulated, goal-directed, adaptive behaviors, which are responsive to adult redirection. In contrast, problematic noncompliance has been defined as active resistance to control and refusal that is often associated with negative affect. This includes 'doing the opposite' of what was asked, an automatic, reflexive 'no,' and noncompliance in the context of angry outbursts" (Chacko et al. 2009, 634). In this formulation, "good" noncompliance is actually supposed to happen, within certain limits, so children will learn to disagree and choose another option that is still within the structure, in a classic instance of self-management. This problem solving also exemplifies the kind of "critical thinking" skills incorporated in the Common Core curriculum. By contrast, "problematic noncompliance" is associated with a more sustained refusal; the child will not self-manage, which means responding to "adult redirection." It is exactly what children's programming aims to head off by showing children how to disagree within limits.

Disney Jr.'s *Max and Ruby* frequently illustrates how "normative noncompliance" can function as a lesson in eventual compliance. Max is the toddler-rabbit, just learning to talk, and Ruby is his older sister/mother figure (there are no parents present). Max consistently makes trouble for his sister—not listening, defying her wishes, generally getting into trouble in a kind of loveable way. In "Max Misses the Bus," for example, Ruby is trying to get him to stop playing with his toys so they can catch the bus and go to her friend Louise's house to play. Max doesn't want to go; he keeps repeating: "Stay home." Due to his recalcitrance, they miss the bus four times. At last, however, he understands how badly his sister wants to see her friend, and he packs up his toys and leaves the house. They are about to catch the last bus of the day when it turns out Ruby has forgotten her purse, causing them to miss the bus once again. Fortunately, Louise has gotten tired of waiting for them and has taken the bus to Ruby's house. Happily for Max, they get to "stay home" after all, and his last-minute agreement is rewarded.

In "Max's Rainy Day," Max wants to stay out in the rain and play, and Ruby says no at first, pulling him inside. But he insists, repeating, "Outside." Ruby agrees, but only if they put on all their rain clothes. They painstakingly put on one item after another—boots, slickers, hats—with Ruby narrating the importance of staying dry. By the time they get outside, Max is jumping up and down with excitement, and Ruby is also happy to play in the rain. However, the moment they step out the door, the rain stops. Crestfallen, Ruby says they must go back inside and take off their rain clothes. Max has the solution: he turns on the faucet, arches the hose, and sprinkles water on Ruby such that she thinks it's raining, and she laughs indulgently. Even though Max is acting outside the boundaries, he has chosen an option that still displays consideration for others—he has solved the "problem" of no rain.

True to the principles of emotional intelligence, many of these programs also demonstrate that problem-solving approaches rely on an integration of emotional and cognitive skills. The team works together to show that learning these skills makes you part of the team. For example, in an episode of Nick Jr.'s *Team Umizoomi* called "The Elephant Sprinkler," the team of Milli and Geo (sister and brother), and their robot friend Bot get a call from Kayla, played by a real little girl (all the other characters are animated), who is at the water park on a hot day. She is visibly upset and impatient because the elephant sprinkler is not working. The team has to figure out why, using their "mighty math skills." How does water get to the elephant sprinkler? Bot explains that rainwater flows out of the reservoir, into pipes that carry it throughout the city, including the sprinkler in the playground. The team makes a plan to check the lake, the big pipes, and the small pipes. Does the lake have enough water?

The team frequently turns to the audience and asks for their help: "When you see the lake, say, 'Lake!'" How deep is the lake? Milli can measure the lake with her ponytails that grow when a composite audience voice calls out, "Milli measure!" And "How can we get to the bottom of the lake?" Geo offers to make a submarine, with shapes, and the audience helps him put the shapes in the right place in order to make the sub. The questions guide the viewer into staying focused on the narrative: "When you see snails, say, 'Snails.'" Obstacles are confronted: the lock to the gate won't open, until they can figure out the number pattern ("2, 4, 6, 2, 4, 6, 2 . . . what number is missing?") Then there is affirmation: "Umi friend, you did it again!"

The team's happy collaboration is contrasted to Kayla's frustration; she calls them to say that the sprinkler is still not working, and "it's really hot." She is on the verge of demonstrating some serious frustration! The team gets to work to discover what is blocking the water passage, and finally they discover a rubber duck stuck in one of the pipes. They hop on the duck, riding it out of the pipe and unblocking the water. They arrive at the water park to find Kayla happily dancing in the fountain. The team has used their problem-solving skills to find a solution that demonstrates their empathy for a friend in need. Kayla called on her friends to help her before she got too frustrated. Problems solved.

In some programs, the rewards for solving problems are material—along the lines of a behavior modification approach in which the characters get an actual reward for their efforts. This is the case, for example, in Disney Jr.'s pirate show *Jake and the Neverland Pirates*. The altruistic crew of (captain) Jake and his two mates, Izzy and Cubby, battle the evil Captain Hook and his sidekick, Smee; the latter two are quite hapless villains, as usually they just want to join the fun that the three children are having but don't know how to play nicely and often steal something from the kids, which then sets in motion Jake and his crew's efforts to get back whatever was taken. Often, the crew offers to share with Captain Hook or invites him to participate—if he can be nice. At the beginning of each episode, the audience is asked by Jake: "Ahoy maties, do you want to join my pirate crew? Say the pirate password—yo ho ho." At each successful stage of the quest, they discover a number of gold doubloons, and at the end, they count the doubloons and put them in their pirate chest. Viewers are interpellated into a subject position that rewards them for playing by the rules: they are complimented for their math skills, made to feel like a part of the team, and awarded doubloons when they solve the problem. In this case, the structure is overtly capitalist, and the children are happiest when they are counting up their coins; thus, the preparation is not only for school and teamwork but for the workplace environment in which teamwork improves the bottom line.

These programs prepare children to enter the classroom, as they have already been socialized to the benefits of good behavior. They can express themselves, as long as they do so within an already defined structure that the teacher ultimately controls. For young children, this entails a considerable degree of discipline over their bodies; controlling emotions means controlling the affective responses that emerge spontaneously—yelling, burping, jumping, running, climbing. It also means learning the appropriate words; the command of language that is developing at this age is being guided into the proper expression. Responding correctly to answers is part of the appropriate bodily and emotional response—as cognitive, emotional, and physical elements merge into the definition of the well-behaved student. Children are explicitly invited to participate in a situation that has already been defined—they are encouraged to be active, yet this activity comes with embedded limits. No characters on any of these shows question its premises; should, for example, the gold doubloons be saved in the chest? Why not go out and spend them immediately?

As with the example of Ezra's kindergarten classroom that I described in the last chapter, students are asked seemingly open-ended questions that actually have highly circumscribed "correct" answers. If the students diverge from this structured freedom, they will find themselves excluded and perhaps disciplined, as was Brandon in the kindergarten classroom (and Ezra, plenty of times). Their isolation becomes physically palpable, and their frustration grows because they cannot match their feelings with those allowed, even though they are seemingly being given opportunities for expression. Why does everyone else seem happy?

We end up, finally, with a clear recipe for self-management—one that is not devoid of creativity and expression but also one that functions well within a disciplinary space and that relies on mastery of normative language skills. Most importantly for my purposes, it allows no room for alternative feelings—bodily or outside the accepted language—and thus increases the frustration of the nonconformists. Ironically, the very management of emotions intended to head off anger could very well increase its frequency and its volume.

Celebrating Extra Toes

Despite its reliance on a conformist notion of emotional management, children's programming embraces bodily differences—an important message to convey to kids as they enter the years in which judgments about appearances become more common. At a basic level, television helps children feel good about their bodies because there are so many different kinds of animated bodies represented. For example, in Cartoon Network's *Clarence*, the title character is a rotund ten-year-old with an unusually shaped head who is completely at ease with himself (see figure 5.1). In Cartoon Network's *The Amazing World of Gumball*, the "nuclear family" is composed of two anthropomorphized cats (the mother and one son, Gumball); a fish (one son, Darwin); and two rabbits (the father and the daughter, Anais). Darwin and Gumball have an array of

Figure 5.1. Sumo, Jeff, and Clarence of Cartoon Network's *Clarence*, cartoonnetwork.com.

classmates who, for no particular reason, consist of a cloud, a banana, a balloon, a ghost, and others. In Disney's *Phineas and Ferb*, the family is more recognizably human, but one brother, Phineas, has a decidedly triangular head, and the other, Ferb, has an elongated body and head, with protruding ears and a mop of green hair. It's simply impossible to define any kind of normative body when there are dozens of different shapes circulating across the channels. Furthermore, in the shows featuring family configurations, children often do not resemble their parents or their siblings.

Difference is empowering. Due to the magic of animation, these bodies are malleable, flexible, reconstitutable, and largely impervious to physical injury. Arms and legs can stretch to unfathomable lengths; bodies can fly off roofs and slam into the ground, then get up and run away; heads can swivel 360 degrees. For kids, such physical prowess is likely appealing when, in their "real lives," they are beginning to understand the limits of their physical agency—living in a world constructed for adults. And these are not superheroes—these are the physical capabilities that every character possesses, in some fashion. In fact, superheroes, such as the Teen Titans on Cartoon Network, are represented as just ordinary kids rather than infallible (adult) heroes. Each of the teens has a distinct personality more than a power. Starfire, for example, comes from the planet of Tamaran and while ostensibly sweet and kind, quickly angers and shoots fire out of her fingertips. Beast Boy can transform into various animals; Cyborg is, not surprisingly, a robot; Raven is a bookworm sorceress; and Robin is the ambitious entrepreneur who really has nothing remarkable about him.

The narrative introduces the channeling of these bodily differences into the naming of emotions that are part of a social situation. The shows help children clarify feelings about bodily differences during the crucial period of entry into school and other sites where differences become more intensely labeled and scrutinized. In other words, at a key moment when children are beginning to see themselves in relation to peers, to compare themselves, and to form social networks, they are learning from much television programming to appreciate differences without creating hierarchies based on appearance. Take, for example, the *Clarence* series, in which Clarence and his two best friends represent three seemingly odd ducks who seem to get along just fine. One of the friends is Jeff, whose square head symbolizes his uptight, orderly character. The third of the tight-knit trio is Sumo, a tough, scrawny kid who comes from a large, low-income family who seems to love him but mainly ignores him. As a result, he seems much older and tougher than his ten years. Encouraged by his single mother, Clarence always says how he feels, which sometimes gets him in trouble but also indicates his lovable honesty, sometimes in contrast to his friends and teachers.

Occasionally, the show applies this openness to the topic of physical differences, as in the episode entitled "Jeff's Secret." In the opening scene, Clarence and Jeff are running through the sprinkler. Jeff is wearing socks, which goes unremarked until he sees a hole in one sock and goes inside to change, telling Clarence not to follow him into the room where he is changing. Clarence follows Jeff's injunction initially but then, forgetting himself, opens the door and discovers Jeff's secret—that he has an extra toe on one foot. He counts, "2, 3, 4, 6—Jeff you have an extra toe! TOE! TOE!" Jeff is extremely distressed and worried that someone else will find out. The scene shifts to Jeff's living room, where he sits shivering and worried on a chair with Clarence across the room from him. On the couch are Jeff's two moms—another sign of the show's embrace of difference. This conversation ensues:

MOM #1: Clarence, we brought you here today because we want to tell you something about Jeff.
MOM #2: You see, Jeff is a special boy.
CLARENCE: Oh, I know he's special. I mean he is my best friend.
MOM #2: What I mean is—he was born with a little something extra. An extra toe.
CLARENCE: Why didn't you just snip it off when he was born?
MOM #2: We can't make that decision for him. Maybe he would want to keep it later on.
JEFF: Clarence, it goes without saying that this stays between us.

Clarence wonders why he has never noticed the extra toe before, and Jeff shows him the plastic cover he wears that holds the two smallest toes together, making them look like one.

At school the next day, Clarence is bursting with the secret; they watch a nature documentary in class, and it happens to be about animals with various kinds of claws and toes, and Clarence imagines Jeff's face in the place of the animals' faces. Jeff is getting paranoid, seeing toes everywhere. At lunch, he imagines his Jell-O saying, "You're not a freak if no one knows about it."

Suddenly, Clarence jumps on top of the cafeteria table and says, "I've been entrusted with someone's secret. A secret about something extra. And I'm going to reveal it right now. There is one with extra parts among us—that someone is right here. [dramatic pause] I've got an extra arm. Thank you for accepting me." He wraps a sweater around himself in a way that makes it look like he has an extra arm. Initially stunned into silence, the students then begin talking. One boy reveals that he doesn't have any eyelashes. Clarence says, "That's OK—everyone is a little bit different." Another kid says he has three nipples. A girl says, "That's not so weird, I have hair in my ears." A child has one eyebrow, another a long tongue, another only eats cheese, and so on.

Jeff is inspired to pull off his toe cap to reveal his extra toe; the kids rush over to see and exclaim in admiration. Clarence says, "Well, it looks like my work here is done." Another kid comes up to Clarence and says Jeff's courage has been an inspiration to him and reveals, "I'm double-jointed," and the kids leave Jeff to run over and see his joint tricks. Jeff runs after them to show him his toe again, and Clarence says, "Don't worry, buddy, your freaky toe is still my favorite." The episode ends with Jeff and Clarence back at the sprinkler, Jeff sans sock and placing his toe cap onto the sprinkler, catapulting it into space.

The episode shows that it is actually the adults—Jeff's moms—who have assumed that his difference will be a problem. Clarence is surprised by the toe, but his main question after the initial surprise is why he didn't know about the toe until now, suggesting that there would be no reason to keep the toe a secret. The cafeteria scene reveals, of course, that the toe is actually cool; everyone wants to be different. "Coming out" in the open with one's secret is a huge relief to Jeff and prompts a wave of self-revelation that brings the students together.

This episode seems tailored to coincide with the endeavors of both empathic education and emotional intelligence insofar as it shows Jeff learning how to name his feelings of shame and then rename them, thanks to Clarence, who openly expresses his love of his own body and of his friend's. The episode does introduce a new element: adults are responsible for creating the very notion of normativity that leads to treating difference as a problem. One might conclude, then, that the show is giving kids practical advice on how to adapt in an adult world that relies on differences in order to define itself. In this interim, in-between space and time, however, kids can revel in all kinds of bodily differences, without channeling them into identity categories. This leads me to my next question: is growing up inevitable?

Farts Are Musical

Some kids' programming subverts the management/developmental narrative by valorizing bodily habits that adults call disruptive—nose picking, farting, burping, pooping, blowing your top in anger. I call this the "growing sideways" genre, drawing on a concept put forth by Kathryn Stockton in *The Queer Child*, as described in the introduction. To reiterate, Stockton argues that children have a different relation to time than do adults; she calls this "growing sideways" in contrast to growing up. Lateral growth better captures a brain's potential, with its "capacity to make neural networks through connection and extension." If one thinks about the brain's lateral explorations, then "'growing up' may be a short-sighted, limited rendering of human growth, one that oddly would imply an end to growth when full stature (or reproduction) is achieved. By contrast, 'growing sideways' suggests that the width of a person's experience or ideas, their motives or motions, may pertain at any age" (11).

"Growing up" corresponds with the linear model of child development, in which children are assumed to move from the largely sensory world of infants and toddlers into the more cognitively defined realm of school and general socialization. They move from a period in which they are fully immersed in the physical world to one in which they are taught to regulate the sensorial. They are also taught to see their bodies in relation to other people and to anticipate others' reactions to acts that might previously have been done spontaneously. As two experts in early childhood education describe this "civilizing" process:

> As "uncivilized bodies," infants and young children are unconstrained by behavioral norms, prone to immediate physical expression of emotions and to satisfying bodily desires without constraint or regard for others.... The teachers' task is to "civilize" children as they care for them. Becoming civilized requires learning to monitor, control, and restrain one's body and bodily expressions. It also requires the deferment and denial of bodily, sensory, and emotional gratification. The civilizing process involves the inculcation of societal norms, conventions and standards, rules, and codes of conduct with respect to behavior and body management. (Leavitt and Power 1997, 43)

While Leavitt and Power treat this process as normal, the "growing sideways" genre resists the transition into a civilized world, defying manners and glorying in what Bakhtin called the "bodily lower strata." Donna J. Grace and Joseph Tobin, theorists of childhood pedagogy, use Bakhtin's notion to critique the lack of bodily pleasure allowed in elementary schooling: "Where the classical body is pure, clean, finished, beautifully formed, and with no evident openings or orifices, the sensual, earthy, grotesque body is protuberant, excessive, impure, unfinished. It emphasizes the parts of the body that open up to the world: flared nostrils, gaping mouth, the anus, and what Bakhtin termed 'the bodily lower strata' (belly, legs, feet, buttocks, genitals)" (1997, 172). Grace and Tobin call for a pedagogy that allows children to revel in the "grotesque," and to delay the moment when they define their bodily pleasures as "grotesque." Tobin describes how he carries through on this theory in his third-grade classroom, allowing students to make videos that other teachers might find questionable, featuring scenes, for example, with "drool, burps, blood, dripping mucus, butt jokes, aggression, violence, and severed body parts. These scenes were enormously appealing to the children and the source of a good deal of transgressive excitement. What was most popular with the children tended to be unpopular with the teachers" (167–68).

One can certainly understand why Grace and Tobin would focus on transgression, and why this may in fact be one of the motivating emotions for children of eight or nine years old, having learned all too well the rules of decorum they are expected to follow and the thrill of transgressing those rules. However, their valorization of transgression suggests that they are seeing children's lives from an adult point of view. They have already sutured them into the affective-cognitive-behavior model, with the behavior figuring as rebellion. The bodily, affective pleasures of the body are named as such within a narrative that posits them as significant only because they signify rebellion of adult norms. Transgression thus hinges kids' pleasures on adults' prohibition of them rather than seeing children's pleasures as autonomously embodied. While this may seem like a fine line to draw, it is nevertheless an important one in terms of maintaining sideways growth as distinct from delayed development. Sideways growth posits a liminal space where one is not expected to move forward or risk being deemed backward; rather, one's movement is dispersed across sites of pleasure.

Children's television in the "sideways growth" genre illustrates a tension similar to what Grace and Tobin describe in the classroom. A considerable number of programs in this genre focus on the butt—an irresistibly provocative zone of pleasure. In Nicktoons' *Breadwinners*, for example, SwaySway and Buhdeuce are two ducks who love to eat and deliver bread all over the universe. Mainly, though, they like to show off their large and pronounced butts, doing all kinds of acrobatic moves that involve their rear ends. Here is what Common Sense Media, the review site for parents, has to say about the show:

> Parents need to know that *Breadwinners* is filled with colorful characters and bizarre predicaments kids will like, as well as an extensive amount of

chaos and pervasive potty humor that parents might not. The main characters talk and joke about their butts repeatedly, and they can "level up" their rumps to use them as weapons, throwing punches at their enemies with their plump cheeks. Farting also is popular and the source of many laughs. Expect some mild racial stereotypes in the characters' appearances and dialogue, which aren't meant to be offensive, and a fair amount of cartoon-style peril. The bottom line? This imaginative show has plenty of sights and sounds that kids will enjoy, but if you're looking for some substance in their entertainment, you won't find it here.[3]

The assumptions in this review are illuminating, if not unexpected. The reviewer links bizarre predicaments and chaos with potty humor, suggesting that the lack of a clear plot line is connected to the focus on the butt, and that's a bad thing. It may be imaginative, but that doesn't mean it is "substantial."

For young children, however, an interest in the lower bodily strata may not be a form of transgression or rebellion—it's just what gives them pleasure. I argue, then, for two possible responses to the many children's shows that celebrate the "lower bodily strata." The first is this realm of transgression—this kind of rule violation can itself produce an affective response—the "thrill" of rejecting adult rules about controlling the body. Second, it's possible to ignore the adult world of rules and simply inhabit the body, especially for children who are closer to four and five years old than seven and eight.

Take, for example, an episode of Nickelodeon's *Sanjay and Craig* titled "Fartwerk," in which young Sanjay and his pet snake, Craig (who can talk and basically acts like a kid), decide to create a "symphony of farts." Sanjay's love interest, an older girl named Belle who is a waitress at their favorite restaurant, admonishes them that "farts are gross. They're not music. They're farts." And thus the bet is on: if the two buddies can make a fart symphony that makes Belle want to dance, she will dance with Sanjay. If not, he will wash dishes at the restaurant.

Sanjay and Craig proceed to traverse the neighborhood, recording the various farts of friends, neighbors, and animals, until they happen upon their archenemy, Leslie Noodman, who, unaware that he is being watched, lets loose an extremely melodious fart. When Sanjay and Craig ask to record it, he responds adamantly, "Farts are personal shames that you keep to yourself... they are evil breezes." To which Craig responds, "Why can't you celebrate it?" Noodman than drifts off into a memory of how his father shamed him for having a musical fart and showed him, by contrast, how a "real man toots," emitting a huge and predictable fart that propels his pickup truck into the air. After getting this story off his chest and receiving assurances of his "manliness" from Sanjay and Craig, Noodman finally agrees to let them record his fart, and the two go on to produce a magnificent symphony to which everyone (including Belle) wants to dance.

This episode clearly valorizes the realm of bodily pleasure, extending the zone of pleasure from the butt to the aural to the movement of the entire body in dancing. Part of the pleasure derives precisely from the violation of rules and from showing adults that they shouldn't be ashamed of their bodily emissions. Sanjay and Craig disrespect the notion of privacy, moving not only from the space of the house to the club but also transforming an individual physical act into a communal one—the fart symphony provides pleasure for a whole group of people! Thus, it's possible to enjoy the farting and dancing and physical pleasures aside from, or at least alongside of, the adult rules, in part because the adults are shown to be misguided. Furthermore, Noodman's father is shown to have antiquated notions of masculinity; the boys reject the idea that they must prove their manliness in favor of proving their "musicalness."

These adult rules of decorum are often revealed to be arbitrary and even impractical. In "Unbarfable," Sanjay and Craig discover that their good friend Hector has never "barfed" in his whole life. They do everything they can think of to induce him to vomit: make him watch a nature show in which a giraffe is giving birth, take him to the "pus bank" in the basement of the hospital, lock him in a bathroom with someone who is having a violent bout of diarrhea—but Hector happily embraces every situation, even using his mouth to blow bubbles out of the pus. When Sanjay and Craig visit Hector's house, they start to understand how he has acquired this immunity: his dad is eating a sandwich off an extremely dirty carpet, his mother is kissing the dog with an open mouth, and his grandma smothers them between her large breasts. Finally, when the grandma brings the boys a snack—*tacos de lengua*—and they eat them, they seemingly acquire the same immunity. What does finally make Hector vomit? When he looks at his own butt in the mirror—something that, of course, Craig and Sanjay are perfectly comfortable doing. Each kid has learned, based on their different household routines, what should induce nausea; however, these rules can also be unlearned. Thus, the lack of household cleanliness in Hector's household is not particular to his Latino culture, nor is Sanjay's obsession with his butt particular to his Indian household. Rather, they are all kids, united in the pursuit of pleasure. The linearity of affect-cognition-behavior that is crucial to emotional intelligence is redefined as a circular movement, with affect then given the potential to redefine cognition and behavior.

SpongeBob and the Drastic Radicals

Recall the study of the nine-year-olds watching the snowman story with which Brian Massumi begins his discussion of affect. The researchers in that situation found that the wordless version of the snowman story was rated as most "pleasant" by the children—more so than the version with either the factual or the emotional voiceover. Massumi argues that "the primacy of the affective is marked by a gap between content and effect: it would appear that the strength or duration of an image's effect is not logically connected to the content in any straightforward way" (84). In other words, an image may well produce strong affective responses without any direct connection to the narrative; this is not to say that the narrative is irrelevant, only that the two may proceed in somewhat disjunctive ways. Children may ignore the storyline for a while as they become immersed in a particularly compelling or pleasing image—say of SpongeBob's eyeballs popping out of his head and then back in.

This is not to argue that children won't understand the narrative—just that they will understand it differently, perhaps not in a cause and effect way. And certainly not in the interest of deconstructing certain ideologies or identity politics, which is the theme of many academic critics of children's programming. In her book on Nickelodeon, for example, Sarah Banet-Weiser focuses on two elements of the popular show *SpongeBob SquarePants*: the campy, ironic nature of the show and the question as to whether SpongeBob may be construed as gay or sexually ambiguous. Similarly, another critic, Heather Hendershot (2004), argues that the show "parodies masculinity and features the most 'out' gay character on children's television," the latter a reference to Squidward.

Banet-Weiser locates her analysis within the context of the show's transgenerational appeal (to both kids and the 18–34 age group); she also connects her reading to the book's larger argument—that ultimately, the consumer appeal of the network works against any kind of critical politics. As she says: "Nicktoons stand out in the television landscape because they are double-edged in meaning, appealing to different generations by employing an ironic social commentary. Yet the critical edge of this commentary needs to be read against the context of the postmodern media economy, where a kind of cool subversion is not so much social critique as a crucial part of a dominant market address" (Banet-Weiser 2007, 180). While these are certainly noteworthy points for an adult audience, they are not issues that most younger kids will take note of, not because they are incapable of understanding social commentary but rather because their frames of reference for what constitutes "the social" are quite different from an adult's. To parody masculinity, for example, a child would need to have a clear idea of dominant modes of masculinity as well as see the need for parody. Perhaps their notion of gender difference is completely different—less about the two categories necessary for parody than a more flexible, still forming exploration of differences between girls and boys. The academic reading, then, perhaps unintentionally inscribes upon children a knowledge of a gender binary that hasn't yet formed and will form in different ways, given the generational difference from academic critics (a difference that was apparent in the *Sanjay and Craig* episode just discussed).

Instead of searching for the parody, *SpongeBob* can be read in relation to an exploration of bodies that does not rely on categories of difference and the naming of identity. Consider, for example, the episode "Extreme Spots" in which SpongeBob and his best friend, Patrick, a starfish, are playing on the beach, building a replica of the Krusty Krab restaurant in the sand. Someone announces that the Drastic Radicals are "tearing it up on Sand Mountain," and everyone runs off to see the daredevils perform their athletic feats. Johnny Krill rides a motorcycle down a steep mountain; Grandmaul Granny and Not Dead Ted perform other death-defying feats. Intrigued, SpongeBob and Patrick ask an "emcee" with a British accent, "What was that?" He explains, while sipping tea through his decaying teeth, that those are the "extreme spots." In doing so, he spits his tea at the two friends, such that they are covered in spots, which

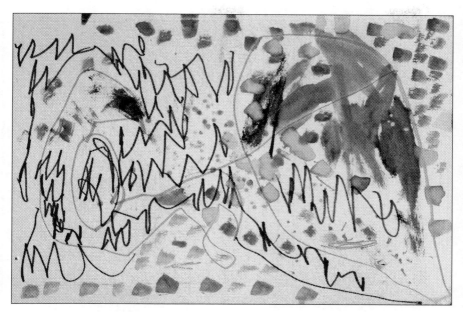

"El Barco," by Fredy, *Arte de Lagrimas* exhibit, Austin, TX.

"La Culebra in Desierto," by Maybeline, *Arte de Lagrimas* exhibit, Austin, TX.

"Manos Fuertos," by Ashley Gabriela, *Arte de Lagrimas* exhibit, Austin, TX.

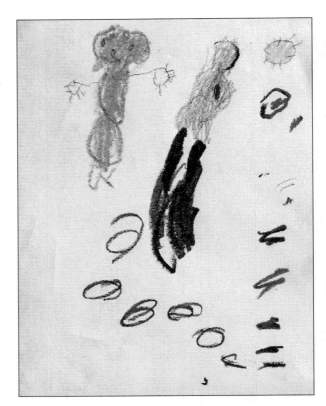

"Amor," by Lesli, *Arte de Lagrimas* exhibit, Austin, TX.

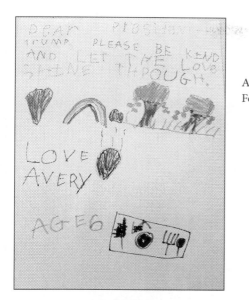

Avery, age six, *Huffington Post*, February 27, 2017.

Osvaldo, age seven, Mighty Writers' Workshop, Philadelphia. *Philly.com*, June 12, 2017.

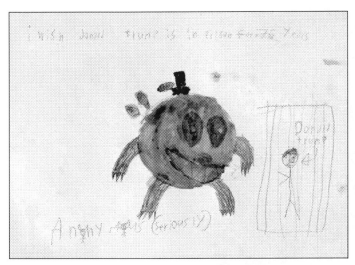

"Anonymous (seriously)," Houston. *Houston Chronicle*, May 23, 2017.

Jonathan, age six, Mighty Writers' Workshop, Philadelphia. *Philly.com*, June 12, 2017.

Anonymous, Austin. *Huffington Post*, March 1, 2017.

Sophie, age nine, Mighty Writers' Workshop, Philadelphia. *Philly.com*, June 12, 2017.

Anonymous, Houston. *Houston Chronicle*, May 12, 2017.

Fanart by artipcon fiziell, Tumblr, http://artifiziell.tumblr.com.

Fanart by Nyong-Choi, Pinterest, www.pinterest.com/pin/416723771752619348.

Stevonnie, Tumblr art by Notice me Senpai, https://stevenkunchan.tumblr.com/tagged/stevonnie.

By Rachel, grade four. Artsonia, www.artsonia.com/museum/gallery.asp?project=1124790.

they believe are necessary in order to be part of the team. SpongeBob already has spots (the holes in his sponge body), but Patrick seeks out some stinging jellyfish in order to be covered by his own spots (jellyfish stings). The two approach the Drasticals and ask to join their "extreme spots," but the team laughs and says, "No, it's extreme *sports*." If they want to join, they'll have to prove they can measure up. A series of body-transforming sports ensues. SpongeBob swallows so much sand while riding the motorcycle that he turns into a large ball of sand. Patrick rides a shell down a mountain and turns into a revolving pinwheel. The team asks them, somewhat sympathetically, "Since our sports are too extreme, what sports do you like to play?"

Jump rope, responds SpongeBob, and they proceed to demonstrate with SpongeBob somehow holding both ends of the rope while Patrick jumps, faster and faster. "My body is leaking!" Patrick exclaims. "It's not leaking, you're sweating from the exercise!" says SpongeBob. "Exercise! I didn't sign up for this!" Patrick responds. SpongeBob suggests blowing bubbles, but the Drasticals are not convinced that is a sport. "Is pillow fighting extreme?" asks Sponge Bob: "Totally!" So he fights a pillow in a boxing ring, but Johnny Krill claims that's not fighting.

There is one sport that Patrick does that qualifies as extreme: he puts on a shower cap and dives head first into a dumpster of slimy trash. To further his case, he finds a toothbrush in the trash and starts brushing his teeth. "That's kind of extreme," concede the Drasticals. Granny climbs up a ladder, says, "Hip don't fail me now," and dives into the trash. Now won over to the "extremeness" of their two new friends, the Drasticals ask what other crazy sport they play. Patrick and SpongeBob show them how they chase jellyfish as if they were butterflies, and the Drasticals join in, getting stung and electrocuted, covered in painful jellyfish bites. They say, "Dude, now we get it. These spots are way extreme."

The episode can easily be read as a parody of the hypermasculine world of extreme sports in which mainly male athletes show off their built physiques. This reading applies, however, only if the viewer is aware of the spoof, and many children—especially younger ones—won't know this genre. It is worth noting here, in terms of narrative, that it is not just Patrick and SpongeBob who are nonnormative in terms of gender types, but also the Drasticals. There is no "us versus them," no setting up of a nonnormative SpongeBob and Patrick versus the normative masculine. Identity categories aren't at play unless the viewer is reading it as a parody of extreme sports.

What happens, by contrast, when one focuses on the images, especially the images of SpongeBob's and Patrick's bodies? The viewer may or may not consume these images in relation to the narrative; my point here is to emphasize the possibility that the characters of SpongeBob and Patrick are so compelling and intriguing in their bodily transformations that they acquire an appeal distinct from the. narrative. Here are some vivid images of bodies and body parts:

> Only Patrick's head is sticking out of the sand, and he says to SpongeBob, "Could you give me a hand?" "Sure thing, buddy," says SpongeBob, and puts his hand in Patrick's mouth, so Patrick can whistle. Patrick's body walks over and pulls his head out of the sand and puts it back on his body.
> As SpongeBob and Patrick watch one of the Drasticals wind his motorcycle down a mountain, their pupils seemingly revolve all the way around their heads, moving in sync with the circling driver.
> SpongeBob pops his eyeballs out of his head and turns them into a set of binoculars.
> Patrick, engrossed in the action, pulls off the top of his head and starts licking his brains as if they were an ice cream cone.
> "Did you see that?" says Patrick, pulling SpongeBob's eyeballs out of his head and then letting them pop back in.
> GrandMaul Granny pushes her walker to the edge of the extension ladder, dives into the dumpster, gets scooped into a trash compactor, dumped out in the form of a large cube of trash, then pops out of the cube, reassuming her former shape.
> The Drasticals get electrocuted by the jellyfish, turn into skeletons, then come back to life.

These bodies are fascinating simply because they are bodies with unusual capacities, not because they are transgressing masculine norms. They are not coded as either weird or normal; there's nothing inherently attractive or unattractive. They are broken down into their parts based on what the character needs or wants to accomplish (seeing better with binoculars), or simply on a whim (eating one's brains). They are leaky and porous, extendable and reconstitutable, the source of tremendous pleasure, fun, and experimentation. Could this body part do this? Try it out! They represent difference without even having to invoke it.

Freaking Out

The malleable and expressive bodies of this sideways growth genre represent to children how their own bodies might be feeling when they are thoroughly immersed in an experience. Unlike the problem-solving programs I describe above, the emphasis here is not on working through an emotion to the point of naming and resolving it. The focus is on thoroughly experiencing the affect, whether it is acceptable to adults or not. Bodily decorum is a bad thing; fully inhabiting your body is a good thing. This irreverence is part of the Cartoon Network brand; even in its programing aimed at younger kids, it sets itself apart from the more didactic programing of Nick Jr. and Disney Jr. In 2012, it introduced new shows aimed at seven- to ten-year-olds, including *Teen Titans Go!*, *Clarence*, *Uncle Grandpa*, and *Steven Universe*.

In many episodes of these shows, characters physically demonstrate their anger, to the point of literally losing it. For example, in the *Teen Titans Go!* episode "Secret Garden," the titans are fighting about who gets "dibs" on the television remote control, and Cyborg starts to "freak out" (see figure 5.2). As he literally loses control, turning bright red and screaming, Starfire (who is from another planet and thus speaks in a somewhat stilted fashion) helps him understand what is happening to his body:

> STARFIRE: You are only in the first stage of your "freaks getting out." Notice your red color.
> CYBORG: I do notice it. I'm like a lobster up in here.
> STARFIRE: And now comes the stage two of the freak-outs. Notice the veins that are doing the bulge on the body.
> CYBORG: (looking in the mirror) It's sick.
> STARFIRE: Yes, but not as sick as the stage three of the freak-outs: the grinding of the teeth.
> CYBORG: (HIS TEETH STARTING TO GRIND LOUDLY, LOOKING AGAIN IN THE MIRROR) This is the worst.

Figure 5.2. Starfire, Robin, Raven, Beast Boy, and Cyborg of Cartoon Network's *Teen Titans Go!*, cartoonnetwork.com.

STARFIRE: No, the worst is the stage four.
CYBORG: What happens at stage four?
STARFIRE: I don't know! No one's freak has ever gone that far out!

To calm Cyborg down, Starfire takes him to her secret garden, a tranquil place with a pond, bunnies, flowers, and music: "This is the place I come to freak in when my freak attempts to get out." Gradually, Cyborg's face returns to its normal color, he strums a banjo, the birds tweet, and the two friends relax on the bench. "This bench really cradles the buttocks," says Cyborg, to which Starfire responds, "Of course, the buttock cradling is essential for the not freaking out."

The newly tranquil Cyborg returns to the house to find the remaining three Titans fighting over cereal and calling "dibs." So he shows them the garden, forgetting about his promise to Starfire to keep it secret, and the others carelessly but unintentionally destroy it, cutting down a tree and turning the pond into a hot tub in which the fish then die. Starfire sees what has happened and rapidly goes through the three stages of anger—then reaches the fourth as a fiery demon escapes from her body. Cyborg says, "Oh no, that must be stage four of the freak out—the freak actually gets out." Starfire is a literal representation of what it feels like to get really angry—the "freak" is a fiery red silhouette of her body with a grimacing face and smoke blowing out the top of her head. Then all the Titans except for Cyborg freak out, and Cyborg realizes he must build a little garden in the middle of the city. He improvises, buying animals from the pet store, using water from the fire hydrant to make a pond, and situating a park bench in the middle. He calls his friends to come and relax, and they all sit down to enjoy "nature." Cyborg apologizes to Starfire for telling her secret, and she accepts. Although the episode does end with a lesson of sorts about making up for your mistakes, the focus is on the feeling of freaking out. The bodies tell the story.

Afraid of the Dark

Young children are allowed and even expected to be afraid of certain things—monsters under the bed or in the closet, ghosts in the attic, water sucking you down the bathtub drain—even though none of these things are "real." As the adult explains, "Nonsense!" Or perhaps, more patiently, he or she will explain why these fears are not rational given the particulars of the situation.

Yet the experience of fear is neither rational nor irrational; it is how one feels, and even if one can process the explanation, the fear may not go away. In fact, the explanation could only heighten the fear, exacerbated as it is now by the feeling of being dismissed or ridiculed. Words do not capture the feeling, and connecting one thing (the source of fear) to another (the reason for not fearing it) does not necessarily follow. Fear registers as a kind of intensity, as Massumi describes it: "[intensity] is not semantically or semiotically ordered. It does not fix distinctions. Instead, it vaguely but insistently connects what is normally indexed as separate." Intensity registers at the "surface of the body, at its interface with things" (85). As was demonstrated in the drawings by the refugee children I discussed in chapter 3, children fear what their bodies will experience if they come into contact with something that could hurt them, or take them away from their family, or even kill them. Their fear may derive from making connections between things that are "normally indexed as separate," but the question is in fact what constitutes "normality." From whose perspective is a situation supposed to make sense?

This adult belief in the power of language to help children "make sense" of things is aptly illustrated on the Common Sense Media site. Consider, for example, this review of Cartoon Network's show *Uncle Grandpa*:

> Parents need to know that although *Uncle Grandpa* is a cartoon, it isn't appropriate for very young kids. Body-related gross-out humor is the main offender, as issues like obesity, farting (including a tiger who passes a rainbow trail from his rear end that doubles as a weapon), and the removal and ingestion of one's own body parts are revisited ad nauseam. There's no semblance of reality to the meandering, fantasy-based plots, and supporting characters are often rude to each other. Despite Uncle Grandpa's craziness, he often proves himself helpful in a roundabout way. Violence is limited to physical exchanges with punching and kicking, as well as the occasional laser gun showdown or stray explosion.[4]

The reviewer transitions from the critique of "body-related gross-out humor" to the lack of reality in the "meandering" plots to the "roundabout" way in which Uncle Grandpa is sometimes helpful. The subtext here is the lack of semiotic order.

At first glance, Uncle Grandpa would seem to be a wise adult; he travels around the world in an RV helping kids "in need" solve their problems. Yet one quickly learns that although he is both an uncle and a grandpa (or perhaps neither), he defies all categories of identity, often showing how ridiculous or inept adults' advice is—precisely because they are too rational or bored to think of anything creative. He is an oddly shaped character, with an elongated head interrupted midway by a furry handle-bar moustache and culminating in a huge, jutting chin. Atop his head is a small helicopter cap that lifts him into the air, and he wears a "belly bag" belt, rather like a fanny pack, whose zipper mouth opens regularly to offer advice. He also wears rainbow suspenders, tightly fitting shorts, knee-highs, and white gloves. His crew includes a slice of sunglass-wearing pizza (Pizza Steve), a laid-back dinosaur man

Figure 5.3. Uncle Grandpa, Pizza Steve, and Mr. Gus on board the Giant Realistic Flying Tiger in Cartoon Network's *Uncle Grandpa*, cartoonnetwork.com.

(Mr. Gus), and the Giant Realistic Flying Tiger (who flies by farting rainbows) (see figure 5.3).

The program illustrates the deconstruction of the binary sense/nonsense posited by Deleuze and elaborated by Liselott Olsson in her analysis of preschool education: children often make up words and play games that make no sense to adults. Yet sense emerges not from predetermined meaning but rather in the process of making meaning: "Young children play with language through inventing it again. They exchange the first letter in a word, they rhyme and sing words and letters and they invent new languages never before heard of. In short, children seem to be using [Deleuze's] idea that all sense words momentarily enjoy a nonsense status. This is often an approach that children have not only towards language but towards most things they learn; everything is potentially otherwise and not static" (Olsson 2009, 114).

Although each episode of *Uncle Grandpa* does follow a somewhat linear storyline, much of the dialogue within the storyline seems superfluous or out of place—some might say it "makes no sense." Yet it's this nonsensical embrace of the sensorial that illustrates Deleuze's deconstruction of the sense/nonsense binary; the route to solving the problem is unpredictable and emerges from the immediate events of the child's life. Uncle Grandpa never lectures or explains but rather joins the child in an impromptu quest.

In the episode "Afraid of the Dark," for example, adults are represented as rational subjects who don't even try to understand the child's perspective. The episode opens with Susie sitting on the bed with her mother, preparing for lights out, saying, "It's so scary, Mom." Her mother assures her that she will be just in the other room, then says, "Just hang in there, kiddo." Susie says quizzically, "Just hang in there?" and her mom repeats, "Yeah, you know, just hang in there," and leaves. Susie tries to reassure herself, repeating the "hang in there" mantra and staring at a poster of a sloth hanging from a tree, with the words "hang in there" written across it.

Then, Uncle Grandpa's foot comes smashing through the wall: "Knock, knock!" he says. When a stunned Susie doesn't answer, a second Uncle Grandpa appears to play out the joke: "Uncle! Uncle who? Uncle Grandpa!" He thus enters not as a hero about to save the day but rather as a jokester—yet not one who makes fun of the child's fears. Uncle Grandpa #2 tells Uncle Grandpa #1 to go see what's in the fridge, then plops down on the bed and tells Susie, "When I was a little girl about your age, I was afraid of the dark too." As he describes his fears, his face grimaces and contorts: "All those wiggly spider monsters, the giant trolls that hide in the closet, the 50-eyed slime-eating bog monster [pulling his eyeballs down so that they multiply and resemble a monster's many eyes], and especially the dark beasts that hide under the bed." Susie responds, "Wow, how did you get over your fear?" And he says, "I didn't! But as a wise man once told me, bologna sandwiches are delicious!" At this point, Pizza Steve appears in a balloon over Uncle Grandpa's head, interrupting what to this point is a fairly linear conversation. The nonsensical idea that a slice of pizza could be a "wise man" and also that his wise advice is that bologna sandwiches are delicious appears to play no role in the lesson, yet its role is in fact crucial in deconstructing the nonsense/sense binary that undergirds the mother's initial attempt to divide the world into rational and irrational feelings.

Uncle Grandpa then continues: "There's nothing to be afraid of in the dark but our own imaginations. So let's start by turning off the lights, and I'll prove to you that there's nothing to be scared of." But he is quickly proved wrong. His arm extends across the room to turn off the light switch, and one by one, the furniture assumes the shapes of horrible monsters—the rocking horse grows fangs and starts rocking wildly, the desk lamp turns into a snapping Venus flytrap, and so forth. Susie exclaims, "I thought you said there was nothing to be scared of but our own imaginations!" Uncle Grandpa responds, "I did, but I didn't know our imaginations were so terrifying!" What could have been a piece of clichéd advice—it's just your imagination—turns out to be a valorization of a realm that cannot be mastered, which in fact does make it terrifying, but something that should be embraced rather than denied or controlled.

Neither—in the spirit of growing sideways—is it a fear that one outgrows. Uncle Grandpa makes it clear that he is still afraid of the dark. The two hide under the bed and then pop their heads out of a dresser drawer, with Uncle Grandpa wiping sweat from his brow and saying, "Man oh man, I'm scared! What do you usually do when you're scared?" Susie says, "I scream for my mom, and she comes and turns on the lights!" so he screams, "MOM!" but the mother is watching television and eating ice cream and doesn't hear him. Uncle Grandpa calls out for Mr. Gus and Pizza Steve, but they are also eating ice cream and watching television and don't hear. Uncle Grandpa and Susie decide to turn the light on by themselves, but now the switch is surrounded by monsters, and the space between them and the switch is filled with gooey lava and flying creatures of all sorts. "I hate my imagination!" despairs Susie.

"We can solve this with teamwork," says Uncle Grandpa. He grabs Susie's pig tails, one in each hand, and uses them as ropes with which to climb down the dresser. "It's a good thing I'm not afraid of heights, or I'd really be in trouble," but then a monster grabs him with its vine-like arms and hangs him upside down, "OK, I'm afraid of heights now." He forms his fingers into a scissors and cuts his own leg off to escape the vine's grip. While Susie is being chased by the snapping desk lamp, Uncle Grandpa distracts the lamp with a dog bone and the two escape together, climbing to the top of a mountain of clothes. He asks his belly bag for directions and the bag gives him a map—which on first glance is not a map at all but a picture, points out Susie, of a "knight fighting a motorcycle." "Maybe to the untrained eye," Uncle Grandpa responds, but then he gets out a magnifying glass and it does turn out to be a map of the bedroom.

Answers are derived only through spur-of-the moment experimentation: "We've got to get past your desk, which is going to be super hard unless you know how to use one of these." Adding "Which I don't," he pulls out a grappling hook and then yanks off his arm and manages to throw both the hook and his arm across the room. Susie "gets on board the Uncle Grandpa express" and he warns her to "get ready, 'cause I don't know what I'm doing." They get past a scary pencil, chomping books, and a creepy giant teddy bear. They continue their journey across a computer keyboard that turns into a snarling cat when Susie says she uses her computer to watch "cute cat videos," then find their way to the gigantic bed/desert, which they trek across for miles, getting so dehydrated that Uncle Grandpa's moustache dries up and falls off. He starts sinking into the sand/quilt, and Susie calls out, "Uncle Grandpa, you're stuck in quilt-sand!" He panics: "OMG, OMG!"

At this point, Susie takes over. She calls out for her pterodactyl fan, climbs aboard, and rescues Uncle Grandpa. Just as they are about to turn on the light, the switch turns into a monster and scares them off. They decide they must turn themselves into monsters, and by transforming themselves into hideously twisted shapes with rows of sharp teeth, they go around the room, scaring the monsters back into their everyday shapes. Finally, back in her usual body, Susie proclaims that, after that, she's not afraid of the dark or her imagination anymore. Susie and Uncle Grandpa turn out to be very convincing monsters. Uncle Grandpa is the paradigmatic example of sideways growth: he does not grow up but rather sideways, insinuating himself into all kinds of situations with a fervor and passion for new experiences.

"Everything is potentially otherwise" opens up a world of possibilities that leads to a solution. The Cartoon Network shows often demonstrate this kind of problem solving, one contingent not on the linear model that proceeds from affect to linguistic command to bodily control but rather one in which these realms are intertwined such that they cannot be discretely identified. These programs lay the groundwork for kids' conversations with each other, showing them that adults can be most helpful when they don't purport to know all the answers.

6

The Steven Universe, Where You Are an Experience

Steveonnie, listen to me, you are not two people, and you are not one person. You are an experience. Make sure you are a good experience. Now—go have fun!
—Garnet, to the fusion of the characters Steven and Connie

In the popular Cartoon Network show *Steven Universe*, characters fuse together when they experience a connection so intense that they physically blend into a hybrid form. They are the embodiment of an affect that erases the normative developmental assumption of a progression from emotions to cognition to proper behavior. Their pleasure is enabled precisely because they transcend labels, categories, and words themselves.

The Stevonnie fusion occurs first in the episode "Alone Together," when Steven dances with his best friend, Connie, on the beach. She admits she has never danced in front of anyone before, so Steven takes out his iPod, puts on some music, and holds out his hand. As they dance and then nearly kiss, without talking, they fuse into one tall, elegant, androgynous being with dark brown skin and long, flowing black hair. Elated at their union, they return to the house to show the Crystal Gems, three female-identifying aliens who take care of Steven. While Amethyst and Garnet are happy, Pearl is taken aback. This conversation ensues:

> PEARL: This is unprecedented—a Gem fusing with a human being. It's impossible, or at the very least inappropriate!
> AMETHYST: Wow! You two look great together! How does it feel, Steven, Connie—Stevonnie!
> STEVONNIE: It feels amazing!
> PEARL: Yes, well, I'm glad you're enjoying yourselves, but you two should unfuse this instant.

STEVONNIE: Wait, what? Pearl, you were so worried Steven wouldn't be able to do this, aren't you proud of him?
PEARL: (stammering) Of course, I am. Garnet, help me out here.
GARNET: Steveonnie, listen to me, you are not two people, and you are not one person. You are an experience. Make sure you are a good experience. Now—go have fun!

This episode speaks powerfully to kids who find themselves in similarly in-between positions, giving them a representation that does not have a name other than "fusion." Stevonnie is racially mixed, both in terms of skin tone and physical features (see figures 6.1, 6.2, and 6.3). They could be said to have a mixed legal status, insofar as they are both human and "alien"—in fact, they are the first human/Gem fusion ever. They resist gender categories, using "they" pronouns and refusing to see themselves as two people and embracing a sexuality that cannot be defined. For kids in between races, genders, and sexualities, Stevonnie represents the hope of passionately occupying an in-between space and making it their own experience. Garnet's encouragement easily trumps the concerns of Pearl, who represents the parent who might say of their nonconforming child: "I don't want life to be hard for them."

The show's appeal to kids is reflected across media, as I will describe in this chapter—on the Common Sense Media kids' review site and in fanart on Tumblr, Instagram, and other platforms. The show's director, Rebecca Sugar, has a fervent fan club of her own. As the first woman director of a show on Cartoon Network, she demonstrates what is possible when adults collaborate with kids. At the 2017 Comic-Con International, she was asked whether a new character on the show, Fluorite, a fusion of six Gems, was polyamorous, and she said "absolutely." She then explained where she got the idea: "It was a little over a year ago, I got to visit this incredible place called The Center, an LGBTQ center in Long Beach, and talk to some of the kids there. We were all chatting together about some things we'd just love to see on the show. That was one of the things that we all agreed we really wanted to find a place for in the show."[1] She has also commented on the gender representation in the show: "My goal with the show was to really tear down and play with the semiotics of gender in cartoons for children because I think that's

Figure 6.1. Steven of Cartoon Network's *Steven Universe*, cartoonnetwork.com.

Figure 6.2. Connie of Cartoon Network's *Steven Universe*, cartoonnetwork.com.

Figure 6.3. Stevonnie, the fusion of Steven and Connie, on Cartoon Network's *Steven Universe*, cartoonnetwork.com.

a really absurd idea that there would be something radically different about a show for little girls versus a show for little boys."[2]

Even as it embraces a passionate fluidity, the show also addresses the ongoing forms of discrimination against kids who don't fit neatly into categories. In this episode, for example, Stevonnie goes to a party, where they elicit admiration from the crowd watching them dance. Kevin, the "cool kid," decides he wants to dance with them, but he mistakes "them" for "her" and calls Stevonnie "babe." Stevonnie starts to feel confused, the fusion starts to unravel, and Steven's and Connie's distinct voices begin to reemerge. They are no longer "in sync" and need to try to communicate their differences. Stevonnie gets angry and tells Kevin, "You want to dance? Let's go. And it's Stevonnie. I am NOT your baby." On the dance floor, Stevonnie dances frenetically, eventually dividing into Connie and Steven, indicating that they have been overwhelmed by conflicting feelings. They are no longer "an experience" but rather compelled by Kevin's assumptions and their own confusion about social norms to become two people again. Still, they end the episode giggling and jumping around the dance floor, while the other kids drift away, following Kevin's lead, who exclaims in shock, "It's two kids! I'm out." The situation is left unresolved, yet Steven and Connie are still optimistic, and Connie seems poised to return to her school with greater confidence in her body.

Steven Universe has a special appeal to kids growing up in complex family arrangements—interracial, blended, mixed legal status, various genders and sexualities. Yet the show also transcends identity and appeals to the more generalized realm of feelings. As one 12-year-old girl on the Common Sense site put it:

> It is the only cartoon that regularly brings a tear to my eye, and makes me want to love everyone (which is not something I can do). I don't always cry for sadness, sometimes for just how the show gives me a sense of human warmth, and that alone is worth crying about. Another bonus is that the leader of the crystal gems is a lesbian black woman and she is still a favourite of the fandom! Also I dont care what the fan base is like so don't call me out on it. Anyway, see what I mean about how it handles love? It puts lesbian couples in the show as a part of everyday life! I love it for that. Cannot recommend enough.

This comment speaks poignantly to the notion of emotion (what I am calling "feelings") as something that "moves one" (see Ahmed, chapter 2); the show moves this girl to cry, to want to love everyone, to feel a sense of human warmth. These feelings seem more powerful to her than the inclusion of a black lesbian couple (that's the added "bonus"); furthermore, what she likes about the couple is that they are integrated into the show rather than highlighted for their diversity.

In the first part of this chapter, I analyze kids' reviews, in juxtaposition to the Common Sense adult reviewer's critique of the show, then shift my focus to slightly older kids, ages nine to 13—the tweens—who are likely beginning to grapple with their identities in a somewhat different fashion than younger kids (though, of course, there is no clear dividing line). In the second part of this chapter, I turn to *Steven Universe* fanart on Tumblr to show that these artists explore their feelings in a way that is not based on a so-called rational form of communication, and to share these feelings with each other in a supportive and collaborative community. This fanart also does not rely on the identity categories that teens are often encouraged to use as they enter adolescence—identities that can be helpful but that also rely on the very categories that some tweens find restrictive.

Common Sense?

Common Sense Media is an independent, nonprofit organization that reviews a wide range of media texts for parents, teachers, and policymakers. While kids also post reviews on the site, the main contributors are adults—the Common Sense reviewers as well as other adults who turn to the site for information. It is thus an apt place for illustrating the gap between adult perceptions of what's "appropriate" for kids and kids' sense of what's meaningful and why.

This gap was made evident in the review of *Steven Universe* by Common Sense Media critic Rebecca Ashby and the kids' responses to it. Ashby said the following in her review:

> Created by former *Adventure Time* artist/writer Rebecca Sugar, this is a quirky cartoon whose off-kilter comedy sometimes leans on stereotypes and crudity for effect. None of it is intentionally harmful, but parents may question the need for recurring potty humor and junk food consumption (ice cream and "fry bits" are a couple of the characters' favorites) that's mostly limited to the show's portlier—and, it's implied, less healthy—characters. On the upside, as the series evolves and Steven matures, more attention is paid to his assuming equal status and responsibility among the Gems, and Greg takes on a more significant mentoring role for Steven's character development, to surprisingly positive results.
>
> As in *Adventure Time*, *Steven Universe* is a cartoon that isn't really meant for younger kids, thanks to some mild sexual innuendo and general

crudity, among other snags. Its bizarre premise and throwback animation style may appeal to tweens looking for something that's off the beaten cartoon path, though, and they will be able to see past the characters' flaws to recognize their positive traits better than younger kids would.[3]

The review met with a torrent of dissenting opinions by kids ranging in age from nine to 17, most of whom said, in varying ways, that Ashby was getting it wrong because she was looking at the show from an adult perspective. As one 11-year-old put it, "In this day and age, most kids cartoons treat us like we have the intelligence of an embryo. *Steven Universe*, however, attempts to challenge kids to understand very adult issues, like that everyone has real struggles and copes in different ways." Said a 12-year-old who watches the show with her two younger sisters, "I'm really upset that this got a bad review, like most things on this site, caused by overprotective parents. The characters aren't 'stereotypes,' they're showing diversity." Other kids applauded the show's embrace of strong female characters, LGBTQ themes, and racial diversity. Most often, though, the kids praised the emotional range and intensity of the show.

Steven himself is the catalyst though not the only source for this emotional expression (in this chapter, I will use "emotions" interchangeably with "feelings," since that is the language most often used by Steven and the Gems to refer to his feelings). For Steven, understanding the power of his emotions is central to figuring out what superpowers he possesses as a half-human, half-Gem boy. Understanding and marshalling his emotions allows him to deploy considerable powers to protect humankind, as both a nurturer and a fighter; he thus embodies both the masculine and the feminine (though these categories are not referenced in the show). Due to his keen powers of empathy, he is able to discern people's injuries and illnesses and heal them with his saliva. He can also resurrect the dead with his magic tears, grow sentient flora by licking the seeds, and summon a bubble that encases himself and whoever needs his protection.

He is being taught and raised by three guardians, Garnet, Amethyst, and Pearl—the Crystal Gems, ageless, humanoid aliens who appear as women and use the feminine pronouns but who also confound categories of gender and sexuality. Steven's mother, Rose Quartz, was the leader of the Crystal Gems; she gave up her human form in order to give birth to Steven. Greg is Steven's human father, which makes Steven half-Gem and half-human. Greg continues to be a positive presence in Steven's life, but Steven lives with the three Crystal Gems, and they teach him how to use his powers as they protect the earth from the evil Gems who live back on their home planet, Homeworld.

The science-fiction elements of the show provide the constant potential for excitement, and Steven accompanies his three caretakers on all their missions, often running into serious, even life-threatening dangers. These dangers are not disconnected from the real world, since, as viewers learn in the first season, the evil Gems wanted to conquer the earth using a weapon of mass destruction and then incubate new Gems on the planet. Rose Quartz led the rebel force of Crystal Gems against this attack, in the interest of protecting earth and its inhabitants. While defeated at that time, Homeworld remains a hostile presence, occasionally sending its representatives to find out what is happening on earth.

The stage is thus set for a somewhat predictable source of empowerment: Steven's superpowers inspire kids to confront obstacles in their own lives. His superpowers, however, do not help him solve every problem (nor are they "typical" superpowers, as I describe above). *Steven Universe* is unusual within kids' programming insofar as it acknowledges that at times, there are no answers; it thus works against narrative resolutions in the form of happy endings, even though most episodes do indeed have a narrative. Some problems simply can't be solved, such as the death of a loved one, the loss of a biological family, the longing for one's homeland, and the feeling that one will never "be normal." Home and the sense of belonging conferred by domestic security is never guaranteed. *Steven Universe* acknowledges all of these dark feelings; as one 12-year-old said in their review, "Best show ever! This show really teaches kids about growing up, how to overcome situations, and also how everybody's perfect in their own way. This show got me through last year when I was ignored at school and sometimes at home. If you're sad, WATCH THIS SHOW. WARNING: Sometimes this show can make you cry. *A lot.*"

"Overcoming" situations, in other words, does not negate sadness and other dark feelings. As one 11-year-old puts it:

> This Show is AWESOME!!!!!! This show is the best! Steven is so optimistic in situations and always can cheer someone up. I do have to say there

is some tragic back-stories, though Steven always finds a way to cheer up that person. Pearl is like a motherly figure to Steven (along with the other gems). Although Steven's Dad's life is sorta bad he always cheers up when he sees Steven. Steven believes in himself and everyone. Not really to much violence but once Steven got a black eye (wasn't that much). Also Steven and Connie have a relationship but as just friends (not as what the shippers think). Over all it's a great show that will give you the feels. Bueckatı signing out!

Notably, this fan admires Steven's relational skills, commenting on his effect on the other main characters. Steven's ability to make other people feel good gives this fan "the feels," an apt phrase for describing an affective, embodied intensity that doesn't correspond to a singular word.

Fusion Cuisine

What does it feel like to experience belonging? The family no longer—if it ever did—provides one definition of belonging, a situation many adults cite as a risk factor for children. Yet kid fans of *Steven Universe* see his nonnormative family situation as a reason for hope. As one 13-year-old fan of the show put it:

> Shows the 21st century at it's best. This program introduces children to new standards that we hold these days. 200 years ago a step-mother would not have ever existed, but today not everyone has a nuclear family. He struggles about his passed away mother, but has a carefree attitude towards everything. Teaches even adults about how to live in the 21st century with passion. Follow Steven Universe's path.

This sense of struggle and pain combined with optimism and joy shows up frequently in fan comments about family. One 11-year-old, calling the show one of his favorites and "very funny," adds that "the only real concerns I have for parents would be that there is violence and Rose, Steven's mom, died giving birth to Steven. And his alive dad said that Rose 'gave up herself to bring Steven into the world.'" And a 12-year-old comments that while "the show has a good amount of action, humour, and even some deeper stuff, and tends to be a very fun, lighthearted show. But be aware, there are some darker episodes, for example, 'So Many Birthdays,' or 'Steven The Swordfighter,' in which certain characters almost die, or sort of die for a small amount of time." The fan refers to the "So Many Birthdays" episode in which Steven discovers that while the Crystal Gems do not age, they can get injured and die. He starts to worry, thinking that he should grow up quickly so he can take care of them, and inadvertently casts a spell on himself that makes him age rapidly. The upshot: he learns that it's OK to be a kid for a little longer.

Many children in the U.S. find themselves in different family formations. The Pew Research Center found in a 2014 study that "fewer than half (46%) of U.S. kids younger than 18 years of age are living in a home with two married heterosexual parents in their first marriage," compared to 73 percent in 1960 and 61 percent in 1980. The percentage of children born outside of marriage is now 41 percent, compared to 5 percent in 1960. Also, 15 percent of children are living with two parents who are in a remarriage, and 34 percent of children today are living with an unmarried parent—up from just 9 percent in 1960, and 19 percent in 1980. Adoptions, by both heterosexual and gay parents, are also on the rise (Krogstad 2014).

Despite the data, the nuclear family persists as a kind of normative standard against which these "deviations" are measured, even as the measurement becomes less stigmatizing as the percentage of nonnuclear families grows. How do children see this norm that no longer represents even half of all U.S. families? At what point do they recognize it as a norm? And at what point does it significantly shape their everyday lives? While these questions are too general to answer in comprehensive terms, they can be approached from a kids' point of view by looking at their reactions to *Steven Universe*, a show that itself both represents the norm and its dissolution.

Because he hasn't gone to school or been socialized in the ways that most children are, Steven is largely unaware of norms and conventions, including the notion of a nuclear family. When he becomes friends with Connie Maheswaran, a human girl whose parents are quite traditional in their definitions of family, it becomes the ideal moment for questioning what counts as a family. In the episode "Fusion Cuisine," Connie's mom calls her daughter when she is at Steven's and asks to talk to his mom. "That's going to be pretty hard, since my mom gave up her physical form to make me," Steven says to Connie matter-of-factly. "I can't tell her that!" exclaims Connie. Unsure what to do, Steven gives the phone to Garnet and says, "Garnet, you have to pretend to be my mom to Connie's mom." In her usual deadpan voice, Garnet says, "Hello, this is Mom Universe. The children are playing swords. Sorry, playing with swords. They're bleeding. Oh, no. They are dead. Don't call again." And then, to Steven, "Sorry, I panicked."

Later, Connie tells Steven on the phone that her mom won't let her come over and says she can't see him again until her parents meet his parents. Her parents want them to go out for dinner all together, and Steven wonders out loud if a restaurant will take reservations for eight. Connie responds that he can't bring everybody because she told her parents he had a nuclear family. This conversation ensues,

> STEVEN: Nuclear! Sure, they make stuff blow up sometimes, but that's because they're magic, not radioactive.
> CONNIE: Steven, nuclear means two adults and their child and/or children. My parents think you live with your mother and father.
> STEVEN: But none of that is true! You never told your parents I live with the Crystal Gems?
> CONNIE: No, and it has to stay that way. If they found out I lied to them, they would never let me hang out with you again.

So Steven tries to decide which of the three Gems "would make the best and most nuclear mom." Turning to the stoic Garnet, he says, "Garnet, you keep us safe by scaring off the bad guys. Just like a mom would. But . . . you're not the best conversationalist." Then to the rebel Amethyst, who is eating chips and picking her nose while he talks to her, "Amethyst, you would be a super fun mom. Can moms be gross?" Then to the anxious and responsible Pearl: "Pearl, you're always worried about me, you teach me lots of stuff, you're approachable, and you're totally not gross. But, you can't eat dinner" (because Gems don't have to eat, and food makes Pearl nauseous).

Discouraged, Steven sits down on the couch with his dad Greg, who is visiting the household (he lives in an RV that he parks outside the car wash he owns). Steven ponders the arbitrariness of the nuclear family: "Man, why did Connie have to say I have one mom instead of zero, or three?" When Greg says that they'll "figure it out, we just have to put our heads together," Steven gets an idea: "You can all come to dinner, all three of you, fused into one!" The Gems desist, saying fusion is only to be invoked in serious situations. Glumly, Steven accepts their decision, but seeing how dejected he is, Garnet says "We have no choice." The three Gems fuse into one very tall "mom" with six arms and a complicated face and go out to meet the Maheswarans—who are rather surprised to see the large creature approaching the outdoor patio where they're awaiting them. Greg introduces himself and then turns to the fusion and says, "And this big drink of water is my wife, Alexandrite."

Connie's parents try to maintain the illusion of a polite dinner party, asking how the couple met and what they do for a living, but it quickly becomes clear something's not right. Unable to maintain the pretense of being one woman, the three Gems start disagreeing with each other and "de-fuse," reverting to their three separate selves. An upset Connie runs off and Steven follows her, and they decide to board a bus and run away to a place where they can be friends, where no one cares what kind of family they're from. The three Gems fuse together again in order to catch the bus, however, and proceed to scold Steven for putting both himself and Connie in danger. In front of Connie's parents, they mete out his punishment: "No dinner for 1,000 years!" says Garnet. "We would never starve you, Steven," says Pearl, correcting Garnet, but then adds, "No television for 1,000 years." Connie's parents are so impressed by the severity of the punishment that they revise their opinion of the Gems and decide that Connie can be friends with Steven after all. Says Connie's mom, "I did not know what to make of the two, excuse me, four of you, but I see that you are responsible parents, uh, caregivers, uh, guardians."

A few of the kids commenting on the family follow in Connie's mom's lead, rearticulating the normative notions of family to fit this new model but retaining some semblance of the norm—as in the quote above: "Pearl is like a motherly figure to Steven (along with the other gems). Although Steven's Dad's life is sorta bad he always cheers up when he sees Steven." Most often, however, fans express their confidence that Steven feels loved, regardless of the family formation. Fan comments quite often noted this "unconditional love" without even linking it to a nonnuclear arrangement. One 12-year-old says, "They all really care about Steven and want to help him through the issues he deals with every single day." And another 12-year-old writes: "Steven Universe also has great action, characters and as scary as this show can be it is all about loving unconditionally, no matter what."

Despite this unconditional love, Steven still misses his mother, Rose Quartz, and he feels her loss as a very embodied, affective longing. His belly button is a rose quartz gem, and numerous episodes comment on his feeling that she is physically part of him. In "Lion 3: Straight to Video," Steven's friend Sadie gives him the sack lunches her mother had packed her, saying she's too old for them. Steven eagerly takes them home and unpacks them, finding a star-shaped cookie and biting into it as he looks up at a picture of Rose on the wall and asks, "I wonder what kind of lunch my mom would have made me. Maybe actual space cookies! [sigh] I just wish I knew a little more about her." Then, he discovers a video in his pet lion's mane that his mother left for him; in it, she looks at the camera and addresses her son:

> Isn't it remarkable, Steven? This world is full of so many possibilities . . . each living thing has an entire unique experience. The sights they see, the sounds they hear, the lives they live are so complicated and yet so simple. I can't wait for you to join them. Steven, we can't both exist. I'm going to become half of you and I need you to know that every moment you love being yourself, that's me loving you and loving being you. Because you're going to be something extraordinary. You're going to be a human being. Take care of them, Steven.

Not only, then, does Steven feel cared for by his mother, but he also feels the responsibility of caring for others, making him both mothered and mothering. Yet Rose does not link his powers to gender but rather to his humanity—his extraordinary humanity.

The fact that Steven knows Rose is always with him is a source of both comfort and anxiety, as the show once again illustrates its respect for the complex range of children's feelings. Because Rose was a fearsome warrior, Steven worries that he can't live up to her legacy. In the episode "Steven vs. Amethyst," he and Amethyst are practice fighting, and she complains that he is better with his powers than she is. He responds, "Why do you think I've been working so hard? I'm not Rose Quartz." This feeling of inadequacy manifests itself again in the episode

"Earthlings." Amethyst is battling the evil Gem Jasper and losing, with Steven looking on. Amethyst is about to give up:

> AMETHYST: I can't win, no matter what I do, no matter how hard I work, she [Jasper] came out right, and I came out wrong.
> STEVEN: That's just what Jasper thinks. She's the only one who thinks you should be like her. Stop trying to be like Jasper. You're nothing like Jasper. You're like me. Because we're both not like anybody. And yeah, it sucks. But at least I've got you. And you've got me. So stop leaving me out of this.
> AMETHYST: Us worse Gems stick together, right?
> STEVEN: That's why we're the best.

The two hug and in the process fuse into a hybrid—a creative combination of Amethyst and Steven—three arms, floppy black hair, Steven's T-shirt not fitting over their large combined torso. The fusion belts out: "What a beautiful day!" Jasper asks, "Who are you supposed to be?" And the fusion answers, "A Rose Quartz and an Amethyst make a Smoky Quartz." Steven's comment that "we're both not like anybody" indicates his feeling of being different, of not fitting in—a feeling that is both difficult and empowering. The empowering aspect is intensified when Connie says, "Us worse Gems stick together," and Steven affirms that this outsider status makes them "the best." In this episode, Steven finds a way to incorporate his mother's identity into his and Amethyst's, producing a rare fusion of three entities, indicating at least a temporary coming to terms for Steven of the multiple parts of his identity. The fact that this affirmation comes without denying the difficulty of being different is not lost on some kids, including these two fans, who comment in different ways on how the show makes them feel better about themselves:

> Amazing show. The show has amazing characters and they are very alike people in the real world. Also this show can teach anyone how to get over things, and how to feel special about them selves (11-year-old)

> WATCH IT NOW. All I can say is YES this is an amazing show full of great messages and role models, that comes with it's own worldwide

fanbase. Watch out for the later seasons though, they're full of emotional moments of friendship. (11-year-old)

Strikingly, each of these kids comments on the affective experience of watching the show—that it makes them *feel* special and that it is "full of emotional moments." The second fan also feels connected to other fans—to a "worldwide fanbase" that constitutes an imagined community.

Steven's strength is seen by fans to derive from his in-betweenness, as a child who is often treated as an adult—since he is living with adults who are teaching him to use his superpowers to battle their enemies—and as a half-human, half-Gem mixture who can fuse not only with another Gem (Amethyst) but also with another human (Connie). Fusions, as I noted above, form when two beings are completely in sync with each other; the combined form draws on the strengths of each in order to overcome an enemy. According to the fan commentary on the Stevonnie wiki, "Stevonnie, like all fusions, possesses an extreme amount of super-human strength and agility. Despite being more human than Gem, Stevonnie is much stronger than Steven by himself, most likely stemming from Connie's strength and athleticism combined with Steven's superhuman abilities. Stevonnie is strong enough to fight equally with a powerful quartz warrior." We can identify here a connection to the neurodiversity I discussed in the introduction insofar as an alternative kind of growing up—Steven's hybridity—is seen to be a source of strength rather than an anomaly or a disorder.

Made out of Love

Many kids who identify as *Steven Universe* fans are taken with the idea and practice of fusion. It speaks to kids' refusal of clear-cut categories, whether they be related to age, gender, sexuality, race, or other boxes into which differences are channeled. Kids in the U.S. today, after all, are more defined by mixture than ever. To take just one indication: *The New York Times* reported in 2011, drawing on the 2010 census data, that "among American children, the multiracial population has increased almost 50 percent, to 4.2 million, since 2000, making it the fastest growing youth group in the country. The number of people of all ages who identified themselves as both white and black soared by 134 percent since 2000 to 1.8 million people, according to census data released Thursday" (Saulny 2011). In addition, mixed-legal-status families are becoming more prevalent in the U.S.; according to the Pew Research Center, "a substantial share of the undocumented population of this country lives in a so-called mixed-status family—that is, a family with at least one unauthorized immigrant parent and at least one U.S. citizen child" (Passel and Taylor). Furthermore, legal status cannot be divided simply into citizen and noncitizen; there are many variations, including legal permanent residents and those with different kinds of temporary legal permits, meaning that family members may pass into and out of various stages of having authorization to live and work in the U.S.

The very premise of *Steven Universe* lends itself to a questioning of belonging and borders, as the Gems must constantly be on the lookout for evil Gems from their home planet of Homeworld, and they frequently battle former friends. The Gems are outsiders, protecting the humans, who are unaware of their benefactors. While these two populations seem distinct, there are signs of these distinctions breaking down, in the phenomena of mixture and fusion. Steven is the child of a mixed couple, since his father, Greg, is human and his mother, Rose Quartz, was a Gem. In the episode "Story for Steven," Greg tells Steven the story of how he met Rose, while playing his guitar at a public performance, where she was the only one in the audience. She slips out before he can talk to her, and he starts "looking for the mysterious pink lady, really tall, lots of pink hair." His manager Marty asks him how tall she is, and Greg says, "About eight feet." Marty tells him, "This is your problem. You want one huge woman when you could have multiple smaller ones." Greg wants to go back and serenade Rose, while Marty wants him to continue on to his next gig. Greg kicks Marty out of his van and goes back to profess his love for Rose. She says he's "awfully cute," but that they aren't meant to be together, and Greg disagrees, saying, "You're all I want." Rose laughs. The episode then cuts back to the present, with Steven laughing and saying, "You loved her!" Since it turns out that Marty did Greg a favor, Steven puts a picture of Greg and Marty beside the one of Greg and Rose next to his bed.

Pearl never approved of Greg—and as we find out, it's because she also had feelings for Rose. Pearl's antipathy for Greg is due not to the fact that he is human, although perhaps that is part of it, but because Rose chose him over her. Steven engineers their reconciliation, demonstrating his belief in people's ability to get along no matter their makeup. This trait is compelling to one 11-year-old fan, who comments that Steven is an "always-wants-to-make-people-smile kind of kid." This fan goes on to explain that Steven "originates from his human father and his alien-warrior-refugee mom who gave up her physical form for Steven and her magical powers which all gems have." These powers include, says the fan, "summoning a weapon . . . that depends on which kind of gem they are, shape shifting, and fusing with other gems to make a being better than both of them combining their powers and making a weapon also combining both of theirs." This fan reads the show as a coming-of-age story: "The whole story is about him developing, maturing, and learning how to control his powers with the help of his mom's former comrades in battle." For this fan, Steven's status as half Gem, half human is closely connected to the Gems' ability to fuse; both mixture and fusion indicate a combination of strength and vulnerability. The fusion makes one strong and can happen only if both parts of the fusion love each other.

Garnet is a fusion of Ruby and Sapphire, as we learn in the "Jail Break" episode, in which Garnet sings a song called "Stronger than You" while she is battling the evil Jaspar from her planet of Homeworld.[4] This song is frequently referenced by fans as a kind of theme song for the power of fusion, especially because Garnet sings it just after Ruby and Sapphire have been reunited into the "one" that battles Jaspar:

> This is Garnet / Back together / And I'm never going down at the hands of the likes of you / Because I'm so much better / And every part of me is saying "Go get 'er." / The two of us ain't gonna follow your rules. / Come at me without any of your fancy tools. / Let's go, just me and you. / Let's go, just one on two.

Then, in a testimony to what true love can effect, Garnet continues,

> Go ahead and try to hit me if you're able. / Can't you see that my relationship is stable? / I can see you hate the way we intermingle. / But I think you're just mad 'cause you're single. / You're not gonna stop what we've

made together. / We are gonna stay like this forever. / If you break us apart, we'll just come back newer. / And we'll always be twice the Gem that you are. / I am made o-o-o-o-of Lo-o-o-o-ove o-o-o-o-of / Lo-o-o-o-ove / Lo-o-o-o-ove / Lo-o-o-o-ove.

Garnet is not only made of love, she defines herself as a feeling rather than an identity: "This is who we are. / This is who I am. / And if you think you can stop me / Then you need to think again. 'Cause I am a feeling / And I will never end. / And I won't let you hurt my planet, I won't let you hurt my friends." The feeling, she then elaborates, is complex: "I am their fury. / I am their patience. / I am a conversation."

Garnet's self-definition as a feeling transcends identity categories. Her fans pick up on this idea yet also see her as a lesbian role model; in other words, they value her amorphousness while also identifying her as a lesbian in a televisual world that has very few lesbians. These feelings are conveyed in comments by three 13-year-old fans:

> Garnet the fusion of Ruby and Sapphire are in a relationship, possibly sexual. In the Episode Keystone Motel Garnet breaks into her different parts Ruby and Sapphire. Near the end of the episode, after Garnet unfuses, Ruby swoops up Sapphire in her arms and kisses her on her face and around her breasts. While most kids won't notice some might see it. I have no problem with this, but most over protective parents might get worried about their children seeing it.

Another 13-year-old says:

> First of all, I love this show's diversity! We have strong female characters with real character depth, a wide variety of body shapes (no one is shunned for this either), and LGBT+ positivity. The violence is nearly bloodless (Gems get "poofed" and return to regenerate inside their gem) and though there are occasional sexual innuendos, such as the fusion dances being occasionally interpreted as intimate actions, it's nothing too inappropriate. It has a rather complex plot and some creepy elements such as the prototype cluster gems that may scare small children (hence the 6+ [age rating]), but it's not too much. But my favorite part would be how positively the show portrays LGBT+ characters. I am a Lesbian

myself, and I was overjoyed to see representation in a children's TV show. Some examples are the relationship of Ruby and Sapphire, Pearl's love for Rose Quartz, and the androgynous Stevonnie who uses They/Them pronouns and is adored by males and females. It's a lovely show, and I'd recommend giving it a watch.

Another 13-year-old, identifying as a lesbian, also focuses on the sexual possibility of the Garnet fusion:

> One of my favorite aspects of the show is the "fusion" of gems. A fusion is where two gems will join together and become one, new, entity. Two of the most notable fusions are Stevonnie and Garnet. Yes, Garnet is a fusion (spoilers, I guess). She is a combination of the soldier, Ruby, and the higher-class gem, Sapphire. Although all the gems on homeworld look down upon the Garnet fusion, as it is seen as something "disgusting" and "wrong" (hmm . . . kinda reminds you of some real-life issues, huh? And, as a young lesbian I love the representation that is Garnet) causing characters like Jasper and even Peridot, at first, to look down on her like she is an abomination. But, Garnet doesn't let that stop her, she is in love, and she proves it through the song "Stronger Than You" (which is an overall great song about love that I have caught my friends singing on multiple occasions).

This fan attributes to the show a critique of homophobia (the perception of an abomination) while also seeing in Garnet the potential of fusion to move beyond identity categories into the realm of feeling and love.[5]

In fact, Garnet does not *have* feelings; she *is* a feeling. In singing these lyrics, Garnet completely deconstructs the therapeutic discourse that distinguishes between feeling, thought, and action and that encourages kids to find a name for their feelings. Words actually get in the way. For example, in the episode "We Need to Talk," Greg recalls how he tried to figure out how he might fuse with Rose. He remembers telling Amethyst that he was "trying to get his head around this fusion thing." Amethyst laughs and tells him, "A fusion dance ain't about your head." And Garnet gives him further advice: "First you need a Gem at the core of your being. Then you need a body that can turn into night. Then you need a partner you can trust in that night." Greg asks, "Metaphorically?" Garnet responds, "Literally." Greg despairs, but Amethyst tells him she thinks he can do it, "but it won't work if you dance like Pearl. You have to dance like you. You have to fuse your way. Get open. Get honest. Invent yourselves together. That's fusion."

"My Narrative Falters"

Words aren't necessary for the hundreds if not thousands of *Steven Universe* fans who have posted their artistic renderings of the show's characters on different platforms—Tumblr, Pinterest, Facebook, Instagram, and their own blogs. Many of these fans build on the idea of fusion, blending characters in different ways, some more closely linked to the show (the canon, in fandom parlance) than others. These fusions speak to how a nonlinguistic, affective intensity can lead to relationships that are, in Garnet's words, open, honest, and experiential. The path to reciprocity is not through language, in other words, in the form of the problem-solving approach I have described in previous chapters. Rather, the path is through a vulnerability to one another that exceeds language.

This kind of bodily mutuality recalls recent work in feminism on vulnerability. Judith Butler, for example, describes the inadequacy of language to capture the relation between self and other:

> I might try to tell a story here about what I am feeling, but it would have to be a story in which the very "I" who seeks to tell the story is stopped in the midst of the telling; the very "I" is called into question by its relation to the Other, a relation that does not precisely reduce me to speechlessness, but does nevertheless clutter my speech with signs of its undoing. I tell a story about the relations I choose, only to expose, somewhere along the way, the way I am gripped and undone by these very relations. My narrative falters, as it must. (2004, 23)

The "I" of the story inevitably posits itself as autonomous, in other words, even when it relates its connectedness to others. By contrast, the images of fusion do not rely on the autonomous storyteller because the image itself tells the story; it does not rely on a distinct "I" and "you" but rather represents their mutual undoing.

This sense of collaboration is enhanced by the practices of fandom—the constant reblogging of images from one fan site to another—which

Figure 6.4. Fanart by Nyong-Choi, Pinterest, www.pinterest.com/pin/416723771752619348.

contribute to the erasure of the notion of origin as well as to the formation of a collaborative community. Although the artists share an affinity for *Steven Universe*, their interpretations of the characters are so diverse and so intertwined as to become part of a collective rewriting of the original show. It's important here to note that there are exceptions to this spirit of collaboration. I am not romanticizing fandom as a community devoid of conflict; there are plenty of examples of flaming and trolling to demonstrate that fan communities can be as vicious as any other, including the *Steven Universe* fandom.[6] These conflicts themselves speak to the power of affect. However, I am focusing here on the potential of fusion fandom to provide routes of communication that allow for vulnerability and community. Here are some examples to illustrate.[7]

This artist, Nyong-Choi, posting from South Korea, draws on the *Steven Universe* notion of family that I discussed above.[8] In each of these images, one of the Gems holds baby Steven so closely to her body that they seem physically connected. This is a powerful commentary on the affective intensity of nurturing that is produced outside the nuclear (biological) family norm; no words are necessary to convey this love, so the critique operates without invoking the norm.

Although there is no way to generalize about the fanart, one characteristic that does stand out is the wide variety of body types, ranging in size from small to towering, and in shape from sticklike to curvaceous. Fans take their inspiration from the canon Gems, who are similarly diverse—from number of arms to shape of face to size of feet. When Gems fuse with other Gems, body types again proliferate, defying any attempt to categorize or create norms. It thus follows that fans build on this embodiment, creating characters of so many body shapes and sizes that any concept of a bodily norm is exploded. The show thus acts as a source of affirmation for its many fans who see themselves as producing nonnormative art—a kind of archive of feelings grounded in pleasure in one's body and affirmed through fans' many (and mainly supportive) interactions with each other.

Take for example, art produced by "artifiziell" on her Tumblr blog (see figure 6.5). Here, as she explains on her site, are six fusions produced by these combinations of Gems from the canon: "Titanium Quartz—Steven + Bismuth / Tangerine Quartz—Steven + Peridot / Smoky Quartz—Steven + Amethyst / Cherry Quartz—Steven + Garnet / Rainbow

Figure 6.5. Fanart by artipcon fiziell, Tumblr, http://artifiziell.tumblr.com.

Quartz—Steven + Pearl / Spirit Quartz—Steven + Lapis." Followers of artifiziell seek her advice on other combinations, such as this question from an anonymous admirer: "Hello love, hope your having a good day. If it's not to much trouble I was kinda hoping you could help me find a fitting gem for a hiddenite and peridot fusion I've been kinda stumped and would really appreciate it." Other followers come up with many possible combinations, developing a vocabulary of gems and fusions that is particular to their community. In this exchange, not once did I see a negative comment. More likely, they are similar to this one from an anonymous admirer of artifiziell: "hi! what would be a fusion between my absolute respect and adoration for you and your art, being happy seeing new gemstones thanks to you, and the knowledge that you're a fantastic person? thanks in advance! :)"

This affirmation and collaboration through art is one defining characteristic of the Tumblr social networking site, especially in relation to how it defines community.[9] Here's how Tumblr advertises itself: "As a global platform for creativity and self-expression, Tumblr is deeply committed to supporting and protecting freedom of speech. At the same time, we draw lines around a few narrowly defined but deeply important categories of content and behavior that jeopardize our users, threaten our infrastructure, and damage our community."[10] This emphasis on community and self-expression has drawn advertising interest, even though its 345 million users are known to be young and outside the mainstream market. For example, Business News Daily advises its readers that if they want to advertise on Tumblr, they should be aware that "Tumblr users are very community-oriented" and then elaborates in quite specific fashion:

> The community is very supportive. Many Tumblr users identify as social outcasts. Tumblr has become a safe place for bloggers to share things they can't share on other networks. They find people they can relate to, and they can remain anonymous if they so choose. The Tumblr community is also a huge proponent of mental health awareness, and it's not uncommon to see posts sharing hotlines and inspirational advice go viral on the platform. Many Tumblr users have formed real friendships thanks to the supportive nature of the network. (Driver)

Three academics who spent three months observing Tumblr fandoms, surveying its users, then interviewing 17 users in more detail, found that "the sentiment of most of our participants was 'absolute' love for the Tumblr community. They appreciated that they have common interests with other Tumblr users and that other people are willing to analyze, and generally obsess over the same things that they do" (Hillman, Procyk, and Neustaedter 2014, 287). Two other findings in their study make the Tumblr community especially relevant for my purposes: the community relies heavily on GIFs, or animated images, and its members have developed their own language for describing their intense feelings about the relationships they create in their fanart. These relationships, or "ships," are referred to as OTPs, or "one true pairings," which are "very important to the Tumblr fandom culture because they often drive what users call feels. Feels describe when a user has high emotion towards any fandom-related event. When a user experiences an overwhelming amount of feels, they can express themselves by typing: alksjdf;lksfd. This text is meant to represent a user pressing random keys in uncontrollable excitement" (Hillman, Procyk, and Neustaedter 2014, 287).

This ability to express one's intense feelings without relying on language—or with a made-up language—fits the definition of affect I have been valorizing throughout this book, as "unqualified intensity," in contrast to the "qualified intensity" of emotions. The excitement is too intense to be articulated in words yet it still must be expressed. Because the affect is unqualified, it is also not "recognizable" in the usual terms of naming, and is thus "resistant to critique" (Massumi 1995, 88). In the case of Tumblr bloggers, this resistance to critique is part of the culture of the community: many bloggers offer each other unqualified support, sometimes explicitly contrasting the Tumblr ethos to less supportive platforms. If one does a search on the Tumblr site for "depression" and "mental illness," this pops up:

> Everything okay? If you or someone you know are experiencing any type of crisis, please know there are people who care about you and are here to help. Consider chatting confidentially with a volunteer trained in crisis intervention at www.imalive.org, or anonymously with a trained active listener from 7 Cups of Tea. . . . It might also be nice to fill your dash with inspirational and supportive posts from TWLOHA, Half of Us, the Lifeline, and Love Is Respect.

Tumblr users reported that the platform was for them an "'always on' technology. That is, they described the process of engaging with Tumblr as an experience that continuously occurred, telling us, for example, 'I always have a tab open'" (Hillman, Procyk, and Neustaedter, 288). This emphasis on the ongoing experience of interacting via images with other young people suggests the ideal space for affective encounters, especially, according to the study, encounters dealing with issues related to sexuality and gender.

This is an especially relevant space for tweens such as 13-year-old Emery, whose Tumblr blog "Hot Diggity Damn" features some *Steven Universe* art as well as many images drawing on other sources. Emery identifies herself as "pansexual," and one can see a connection between this refusal of categories and the art she bases on the *Steven Universe* character Lapis (see figure 6.6). In the show, Lapis is a feminine-appearing Gem who wears a flowing blue skirt and a short-cropped halter top, revealing a blue lapis lazuli gem embedded in her back from which emanate her wings. She is a passionate, stubborn character who is generally skeptical of humans but open to friendship with Steven, who freed her from imprisonment in a magic mirror. She finds life on earth confusing and wants to return to Homeworld.

Figure 6.6. Lapis of Cartoon Network's *Steven Universe*, cartoonnetwork.com.

Under the hashtag #Lapis, Emery posts an image that appears as a more androgynous version of the canonical Lapis. Emery's Lapis has shorter hair, a more angular face, and a flat chest. Emery's Lapis, which she calls Purpkins, receives a lengthy positive comment from an anonymous poster who expresses her support and begins a conversation:

> Your art is amazing! I would suggest doing more backgrounds though, but i know that when you will do some it will be absolutely stunning! Could you by any chance draw Malachite from SU? I think it would look great in your style, maybe even as a palette challenge or in a minimalist palette like your icon! (You could even do Jasper with it and make it a set or something!) Question, what/who inspired your art style?

Emery responds in a manner that adds members to the community:

> ahhh thank you so much! especially for the advice; i'd love to try to do more backgrounds and landscapes in the future. here's a quick malachite, i tried to make it somewhat similar to the lapis one. i'd love to do a jasper one in the future as well :O
>
> as for the question; a number of people and things actually! a lot of other talented artists, including but not limited to; trackalaka, spibbles,

bunblevee, kiwi byrd, all of my arty friends, many more i can't remember right now. I'm also super inspired by a lot of webcomics and cartoons like SU. thanks again for the ask, anon!

This exchange demonstrates the importance of a supportive fan community in affirming Emery's sense of herself, one which defies identity categories even as it seeks definition. It assumes even more significance when one considers what Emery has posted on her home page: sayings and artwork about depression, including a drawing that says, "I thought things would get better but they didn't/I have no hope left"; a comic strip urging people to be careful about what they say on social media because it can spread quickly and without recourse; and a post about how more popular artists on the internet can and should support beginning artists by reblogging their work.

The show *Steven Universe* seems to appeal to these young artists because the characters themselves are shifting and in process. This state of identity in flux is a cause for both uncertainty and hope, as can be seen on the Tumblr blog of "Notice me Senpai" (see figure 6.7). This young person posts many *Steven Universe* fanfics, often with the caption "hope you guys like it" or "sorry I haven't posted in a while." The facial expressions in the drawings are often sad and uncertain, or perhaps vulnerable,

Figure 6.7. Stevonnie, Tumblr art by Notice me Senpai, https://stevenkun chan.tumblr.com/tagged/stevonnie.

as in this one of Stevonnie. In fact, this image nicely illustrates the idea that affect is hard to pin down and name: it's not clear what Stevonnie is feeling in this image, though one still feels powerfully a sense of longing and desire for connection. The connections come quickly in the form of brief comments, all of them positive ("like it," "awesome") and rebloggings. While the conversation that ensues is not in-depth—it is a "narrative that falters"—it nevertheless provides for the artist an immediate space of belonging and affirmation.

PART III

The Limits of Digital Literacy

Kids are using the internet at younger and younger ages, perusing YouTube, playing games online, and accessing social media sites such as Facebook. A recent study by EUKids Online, "Zero to Eight: Young Children and their Internet Use," found that internet use by kids under nine years old has increased in most countries around the world (Holloway, Green, and Livingstone 2013). The study found that *Minecraft* figured as one of the most popular virtual worlds for children up to the age of eight, alongside *Club Penguin*, *Moshi Monsters*, and *Webkinz*, with children as young as five participating in gaming.

While there is still concern about the effects of internet usage by young kids, much of the panic has subsided, and an interest in how to help kids safely navigate and use the internet has taken over. The phrase most frequently cited to encompass this approach is "digital literacy," a concept that combines technological expertise with critical thinking skills. The well-rounded student knows how to use social media and other online sites and sources rather than accepting them without question. Furthermore, digital literacy encompasses an ethical approach to the complex kinds of communication that occur online, encouraging an examination of how one conducts oneself online, given the anonymity that the internet allows.

The online gaming world is often seen as a threat to digital literacy, at best mindless and repetitive and at worst encouraging antisocial, at times violent behavior. Parents spend considerable energy trying to ascertain at what age their kids should be allowed to play certain games. Yet some games have been considered worthy of inclusion within the realm of digital literacy—certainly any kind of educational game—but also, recently, "non-educational" games that can be used to teach social skills. These "prosocial behaviors" are closely linked to the skills of emotional intelligence I have been describing throughout this book; implicit in the idea of emotional intelligence is the notion that emotional expression can be taught as a skill, not unlike math or reading, and practiced in certain controlled environments. Hence the link to problem solving—and to the idea, as I mentioned in the introduction, that some policy makers proposed that emotional intelligence become part of the Common Core curriculum.

One of the games receiving considerable attention for its potential in teaching a range of skills is *Minecraft*, a creative building, exploration, and combat game that is the focus of the next chapter.[1] Two information science researchers who studied the game's pedagogical uses say that

> although the media often casts online gaming in a negative light, Minecraft's game play and social dimensions have made it popular with educators, child therapists, and even librarians. These professionals are actively evaluating and incorporating Minecraft into their educational, therapeutic, and community-building programs Even prior to Microsoft's purchase of the original publisher in 2014, the game's creators invested in outreach to educators. Today, the Minecraft Education Program includes the capacity for an education organization to host a Minecraft server specifically for their students. A growing number of constructionist educators and education researchers have embraced Minecraft because it affords a creative space for students, one that allows easy sharing of creative work in a collaborative environment. Some clinics and other support organizations for ND youth have also chosen to integrate Minecraft into their services. (Zolyomi and Schmalz 2017, 3391)

The "ND" refers to neurodiverse youth, who, say Zolyomi and Schmalz, are particularly well served by the game because it allows them to practice social skills that are difficult for them in the "real world." The researchers rely on social learning theory, in which learning is seen as "a cognitive process that occurs within a social context. Learning is influenced by three elements: environment, behavior, and cognition. The learning process consists of a role model exhibiting behavior, which the learner attends to, internalizes cognitively, and ultimately, performs. The behavior is reinforced by positive or negative consequences to the behavior" (3392). *Minecraft* is an effective forum for learning, they found, because it provides positive reinforcement for the kinds of behavior that facilitate social interaction—focused attention, modeling of good behaviors, cooperation, and emotional regulation—within an enjoyable context. The authors and their interviewees acknowledge the realm of emotions insofar as it pulls the kids into the game, and, in turn, the game becomes a way to practice "regulatory skills" (3393).

While I appreciate the attention to the particular needs of neurodiverse kids, I question, again, the need to name and regulate emotions within a context that valorizes cognition. As I show in the next chapter, *Minecraft* seems to me—based on hours of observations of my kid and his friends playing the game as well as watching the YouTube tutorial videos—a game of structured but unregulated affect. In chapter 8, I make a slightly different argument about the game of *Roblox*, which, while still providing an affectively charged space, is more regulated because of its integration of logos and the imperative to spend money within the game. Despite this consumerism, the game illustrates a primary feature of online kids' culture—the use of memes and images to construct a common vernacular that weaves together a wide variety of texts that are open to constant redefinition and recirculation.

Another vein of scholarship on *Minecraft* approaches it from the angle of identity; one study in Australia, for example, focused on eight- and nine-year-old girls and their use of *Minecraft* within a school setting. The authors drew on data that

> was collected as part of a large three-year Australian Research Council Linkage project investigating the use of digital games in 10 schools in Queensland and Victoria, Australia. The project, "Serious Play: Digital Games, Learning and Literacy for Twenty First Century Schooling," aims to explore the ways in which digital games might best be used in the classroom to support formal educational purposes, cognisant of the tremendous potential of games to do so, but also of the need for detailed, nuanced and specific insights into the ways in which teachers and students actually work with games (Dezuanni, O'Mara, and Beavis 2015, 155).

The researchers found that the girls in their focus groups used the game to negotiate their place within a peer group, based on their levels of knowledge and skill. They concluded that "Minecraft players, therefore, undertake practices of social display to achieve recognition within school- and home-based affinity groups and these representational practices are central to the production of learner identities in and around Minecraft" (160). The emphasis on "learner identities" coincides with the overall valorization of digital literacy and self-management within the already defined, albeit fluctuating, space of the classroom.

But gaming is not just about knowledge, skills, and learning, all of which overshadow the primary reason most kids likely play games: to have fun. Kids also play *Minecraft* and *Roblox* to experience a feeling of belonging and creativity, to build and inhabit a shared space that is distinct from institutional spaces. Here is an eloquent summary of what it feels like to enter a new world, from Samuel Evans, a Cornell student (also my research assistant for *Minecraft*). He recalls how he felt when first playing *Minecraft* in high school:

> I always found that I didn't want to go back to old worlds because I wanted to rediscover things/remake everything/experience the excitement of starting off and trying to gather enough things to survive while being vulnerable. After leaving the world for some time, I started to feel a loss of ownership on that set of fully enchanted diamond armor (and on all the stuff I have built or found), since even though I did in fact work for it a long time, it doesn't feel the same as soon as I take a long break from playing in that world.

I am struck by Sam's emphasis on his feelings, even in this brief response to a question I asked him about why Ezra doesn't want to return to previous worlds he has constructed (Ezra's response was "I can't find my house again," which may be more typical for a younger player). Sam experiences excitement, vulnerability, and loss, and these feelings intersect and overlap. This is the *Minecraft* experience—one that cannot be distilled into a set of skills, though these skills are clearly part of the affective experience.

7

Minecraft's Affective World Building

The scene is one of controlled chaos: a birthday party, where a dozen boys and girls, ages six and seven, lick frosting off their fingers and suck loudly from their juice boxes. Seated around a table in the party room at the science center, one kid starts humming, and pretty soon the whole gang has joined in, quickly switching from humming to singing, to the tune of the pop song "Dynamite," these words:

> I came to dig, dig, dig, dig / A city that's so big, big, big, big/ Just wait a sec, gotta kill this pig, pig, pig, pig / Cook me some bacon, take a swig, swig, swig, swig / Yea, there must be something I can craft / To ease the burden of this task. . . . I shoot my arrows in the air some time, saying a-o, creepers, K-O'ed, saying a-o, not today-o. Then I go to work under the birch tree, and I'll make myself tons of TNT / and I'll use these blocks to build a big city, / and I'll mine it all using TNT/ I came to blow, blow, blow up everything you know, know, know.

As the sound crescendos and the energy amps up, with kids now marching around the table, the parents look at each other, at first smiling, then grimacing as the lyrics become a bit more gruesome. "What are they singing?" one mother murmurs to me. "It's a song about *Minecraft*. It's one of those YouTube parodies," I explain. "Does your son play the game?" She answers, "No, I'm not sure how he knows the song. Is the game violent?" "Not really," I say, though I can't fully explain why blowing up cities with TNT is not really violent.

In this chapter, I show how the gaming world of *Minecraft* and the related tutorial videos on YouTube represent the formation of a kids' cultural space that is largely (to the degree possible) independent from adults (and often inscrutable to them). The game fosters a creativity that is lateral, winding, and expressive, as it enables kids to build anything they want and explore the environments they create. Furthermore, the language kids use while playing and talking to each other about the game describes this exploratory movement, often in nonlinear, exclamatory terms. Given what I argued in the first section about the limited control children have over their physical environments, the game and its related activities provide sites where children exercise a considerable degree of agency in building and navigating their own worlds. In addition, it is often a collaborative world, in which children share information and tips about the game as well as create para-texts like the one at the birthday party.

The *Minecraft* world building illustrates Raymond Williams's notion of "structures of feeling," which, to recall, describes how feelings acquire a certain conceptual force, and vice versa—"not feeling against thought, but thought as felt and feeling as thought" (132). As I argued in the introduction, structures of feeling are shaped by and reshape both time and place: a cultural production can define a temporary home as an affective, embodied, felt place. This happens even when the home is a virtual home and the child's embodiment takes place through an online avatar. *Minecraft* is an especially relevant example of world building insofar as it invites players to design and build their own homes and go out mining, hunting, and fighting in order to protect their homes and themselves. This simultaneous appeal to both the domestic and the public may be one reason the game appeals to both boys and girls in equal numbers. Through multiplayer gaming and online forums, players extend this virtual space to include friends and other players, enhancing agency as they collaborate in the construction of non-adult spaces. This is not a static place but rather a moving, constantly redefined space in which kids can evade parental regulation. They must still adhere to parental rules about screen time and content, but because many parents will not understand the gaming world, kids can subvert the rules to varying degrees, depending on the home situation. The language with which they negotiate the *Minecraft* world—full of expressions and exclamations that do not adhere to "proper" speech—helps construct these alternative spaces.

While there is a large archive of *Minecraft* worlds—both saved on a child's iPad or computer and in the form of YouTube videos—every *Minecraft* world is a fluctuating one. There is no singular emotion given primacy but rather varying experiences of intensity as one roams through the various terrains. It is, in many ways, a Deleuzian world, and I will be drawing on some of the philosopher's ideas to show how *Minecraft* presents an alternative to the naming of emotions that I have questioned in earlier chapters. This is not a game about finding one's identity—i.e., defining an avatar that fits who you are before you begin and seeing him or her through to the completion of the game. Rather, *Minecraft* embodies the Deleuzian notion of "becoming," in which subjectivity forms with movement through a space and is ongoing. This process is both psychic and physical: movement prompts descriptions, elicits affective responses, and shapes subjectivity, as I show by recounting narration of the game by children who have set up their own YouTube tutorial channels as well as Ezra's monologues. "Children never stop talking about what they are doing or trying to do: exploring milieus, by means of dynamic trajectories, and drawing up maps of them," writes Deleuze in his essay "What Children Say" (1997). These maps build on each other, but not in the linear fashion of a story with beginning, middle, and end; rather, says Deleuze:

> maps... are superimposed in such a way that each map finds itself modified in the following map, rather than finding its origin in the preceding one; from one map to the next, it is not a matter of searching for an origin, but of evaluating displacements. Every map is a redistribution of impasses and breakthroughs, of thresholds and enclosures, which necessarily go from bottom to top. There is not only a reversal of directions, but also a difference in nature: the unconscious no longer deals with persons and objects, but with trajectories and becomings; it is no longer an unconscious of commemoration but one of mobilization, an unconscious whose objects take flight rather than remaining buried in the ground. (63)

Children's desires, in other words, are not waiting to be uncovered by intrusive adults who hope to better understand their unspoken emotions. They are constantly being produced, in all the maps that are constantly being drawn (Ezra at the age of seven already had more than 300 *Minecraft* worlds stored on the iPad). It is not simply that children are being shaped by these spaces, or that they are constructing these spaces; there is not a clear delineation between space and subject. As Deleuze says, "The trajectory merges not only with the subjectivity of those who travel through a milieu, but also with the subjectivity of the milieu itself, insofar as it is reflected in those who travel through it" (61). The "milieu itself" has a subjectivity—something that *Minecraft*'s millions of youth fans attest to as they describe their encounters with the villagers, creepers, endermen, and spiders of their various worlds.

One strong piece of evidence that speaks to *Minecraft*'s divergent paths is the fact that many kids diagnosed with autism have been drawn to the game. Therapists and teachers speculate, drawing on feedback from these kids, that the game allows them to use their imaginations yet still provides structures and rules. Recognizing the appeal, one father of a child with autism set up a server—Autcraft—just for kids with autism and their family members that now has more than 8,000 members. The autism community that has grown around the game of *Minecraft* includes the server, blogs, live-streamed videos on Twitch and YouTube, and community forums. Kids in this community find *Minecraft* appealing because it gives them a way to interact socially without having to rely on conventional routes of interaction predicated on face-to-face verbal communication. As the authors of an ethnography of the Autcraft community say,

> Some assistive technologies address difficulties surrounding social interaction by supporting discrete kinds of communication (e.g., verbal speech). This focus on a single avenue for communication, however, may be inadequate in addressing the myriad ways in which people with autism can be expressive and social that extend beyond a singular medium. Alternatively, online communities, including social networking sites, can create multiple avenues for communication for those who struggle with face-to-face interactions, such as those with autism. (Ringland et al 2016, 1256).

This explanation could very well apply to many kids who enjoy the game for its nonnormative mode of expression, who are drawn to the combination of freedom and structure that ultimately produces a kind of controlled pleasure. This is what Keith Stuart, whose son Zac was diagnosed with autism, discovered in the game—and which prompted him to write a novel called *A Boy Made of Blocks,* describing how playing *Minecraft* with his son helped them form a closer relationship. Stuart, also a gaming editor for *The Guardian,* writes that "most games have missions and objectives, pushing you in certain directions. *Minecraft* presents you with a world and a bunch of tools and you can do what you want. If Zac just wanted to roam the landscape hunting sheep or digging holes, he could. He is free to express himself. There are rules but they are very clear and don't change. The powerful combination of openness and clear rules definitely appeals to my son" (quoted in Rutkin 2016).

"A World of Trial and Error"

Minecraft has gained a reputation for being an unconventional game, and one immediately visible testament to this distinction is the insignificance of one's avatar. In most games, such as *Roblox* (next chapter), the avatar embodies one's fantasy self—a fantasy that can shift constantly as players acquire, in different ways, different kinds of bodies, skin colors, hairstyles, and so forth. While the fluidity of avatars allows for experimentation with identity, it also keeps the self at the center of the game. This centering is magnified by the visible presence of the avatar within the gaming world, as the game is played in a third-person, over-the-shoulder perspective; the player is always looking at him- or herself playing (see figure 7.1).

By contrast, in *Minecraft* the default avatar is Steve, a brown-skinned man, and many players simply keep Steve because changing one's appearance is not an integral part of the game. It is possible to change, through the purchase of "skins," but there is no in-game skin editing, and getting a skin requires downloading a file, then correctly telling *Minecraft* where to find it. Furthermore, the default mode is *Minecraft* is first person, so one does not see oneself while playing, even as one sees the terrain from his or her character's point of view (see figure 7.2). *Minecraft* is difficult to play in third person/over the shoulder. Thus, the avatar assumes much less significance, encouraging a less self-absorbed wandering through the spaces and discouraging a reading of the game through the concept of identification—a notion to which I will return below.

Minecraft offers multiple ways for players to create and control their worlds; although one is never sure when an enemy or an opportunity might pop up, players can anticipate these events with greater certainty the more they play. As Sam, the Cornell student who has played the

Figure 7.1. A third-person perspective in *Roblox*, where one's avatar is viewed on screen.

game for seven years, told me, "I can give you a complete list of the enemies in Minecraft, and tell you approximately when I should be careful about running into which ones. Also the terrain/obstacles MC constructs are made in a somewhat intuitive manner (e.g. so that there are cave systems and tunnels rather than random blocks missing in random places with little structure)."

While there is a loose structure, there is much room for maneuvering and unpredictability. Thus, the sense of control that players feel is not gestural or contrived; they are actually making decisions that shape their lives, from the everyday (building a house) to the fantastical (fighting the mobs). As the *New York Times Magazine* writer Clive Thompson (2016) describes it:

> It's a world of trial and error and constant discovery, stuffed with byzantine secrets, obscure text commands and hidden recipes. And it runs completely counter to most modern computing trends. Where companies

like Apple and Microsoft and Google want our computers to be easy to manipulate—designing point-and-click interfaces under the assumption that it's best to conceal from the average user how the computer works—Minecraft encourages kids to get under the hood, break things, fix thing, and turn mooshrooms into random-number generators. It invites them to tinker.

Each time a player begins a new game, notes Thompson, "Minecraft generates a unique world filled with hills, forests, and lakes. Whatever the player chops at or digs into yields building blocks" that are then used to craft tools and build an endless variety of structures and contraptions. Thompson situates *Minecraft* within the history of children playing with blocks, observing that European philosophers "have long promoted block-based games as a form of 'good' play that cultivates abstract thought."[1] Thompson lauds the game and quotes numerous supporters from both the tech and parenting worlds who credit *Minecraft* for helping a generation of kids learn the art of computer coding.

My interest here is less in the issue of skills and more in the affective realm—something Thompson touches on with the theme of "randomness" that he notes recurs through his interviews with kids who love the game. An unusual element of the game is that it does not come with a

Figure 7.2. A first-person perspective in *Minecraft*, where there is no visible avatar.

guide or player manual. When Ezra began playing upon just turning six, he had no idea how to go about it. He just began pushing buttons and trying things out, gradually becoming more and more engrossed. I struggled to keep up and understand, but he simply ignored my questions. Perhaps he could not explain or perhaps he was just impatient with my adult mind. Here is what I learned, via watching Ezra, talking to my student Sam, trying my own hand at the game, and studying the wiki page:

A player must first choose whether to play in creative or survival mode. As the wiki page explains, "When playing in survival mode, you will have many of the familiar requirements of other games. Health, hunger, armor, and oxygen (when swimming) bars will appear, as well as an inventory. You will also need to gather materials for crafting, through mining and other means, as well as gain experience points." In creative mode, "You will have unlimited access to materials in this mode, and your needs (such as health and hunger) will be gone. Also, you can fly."

Within each mode, players can choose their desired level of difficulty: "the difficulty settings determine whether or not monsters, which are also known as 'hostile mobs' will show up at night or underground. . . . Peaceful (for beginners) will prevent hostile mobs from spawning, while Easy will give you a small spawn rate, and Hard will give you a massive one. . . . Also, in the hard mode, Zombies, which are hostile mobs, can break down wooden doors and kill you!" Players can also decide on a particular environment, or "world mode," including superflat, large biomes, amplified (includes mountains and caves), and customized. The amplified mode makes everything more intense—mountains higher, oceans deeper, biomes wider.

In survival mode, making it through the first night is crucial. To do so, players should build a shelter before the sun sets; this shelter will protect them from skeletons shooting arrows and creepers blowing themselves up. Roaming through their environment, players look for building materials, such as trees, which are used to build a crafting table that allows players to build the other tools and materials they need. Tools include a pickaxe, an axe, a shovel, and a sword. A player must also mine some coal in order to build torches for their house; another option is to use a furnace with wood as fuel to turn the trees into coal.

"Otherwise," warns the wiki page, "your home will be dark and hostile mobs will spawn in."

Building a structure involves a series of decisions that are both practical and creative. The player must choose a location: the top of a hill is good, for example, because it is easier to defend. Then, if there is time, one can build an actual structure; if not, one could dig a cave. You need to shut yourself in before nightfall, and there are other threats: spiders can get in if you do not have a roof. You must craft a door by putting planks in certain positions. Then, you must craft a bed, which requires you to kill some sheep. Says the wiki page: "It may seem cruel, but it's how you will survive. They will drop 1 piece of wool if you kill them but if you somehow find iron and craft shears, they will drop 1–3 pieces of wool. Collect 3 pieces of wool and 3 wooden planks to craft a bed. To craft a bed, place the 3 wool in positions 4, 5, and 6 and the 3 wooden planks in 7, 8, and 9." The next task is to find food, since "going hungry will lower your health over time and make you easier to kill. The easiest way to find food is to kill animals. If you are too nice, then use apples or plant seeds to get wheat."

Once players have built their structures and survived the night, they can choose to play the game in one of three styles: role-playing, sandbox, or inventor. Only the role-playing style has a definite end point; in this mode, players collect and craft items and slowly work up to fighting the enderdragon to win the game. In the other two styles, there is an endless process of building new environments (cities, Helm's Deep from *Lord of the Rings*, etc.) and contraptions (elevators, cannons, etc.). The lack of an ending also distinguishes *Minecraft* from most games, which incorporate levels in pursuit of the end goal.

Players must also defend themselves against various monsters who appear unpredictably. Swords are one option, and players experiment with which materials are best (not wood!). Players also craft armor from materials that include leather, iron ingots, gold ingots, and diamonds; the armor includes a helmet, chest plate, leggings, and boots.

Finally, there are mobs (short for "mobiles")—creatures, both good and bad, which move about. There are peaceful mobs, such as cows, chicken, and sheep, who will never attack but can be attacked for food; neutral mobs, which will attack only if provoked; and hostile mobs, including skeletons, zombies, creepers, endermen, and spiders, which will always attack you if they see you (a slight exception: endermen will not attack you unless you attack them or look into their eyes.) Other things you can do: make a map, acquire a horse, get a dog or cat for a pet, breed animals, build a basic farm, and brew potions to heal yourself, make yourself stronger, or turn invisible.

"I'm Feeling Lucky, Mama"

One morning while Ezra is playing *Minecraft*, I ask if I can follow along, and he agrees. Sitting next to him, with my laptop, I record verbatim his narration (my interjections and descriptions are in parentheses). Many of these comments speak to the child's desire to build a home, offset by the desire to roam outside, but then return to the home. It is the perfect combination of adventure and stability.

> I'm flying. Looking for a place to build a house—where there aren't so many trees, but some trees and some grass. Maybe I took a wrong turn.
> (A landscape is unfolding on the screen—trees, mountains, grass slowly unrolling before us.)
> Ooh, a little island! You can build houses in caves or in a wall. I've built a house in a cave before.
> (Does that work well?)
> Yes, as long as there's no mobs.
> (He goes to the main menu "to do something" but can't explain in any more detail. I see the word "seed" appear, and he writes a four-digit number in a blank space on the screen.)
> I wanted to find a flat plain like this.
> (How did you know what number to punch in?)
> I don't know, I just do random things, but it works.
> I'm going to build my house. Oh, there's my horse.
> (A horse appears, and he switches to another page and clicks on a saddle before he returns to the main page. But he then he decides to kill it because "he's not letting me ride it." He begins to build his house.)
> Using oak-wood planks. Mining a tree so I can build my house.

I'm going to use something like scissors, but not technically scissors. Shears. I want to find a good place to build a house. You want to make it big enough so you don't bump your head when you jump but small enough so you can put stuff in it.

I'm going to make a double-decker house, you know, like a two-story house, one of those things.

I'm going to find a mine and see what I can find—a cave. One of these things.

(Are you going to build your house there instead?)

Maybe. If I want to, I will.

Going down deeper and deeper into a mine. Lava means I find diamond. Whoa! I've never found one of these in such a long time. It's an abandoned mine cart place. I found one. A mob spawning, no way! That means I can get finally . . . oh jeez! It's a bad thing, but I always have sponges to help. Sponge, pickaxe.

(What are you doing now?)

Putting sponges in places. So it can soak up the water. Actually, never mind, I'm leaving this place. Going another direction.

What's this way? Gold, that's a good sign that I might find some diamonds. Oh no, not one of these mazes. You can never find your way out. Oh, a chest. What could be in here? Oh my god! You can find things in chests, like what I just found. Lapis lazuli. That is just weird. I've never seen one of those. Oh jeez. I'm glad this isn't survival mode, or else I would have been dead by now. Creative is where you can't really die. Probably by the time I dig upwards, it's going to be nighttime. Whoa, redstone and diamonds. I'm on the hunt for diamonds. You can build diamond armor, which is better than any kind of armor.

(Is redstone good?)

If you like redstone.

Ooh, lapis lazuli! I'm close. I'm very close. You can enchant with that stuff.

I'm building a bridge across the lava so I can get across to the other side. Wow! What an amazing journey.

Oh jeez. If I wasn't careful I would have fallen down into the lava. So that's just where I came. Lapis lazuli.

I'm feeling lucky, mama. I'm feeling lucky.

No, I don't want to go there, I want to stay in here. So I'm back here again. Oh, I just destroyed the spider web. If you get caught in one of those by mobs, you're dead. I'm not lying.

Once you defeat the enderdragon the game is over.

(Have you ever done that?)

Nope!

Time to dig straight up, which is going to be a little problem. Man, I hate water!

This is new. I'm staying on this level. Going to have to dig.

(How does the torch catch on fire?)

Oh my god! Another chest. Some iron. Build some pickaxes.

Oh—give me a second.

(Goes to another screen and increases the "difficult" meter.)

Now even the wither skeletons have their weapons down. There's an enderman. They teleport. See how they teleport. (He makes dozens of them.)

(How do you get rid of them?)

You can't. It's very hard.

Ezra simultaneously constructs and travels through this world; this double process is what seems to increase both his sense of control and his pleasure. When he doesn't know how to do something, he simply tries something else. His exclamations, such as "oh jeez" and "wow," are filled with glee as well as intrigue, as he wonders what new surprise will pop up even as he gains some measure of control over his environment as he builds his house and collects material for his weapons.

This exploration does not hinge on Ezra identifying with Steve, the default avatar; in fact, the question of "who is he" seems not to play a role in the game. Rather, the operative questions are what happens and how does it feel if I move here, do this, change this, encounter this? Yet the "what happens" and the "how does it feel" are not two separate realms but rather intertwined, allowing for expressions that are not available in the linear prose and narratives that are valorized in many arenas of children's lives. These are not free-floating modes of expression but rather the products of a circumscribed space that regulates movement based on the player's decisions; this movement-within-structure builds on itself over time yet not in a linear and predictable pattern. There is no pressure for the *Minecraft* player to conform to a certain predetermined mode of expression, yet there are boundaries and parameters through which they can construct their own homes and paths through their worlds.

I notice that Ezra's confidence builds as he makes new discoveries, to the degree that he is willing to take risks and increase the game's difficulty. This is a new characteristic for him to exhibit; he is generally averse to pushing himself. I could surmise, with some reason, that this kind of learning suits him; it is similar to the Deleuzian pedagogical approach described by Liselott Olsson in her study of a preschool that implemented a nontraditional curriculum (see chapter 4). Olsson describes it as "going in circles, backwards, sideways, forwards, in a mess, [which] draws upon the contours of a different kind of learning and a different kind of knowledge. In this process knowledge is not pre-existing and built in a linear logical way. It is a messy learning process and it is going in all sorts of directions. Totally different things are being drawn in to the process" (167). Still, this unpredictability happens within structures; as Keith Stuart describes his son Zac's attraction to *Minecraft*: "In this universe, where the rules are unambiguous, where the logic is clear and unerring, Sam is in control" (quoted in Rutkin 2016). This sense of setting one's own path—freedom—within a stable environment heightens the feeling of agency—of world building.

The sense of "going in all directions" intensifies the affective possibilities; it is what Deleuze called the "distribution of affects" that "constitutes a map of intensity. It is always an affective constellation" (64). In other words, it is not just one affect experienced in isolation but rather a dispersed range of affects that assumes no necessary order; this randomness amplifies affect, pulling the entire body into the experience. As Massumi puts it, intensity registers "at the surface of the body, at its interface with things." Furthermore, intensity is "outside expectation and adaptation, as disconnected from meaningful sequencing, from narration, as it is from vital function. It is narratively de-localized, spreading over the generalized body surface" (85). Ezra's *Minecraft* narration spreads over the surface of the game as well as his body, creating a constellation that builds on each affect, though also at times diverging in various directions: there is the thrill of finding something, the fear of getting stuck in a maze, the pleasure of anticipated outcomes. One affect flows into the other in a manner that makes it hard to distinguish when one stops and another begins; this stands in clear contrast to the earlier attempts I have described to identify and categorize children's emotions. Consider this narration by Ezra for its flow of affect in the midst of world building:

> I just do seeds so I can find villages and stuff. It's just fun to type in random numbers and see what happens. I have a feeling this is going to be bad. This is a bad place to spawn.
>
> Now I'm in a cave looking for diamonds. The water means I'm going to find lava, and lava means I'm going to find diamonds. Gold means I'm going to find some diamonds. (sing-song voice) Going to find some diamonds, going to find some diamonds. That's a dead end. I mean a deep end.
>
> Let's do 12345. Create world. There's a lot of flowers. That's pretty. Mmmm. I know I should have went with 123. There's a bunch of bunnies getting chased by wolves. Oh my god, I got to see this TV show. This is the best TV show ever. You can do it, wolfie. I've never seen a wolf before. Hey, get back here bunny. I'm going to chase you with a sword. This is my kill, wolf. Die, wolf. You know what, let's go find a wolf to tame. Bunny! Wolfie! Wolf, where'd you go? I got a nice juicy bone for you. Wolves? Oh, wolves! Wherever there are bunny droppings, that's it, I have to find where bunny died. Mmm. Wolves, yes, over here. Yes. No wait, doggie. Come on, come on. I'm going to need you to sit. Now stay there. Sit. Sit. This looks like a good place to make a house. My doggies are sitting down. I made two.
>
> (I thought they were wolves.)
>
> They are wolves, but they turn into doggies for you.

What struck me in this narration was Ezra's sense that although he felt like something "bad" was going to happen, and that he should have tried the "123" combination, he not only kept exploring but enjoyed the unknown, as he slipped into a sing-song voice in saying he was "going to find some diamonds." Another spontaneous combination of expressions occurs in his looking for both bunnies and wolves—first, he wants the wolf to die, then to tame him, then the wolf turns into a doggie that he domesticates. This, he muses, is "the best TV show ever."

Building the *Minecraft* Community

My discussion to this point has focused on the solo player, interacting only with the game and his or her imagination. There are numerous, more social ways to engage with *Minecraft*: multiplayer games online, for example, and many sites for sharing tips and information about the game. Thompson reports that the biggest gaming wiki, Gamepedia, has nearly 5,000 articles on *Minecraft*. He summarizes some of the ways that *Minecraft*'s inventor, Markus Persson, designed the game so players could share their work:

> You could package your world as a "map" and post it online for others to download and move around in. Even more sophisticated players could modify *Minecraft*'s code, creating new types of blocks and creatures, and then put these "mods" online for others to use. Further developments included a server version of *Minecraft* that lets people play together on the Internet inside the same world. These days, kids can pay as little as $5 a month to rent such a server. They can also visit much larger commercial servers capable of hosting hundreds or thousands of players simultaneously. There is no single, central server. Thousands exist worldwide.

Cumulatively, kids are creating a common *Minecraft* culture and mode of communicating with each other; they learn not from adults or a rule book but from each other. These social interactions enhance the potential for shared feelings—feelings intensified precisely because they are shared. This is what ethnographer Kate Ringland found in her 60 hours spent combing through the online forums of Autcraft; she "saw kids expressing their feelings—joy over a good time in the game, and anxiety or sadness about problems in the real world. 'There's a lot of reflection going on,' she says. '*Minecraft* is supporting a lot of these social behaviours'" (quoted in Rutkin 2016).

This community interaction is further produced on the many YouTube sites where kids narrate games as they play them. These communications are far different from the YouTube videos posted by parents of their children's responses to Trump that I described in chapter 3. Exploring the realm of what she calls "lateral engagement," Patricia Lange shows how kids (her focus is teenagers) use YouTube as a kind of civic engagement, sharing information in a nonhierarchical way that "serves as a blueprint for successful future civic discourse" (98). She further describes the process:

> How they engage in civic affairs is influenced by their affiliation to particular technologies (e.g., online and social networking sites) and styles of communication (e.g., documentaries, mash-ups, and video blogging). By discussing their concerns on the global video-sharing site of YouTube, kids can reach broader audiences who may not share their views. Given its agonistic environment, diverse content, and heterogeneous user base, YouTube has the potential to avoid being a stale echo chamber. YouTube's confrontational timbre exposes kids to contrasting opinions that they say are hard to find on- or off-line. Sharing videos enables them to try out opinions, explore world views, and develop civic attachments and empathy. (98)

How does this work for younger kids, for whom "civic engagement" operates at a more everyday level? Specifically, I argue that gaming tutorials function as a kind of pre-civic engagement, in which kids learn from other kids how gaming is a site where they can express themselves freely, and free from adult interference. However, given the fact that younger children do not have easy access to the creation of their own YouTube channels, it is also more likely the case that certain "stars" emerge in the YouTube universe, thus lessening its democratic potential.

Take, for example, the British gamer Ethan, whose EthanGamerTV YouTube channel has built up an avid following since he began it in 2013 as a seven-year-old. On July 9, 2016—his tenth birthday—he passed the one-million mark in subscribers, an event he memorialized in a short video documenting his rise to fame.[2] In the video, we see Ethan "grow up," so to speak, getting glasses, getting bigger, getting more sophisticated in his approach to the various games he plays. Although Ethan makes the practice look easy and doesn't reference the financial expense, the technological start-up costs are not cheap. They include a capture card that records the games as you play them, which goes for around $150; a decent microphone that allows you to record your voiceover while you are playing that runs anywhere from $20 to $120; and video-editing software.

The comments on Ethan's YouTube channel page show that viewers are inspired by the fact that someone their own age could have such success. Some, such as Mason Amburgey, ask Ethan to "friend" them:

> ethan if you missed my first comment on your newest video I could find will you please accept my friend request on *Roblox* my name is titanboy26

Other kids either have or want to have their own channel that has as many subscribers as Ethan does:

> Ethan you inspire me. Now I have my own YouTube channel. Please sub. I have little subscribers.
>
>   hey ethan i want to be just like you im a 9 year old kid and i finally got my you tube channel im hope fully getting youtube gear soon but i want to ask if you can give me some tips for youtube to help me out ;) btw my theme of my channel is da roblox noob :D XD and ethan congrats on a million subs i want to be just like you ;)
>
>   ethan can you help me on my YouTube channel i only do gaming and some art and can you friend me in roblox and i am the same age as you and also i live in Austrailia sorry my spelling is bad. Can i make a video with you plz i need your ergent help please help me please and i only have 7 subscribers i cinda like the same things as you. dantdm red logo roblox minecraft fgteeve and we have two channels but my second channels could iseeyou2boy.

These posts indicate how much kids rely on each other for advice and support, with the ultimate goal of gaining subscribers. These subscriber pools clearly overlap with each other; thus, while there is some competition, kids also recognize that subscribing to one YouTube channel in no way negates but rather enhances the chances of subscribing to a similar one. As "iseeyou2boy" says, "I cinda like the same things as you," followed by a list of game-related interests (DanTDM, for example, is a popular YouTube gamer and video personality, well known for his *Minecraft* videos.) Implied here is the expectation that none of these references needs to be spelled out.

  Not every expression on Ethan's page was positive, illustrating the range of affects kids are "allowed" to express in this relatively unmediated space. Some kids complained that the popularity of Ethan's *Roblox* videos had caused some players to switch from *Minecraft* to *Roblox*; for example, CraftMaster 84 says:

> I HATE YOU SO MUCH BECAUSE YOU ARE THE REASON WHY A BONCH OF MINECRAFT YOUTUBERS PLAY ROBLOX NOW!!! SOME OF THEM DONT EVEN PLAY MINECRAFT ANYMORE!

A number of fans rush to Ethan's defense, saying that plenty of kids still play *Minecraft*. This open airing of conflict speaks to Lange's description of YouTube as a site of "contrasting opinions"; however, the conflict is limited by the fact that the preponderance of sentiments are ones of adoration for Ethan. In this way, the kid community work out their strong feelings without adult mediation (though I am not claiming that always happens).

Ethan's narration of playing the game is not scripted; he describes in real time what is happening, coming upon unexpected turns and failing as often as he succeeds to clear an obstacle. While these games include a wide variety, I will focus on two of his *Minecraft* videos in this chapter, and one of his *Roblox* videos in the next chapter. The first is the "grand opening" of his *Minecraft* hub on the TEI server, for which he invites players to join in an exploration of a replica of his room that he has made within *Minecraft*.[3] All his fans are awaiting his invitation to join him in his bedroom; it is like being invited into Ethan's inner sanctum, where they come across his stinky socks and discarded toys.

Ethan opens the video with this comment: "I wonder who's going to be the first person in. . . . in 3, 2, 1, here we are. . . . now, let's let the fans flood." He opens up the server to his fans, and it does immediately flood with avatars. "Yes, I'm so excited. Everybody's so happy." They are all jumping around wildly, to which Ethan says, "Parkour, bed, desk. Awesomeness. Yeeaaaa. What up? Yes! Look at everyone! So much. What! So many people. Yes! This is awesome. Oh, yes. Whew! Somebody's dressed up as me as well. Oh, best day ever. Best day ever. Oh my goodness. You know what—let's go to the bedroom. Let's go to the bed to bounce."

Productivemr.duck writes, "First on bed!" RoboJack2000 asks, "How u get on?" Aquaries writes, "I can't read." Some of the players are having trouble maneuvering their avatars onto the bed. "Follow me," says Ethan. They jump from the desk to the floor, the tiny figures dwarfed by the furniture. They congregate under the bed, interrupted by various fan comments: "I love you, Ethan"; "congrats on the 1 million subs"; "ethan say hi I'm recording"; wigglybacon123 asks, "why u defriend me?" Soon, dozens of tiny figures are bouncing on the bed together. And Ethan comments, "look at all my fans bouncing on the bed. Hashtag love it."

The bedroom space is a series of maps, in the Deleuzian sense. As players cross the room, trying to figure out how to climb a dresser, go under the bed, climb up on the bed, and jump, "the trajectory merges not only with the subjectivity of those who travel through a milieu, but also with the subjectivity of the milieu itself, insofar as it is reflected in those who travel through it" (Deleuze 1997, 61). The space itself becomes part of their subjectivity; one cannot imagine one without the other.

Many players are not only moving through the space but also simultaneously typing comments that appear in a sidebar on the left of the screen, thus producing a language that matches the energy of the game and furthering the intermixing of subjectivity and space. For example, while playing hide and seek, many of the players are saying, "where's Ethan?" and "I love you, Ethan!" and "Ethan, your my inspiration to play Minecraft." Ethan types directions: "Follow me to the shelf on the left." And they all bop after him. The movement prompts a range of feelings. Inexplicably, for example, StompyDog comments, "I'm gonna cry." TheMasterGamer says, "This is epic!!!!!!" Ethan starts singing, "I believe I can fly. I believe I can touch the sky."

Toward the end of the game, Ethan types, "press the compass and we will do a gigantic screen shot," and the players all gather on the bed for a group photo, like a family at the end of their vacation.

This domestic scenario is further elaborated in Ethan's *Minecraft* video titled "In My Room," though this video differs insofar as Ethan gives specific directions on how to operate in different worlds.[4] At the start, he says, "Hey guys, can you guess where I am right now? I am on my desk, in my room, in Minecraft." Then he talks to his avatar: "Hello me, wielding two enchanted diamond swords." He shows us the EthanGamer Plushy Comfy House, into which we climb. From there, under the bed, then on the bed. He then makes a discovery: "Hallelujah! A light saber? Insane."

The bedroom is also transformed, illustrating Ethan's ability to turn his domestic space into a *Minecraft* site. Under the bed is an explosive crate that goes down a railroad track and hits a target that explodes into fireworks—"Kaboom!" He then shows us the survival world, loading the terrain—"Oh, come on, it's raining. Come on!" Then there's the building world; Ethan goes to the top of a diving board. He also shows viewers the mining world and how to get the resources they need, then go back to the building world, claim their plot, and use the materials acquired in the building world to construct whatever they want. Ethan's expertise allows kids to circumvent any other "authority," relying on each other to navigate worlds and develop their own means of communicating.

"If You Can Fit in It, It's a Home. Duh"

As children build their worlds together, both within the game and via YouTube, they construct a kind of "archive of feelings" to which they can return at any time. Even though the *Minecraft* archive is constantly changing, its large and well-traveled presence on the internet does provide a material space for kids to visit and revisit. It is a kind of public sphere, or, more aptly, a counterpublic sphere, since it evades the kind of institutionalization that can diminish the vibrancy of the affective encounter (Cvetkovich 2003, 17). The construction of an archive through the performance of an activity that, when gathered, acquires some degree of material permanence, allows children a dwelling to return to, again and again. Ezra illustrates in this commentary what he learned about home building from one video:

> I'm making a cool house so if any mobs spawn, they'll think this is just a random cave and they'll walk right past it. I'm using dirt to disguise it. It's not a house, but it's still going to be home.
> (What makes it a home?)
> If you can fit in it, it's a home. Duh.
> So those blocks are made out of dirt?
> Mmhmm. Sounds pretty silly. But if no mobs come in, then I'm safe.

(Have you ever tried this before?)

Nope, so this is my first time making a camouflage house.

What gave you that idea?

I saw a video of someone who made a house that was camouflaged, so no one would know.

I'm going to make a lever so that pistons will pull it back and forth. Same thing, from the video.

(What's the piston going to do?)

Just give me a second, I'll show you. I hope this thing works. So I'm making a secret place where there's a lever. So nobody will know.

(Goes to another page and touches the "Lever" button).

Oh, I see now, I have to pull all of these levers to make it work. See, isn't that cool? Then I just go back here. Bloop. Bloop. What is this one going to do? Oh, wait, I have an idea. This might work. Now all the animals will think this is just a normal thing.

Ooh, I have an idea. What I'm going to do . . . cover the rest of it up. Then go back to here and make it extra secure. Ta-da, all blocked up. Since there's only one piston, to cover up the door. I have extra levers. If I pull that, that goes back. If I pull that, that goes back. Isn't that cool? I cover it up at night time. Ooooh. I should have thought of that.

(Thought of what?)

Ooh, I forgot to do something. It's inside my home. I forgot to put levers on this side, so I can actually get out of my home, in and out, or else I'd actually be trapped inside my home. It's closed up now, see I don't even need to put in a door. And then no zombies will break through. You know what, instead of dirt, since zombies can break through dirt, why not just make it cobblestone? Actually no. No, that would lead to a village. Stone. Just plane smooth stone. Look. Got to close it, close it, close it. Final thing you do. See, isn't that cool? That's redstone creation stuff.

(Let me understand, cobblestone leads to a village?)

Well, no, there's a path that leads to the village. Well, no. Bloop. Bloop. Bloop, bloop. Oh, that works really well. I got to go inside, close this lever. Now to get a pet cat. Watch. Yeah, I got the tabby cat.

(Little red hearts float above the cat; what does that mean?)

That means I fed him, and he likes me. I can't name him.

(Why not?)

> I don't know. You can name horses, but not cats or wolves. It's sad. Oops. Sorry, kitty.

Ezra has figured out how to construct levers within his house through watching other players on YouTube; these videos have led him to a series of trial-and-error maneuvers. His fingers fly over the buttons. His constant movement through this space, albeit on a screen, encourages him to try out new ideas, and he gets to find out immediately if they work out or not. He makes up his own sound effects ("bloop, bloop"). Ezra's affective range extends beyond my attempt to fix a particular emotion to his experience. Although he does incorporate feelings such as "happy" and "sad," they are momentary stops during the overall experience.

The collaboration intensifies when Ezra has a friend over, and they play the game together, each on his individual iPad, yet connected via the same IP address. They are looking for each other in the common world they have designated for this game:

> Just wait, I'm coming.
> Oh, there you are.
> Do you like my skin?
> How cool.
> Whoa—there's a village.
> Let's live here!
> Meet me in the house. I'm just going to do something. This might take me awhile to get the flame sword.
> I got dibs on getting the flame word, 'kay?
> Wait for me to get my stuff, OK?
> OK.
> I'm getting us an anvil so we can repair stuff.
> 'Kay. Dang it, let's try this again. Oh, I think I know why this isn't working. I have a theory. Maybe you need books to get the right enchantment.
> Yes! There, I have fire. Now to enchant my armor. I'll do the projectile.
> Where are you? Are you in the right house?
> I'm not even in the house.

OK, I'm coming. I'm coming, dude. I see your name tag. Where are you? Oh, there you are.

What are you doing? Stop it.

Why isn't it working? Why can't I kill you? Oh, because we're hacking. It's creative.

I'm going to finish working on the house, OK?

OK, see ya.

Villagers keep coming into our house. It's very annoying.

Yes, any villagers who come into our house will be obliterated.

I'm getting some bows, OK?

Got it.

I have the beds, the furnace, the chests. Oh, and wait, I'm going to put the beds down. Are you still doing it? Why are you still doing it? Do you have a book in your hands?

Yes.

Why?

Wrong chest.

Dude, I need your help.

Dude, want to see how cool my sword is? I have three enchantments on it.

Wait, you can get three enchantments on your sword? How did you do that? Could you do that for me? Let me get a different diamond sword for myself. How did you do that? Oh, I think you need a book, right? Isn't that right?

Umm. I think so.

Let me get a book then.

Hey, can you put a ladder down?

Can you put a piece of dirt here? I'm building our house.

Don't just stand there, help me out!

Come on, let's build somewhere else.

I see you! Let's go!

Dude, if I drown, I'm going to lose all my stuff.

No, you won't, 'cause I would get it for you.

Do we need birch wood?

No.

I found a bunch of wood!

OWWW!

I'm sorry, I'm sorry. I tried to hit the piggy. I didn't know you were right there.

Oh my god! I have so much coal!

How much do you have?

65!

We found the sheep but now I have to go back to the house and make the bed.

Each child's sense that he is building a home and a world with other kids who "get it" heightens their feelings of independence and initiative. They create home spaces where they can feel whatever they want to feel, and where these feelings fluctuate as they move rather than remain fixed. Their language emerges from the game and each other and could not be replicated outside this space.

Everyday Life

The *Minecraft* world has produced a common vernacular among kids that exceeds the game, to the degree that one can enter and engage at various levels without any specific knowledge of the game itself. This is illustrated in my opening anecdote about the birthday party, the hundreds if not thousands of music videos using *Minecraft* figures, and the wealth of *Minecraft*-related products available in toy stores and elsewhere. Some teachers have used the game as a pedagogical tool, applying it to math, science, and other subjects.[5]

Other teachers have used *Minecraft* as the basis for kids to draw their self-portraits. At Home Grown Hearts, a home-school collective in Michigan City, Indiana, fourth grader Rachel produced an image of herself in *Minecraft* gear (see figure 7.3). In McKinney, Texas, second-grade teacher Stephanie Mundt had her students make *Minecraft* images that she then organized into an online exhibit, the "Minecraft Monster Gallery."[6] Both of these images can be found on the Artsonia website; the company calls itself the "world's largest student art museum" and allows parents, teachers, and art educators to create galleries for various student projects.

Minecraft fans appear confident that other *Minecraft* players will have an interest in them that extends beyond the game. In other words, they

Figure 7.3. By Rachel, grade four. Artsonia, www.artsonia.com/museum/gallery.asp?project=1124790.

feel connected to other kids, even though they may not ever actually get to hang out with them. We see this belief on the numerous YouTube channels in which kids straightforwardly describe their everyday lives. This approach is exemplified in a video by Shawn Carter, a boy of about ten, who also contributes to a genre called "*Minecraft* in real life" videos. In one video on his channel, he simply describes his life. He is wearing a too-large *Minecraft* baseball cap that pushes down on his ears such that they fold over and stick out from his head. He is sitting on the floor by his bed, on which one can see several stuffed animals. He speaks in a mainly monotone voice as he relates to his 3,352 subscribers what he has been doing since his last video. We get a detailed account of his everyday life; note in particular here Shawn's attention to time and his attempts to reconstruct his life. He talks casually to his subscribers as if they are friends with an interest in what he has been doing, even though none of it has to do with *Minecraft*:

I haven't made a YouTube video in a long-time, so I'm just saying, why not make one right now? And um . . . so . . . let's just cut to the chase and let's do this. So we went to our grandparents' house one, two, three days ago, and umm., oh yea, by the way, I'm using a camera stabilizer, so if I accidentally do that, blame it on the camera stabilizer. We went to my grandparents' house, and they have this inflatable water slide, and me and Emerson were doing cannonballs down it. And I've been doing my gymnastics as usual, my classic six-hour thing every week, umm, well not, like six hours one day, but two hours a day, six hours in all, so I go three days a week. And I don't think I actually told you this, but maybe I did, I don't think I did though. We were watching the Olympic trials, and my coach Chris Brooks made it, and I am so excited for that [pumps his fist in the air but has no expression on his face], but umm I hope he gets a high score in the Olympics. And um, yeah, what else have we been doing? Give me a moment to think about this. speaking of gymnastics, um, I um, ppppffft. I don't remember what day it was, I don't know, umm, I don't remember what day it was, I think it was Friday, I got my run-off back handspring on the tumble track. And the tumble track is hard [smiles broadly and puts his hand close to his mouth as if to whisper and mouths the words "just saying"]. . . . [describes more gymnastics accomplishments].

Shawn speaks with utter confidence and aplomb (he does have more than 3,000 subscribers, after all), and in doing so he establishes his own community of confidantes, a community likely begun in the *Minecraft* world but not exclusive to it. He tells them about a board game he is inventing, with no sense at all that kids will find a board game antiquated: "I've been working on a little board game, which I'm really excited about. It's still a work in progress. I made the game board, I'm still making the characters and stuff. It's called tribes, and I think it's going to be a really fun game." The camera shifts to the game board, and Shawn describes the game in detail while demonstrating how it works. He predicts that "it's going to be the very first game in history—board game, not a video game—to have up to 12 players." Then he returns to his routine, as if he has just recalled a few things: "I think, I don't know, maybe on Monday, I believe, we went to the pool, which was really fun, splashed around, really fun. Just a little side thing I wanted to throw in there. Also, the day after that we went to my grandparents' house, well, we went to my grandparents' house again, that was before the water slide, and my grandpa bought us ice cream, and it was really awesome."

It may seem that Shawn's very ordinariness distances him from the autistic and other neurodiverse kids discussed above and throughout this book. The point of his narration of his everyday life, however, is precisely what neurodiversity appreciates: the desire for connection with other kids with mutual interests, desires, and needs. Shawn is not trying to impress any one, or self-manage for success. He wants to garner subscribers and establish a routine by which they can regularly visit him, learn about his life, and make him feel like part of a community of kids. As he says in the closing of this video, "Please like, comment, or subscribe, and I'll see you guys next time. Peace."

8

From Memes to Logos

Commercial Detours in the Game of Roblox

"NYANNYANYANYANYANYANYANYANYANYANYA."

So go the "lyrics" (repeatedly) to the hugely popular YouTube video of Nyan Cat. To the tune of an equally incessant pop song, the cat with the body of a Pop-Tart flies through the sky, powered by a rainbow fart. The Nyan Cat has been remixed into hundreds of variations: *Minecraft* Nyan Cat, Pikachu Nyan Cat, Mario Nyan Cat, Nyan Dog, Nyan Pig, and many, many more.[1]

In the YouTube video "Kids React to Viral Videos" that focuses on Nyan Cat, eight children ranging in age from six to 14 watch and comment on the video. The older children agree that the video is "annoying"; as they watch it, they comment, with varying degrees of derision, "Shut up!" and "What's the point of this?" By contrast, the youngest child, six-year-old Morgan, leans toward the computer screen as if she wants to hug the cat, and says, "She's adorable! She's dancing in the sky!" When the offscreen interviewer asks why the video was "showing the same thing over and over again," the older kids each say variations of "I don't know," or "to be irritating," but Morgan responds, "They want it to be a pattern. Because patterns are not boring." The interviewer presses her, "Doesn't that get boring?" but she responds, "Nooooo! It's just a kitty. A cute little kitty, people. She's so adorable! Didn't you want to kidnap her, people?" When the interviewer asks, "How long would you watch this?" Morgan responds, "Until I die!" He asks, "What name would you give it?" She responds, "Rapunzel. Cute, cuddly, and soft!" and hugs a pink blanket in front of her.

The affective appeal of the cat is undeniable. Nyan Cat is like a pet, giving kids a sense of ownership. Morgan doesn't say the cat makes her happy; she is not naming an emotion in the way the interviewer seems to want her to do. Rather, she describes how it makes her feel—like she wants to hug the cat—and how she imagines the cat feels—cuddly and soft.

Even though kids didn't originally make the image,[2] they have made it their own. Memes and animated GIFs[3] are part of the participatory culture of the internet; they exemplify what Limor Shifman calls the "constant reworking of texts by internet users," with YouTube functioning as "a central hub—if not *the* central hub–of user-generated bottom-up video content." As a social network, YouTube "plays a central role in divergent practices of community building" (2011, 189). YouTube disseminates videos such as Nyan Cat across multiple videos and games, which cumulatively constructs a common vernacular; the vernacular is constantly evolving to fit the desires of its users. "Like genes, memes undergo variation, selection, and retention," says Shifman. "At any given moment, many memes are competing for the attention of hosts. However, only memes suited to their socio-cultural environment will spread successfully; the others will become extinct" (188–89). The images appeal to younger kids like Morgan because of their smallness, their catchiness, and their repetition ("the pattern" that Morgan identifies)—all characteristics that the older kids find "annoying."

Yet memes are also open to appropriation for the purposes of profit, at which point they become more like corporate logos. The Nyan Cat when merged with the *Pokémon* figurehead Pikachu draws on *Pokémon*'s success, and the *Minecraft* Nyan capitalizes on that company's popularity. When these images and other logos are used in games that are also reliant, to some degree, on spending money, the line between memes and logos becomes even blurrier. The affective intensity that is produced as gamers move through space (as I argued in the last chapter) or as they imagine hugging Nyan Cat is limited by the need to stop and make a purchase, even if it's a virtual or symbolic purchase.

In this chapter, I explore the implications of consumerism and branding within the gaming world for kids, focusing on the popular game *Roblox*. Like *Minecraft*, *Roblox* is a game in which players move through spaces; in its original incarnation, it was also a building game. Both games provide social spaces for kids in the five- to nine-age group as they're just starting to form friend groups yet are still largely dependent on their parents for access to social spaces. YouTubers like Ethangamer and gamergirl bring kids together within *Roblox* spaces, where they can express a range of feelings with little to no adult mediation. Like *Minecraft*, *Roblox* also generates its own vernacular, creating an intertextual

Figure 8.1. Screenshot from a *Roblox* game, roblox.com.

web through references to other games such as *Pokémon* and popular characters like Sonic the Hedgehog and Nyan Cat. This vernacular is further produced through an ongoing chat option on the side of the screen as kids not only play the game but also send friend requests and interact with each other through their own language (abbreviations like "obi" for "obstacle").

There are limits to the freedom, however, that come with *Roblox*'s heavy reliance on branded products and logos, as players often move through spaces interrupted by McDonald's golden arches and the Starbucks logo (or "Sawsbuck," see figure 8.1) or buy shirts with the Nike swoosh. Furthermore, most *Roblox* games encourage players to buy the in-game currency Robux with real money (via an adult's account) in order to advance more quickly or buy weapons, accessories, cars, and other objects in the game. In this manner, the affective flow is interrupted, generating feelings linked to consumerism, such as frustration, desire, and competition, all of which can be momentarily satiated through the purchase of Robux.

Roblox also raises interesting questions about what it means to define a kids' language, and who is a kid. *Roblox* advertises itself as the "#1 gaming site for kids and teens," with "the largest user-generated online gaming platform." The company says it has 1.7 million developers, and that it expects to have paid out $30 million to these creators by the end of 2017. Many of the game developers are in fact the teens and 20-somethings who themselves once played the game and know how to appeal to younger kids, creating a space of entrepreneurialism. On the *Roblox* game development site, the company recruits developers by advertising its "monetization tools" and says that "our shared economy gives you full control of your in-game monetization." Although these "monetized" *Roblox* games still provide a kind of social space to their younger players, this space is less likely to generate the kind of creative flow that *Minecraft* does and more likely to define itself through the language of consumption. As such, it shows the challenges kids face in defining their own spaces in the face of such naturalized socializing forces as the brand image.

Dancing Bananas

A catchy YouTube video song recurs throughout the day, bursting through moments of silence and interrupting conversations. Ezra sings out, and a friend is quick to join in: "It's peanut butter jelly time, peanut butter jelly time. Where he at? Where he at? Where he at? There he go. There he go. There he go. It's peanut butter jelly, peanut butter jelly, peanut butter jelly with a baseball bat." Ezra imitates the dancing banana of the video, rounding his shoulders and wiggling his butt before he ends with a loud, "Where he at?" Another one he loves to belt out upon waking up in the morning: "It's raining tacos, out of the sky, tacos, no need to ask why. Just open your mouth and close your eyes . . . It's raining tacos, no need to ask why. . . ."

These are the kinds of grassroots memes and gifs that Shifman refers to when she talks about a "bottom up" culture. Kids across the U.S. are singing these songs—making them into their own versions, adding their own dance moves. Memes are defined through their repetitiveness and lack of narrative, which, Shifman notes, "may have an important role in encouraging active user involvement in re-making video memes. The meme itself includes a persuasive demonstration of its own replicability and, thus, it contains encrypted instructions for others' replication" (197). Memes usually do not have a concrete theme; rather they are playful and whimsical, which also aids in their remixing: "This combination of human playfulness with lack of concrete content may, in fact, be regarded as an advantage when evaluating the tendency to replicate YouTube memes: users can imitate the playful spirit embedded in the texts, yet inject new themes according to personal preferences" (198). Thus, while the kids themselves are not the original producers of the memes, they make them their own through their creative uses, and the memes lend themselves to such appropriations.

Much of this appropriation is connected to music, which recalls my point in the introduction about the power of music to circumvent language. With music comes movement and the evasion of bodily comportment that characterizes spaces such as schools and parts of the home (chores, rules, etc.). Also, music invariably invites the consumer to make the song their own, through humming, singing, and dancing. Consider two recent examples of internet videos that kids helped make wildly popular.

First, in 2015 the rapper Silento released his single "Watch Me (Whip/Nae Nae)," which integrated two dance moves: the nae nae, which "involves planting one's feet, swaying with shoulder movement, placing one hand in the air and one hand down, and incorporating personal creativity." The move typically follows another move called the whip. The whip involves "lifting one foot off the ground and planting it with a stomp; simultaneously, the dancer twists and extends their opposite arm forward."[4] While Silento's song was not the first to incorporate these moves, it took off across the U.S. in 2015, as kids made up their own variations of both moves (within certain limits, of course, as the new version must still be recognizable). The song and dance were taken up by a variety of kids in different places, ranging from a physical education class at Harvest Elementary in Harvest, Alabama,[5] to kids performing to the song on the street.[6] There are also dozens if not hundreds of YouTube videos featuring remixings of the dance with the likes of Alvin and the Chipmunks, the Minions of *Despicable Me* fame, SpongeBob, and many more. Kids' comments on these sites illustrate how they use the internet, both intentionally and inadvertently, to define themselves affectively and in relation to each other, across dispersed geographies.

A similar phenomenon occurred starting in 2015 with the dance movement/gesture called dabbing, described by Wikipedia: "To perform the move, a person drops their head into the bent crook of a slanted arm, while raising the opposite arm in a parallel direction straight out. The move looks similar to someone sneezing into the 'inside' of the elbow."[7] While the dab had its origins in the Atlanta hip-hop scene, it also acquired purchase in professional sports, especially after Carolina Panthers quarterback Cam Newton performed a dab during a game in a celebratory fashion that was also perceived to be a taunt. He later explained that he had learned how to do it from his 16-year-old brother who had told him to "dab on them folks."

Whether people, or characters such as SpongeBob, were actually dabbing, became a topic of national debate in 2016. Adults revealed their lack of coolness as they (including Hillary Clinton) attempted to dab. Why do adults make weak attempts at dabbing, or, conversely but relatedly, seem threatened when kids dab in their presence? For example, Cal, the 17-year-old son of newly elected Republican congressman Roger Marshall, dabbed while holding the bible during a photo op with his father and House speaker Paul Ryan. Ryan looked quizzically at Cal, who was holding his arm across his face, and asked if he was going to sneeze, then put his own hand on the young man's arm and lowered it. Later, Ryan tweeted: "Just finished swearing in photos. Nearly 300 members. Countless cute kids. Still don't know what dabbing is, though." And Marshall tweeted back: "Just so you know Speaker Ryan: He's grounded."[8] The dab's widespread circulation meant that Cal could be certain that most kids watching would know immediately what he was doing; its subversiveness was also confirmed by Ryan's and his father's response.

At some difficult to determine and likely ever-shifting point, the grassroots internet culture merges with a more mainstream culture, whether that be the halls of Congress or Nickelodeon (numerous YouTube videos attempt to prove that SpongeBob is dabbing). This confluence of the citizen-consumer is what Sarah Banet-Weiser describes in her book on Nickelodeon, which, she argues, has constructed children as citizen-consumers, empowered through their ability to make choices as both consumers and future citizens, two roles which are increasingly conflated. Banet-Weiser argues that the cable channel has been so successful at drawing kids into its generational marketing appeal because of the "structure of feeling" it generates, not only through programming but also through its ads, promos between programs, and highly visible logos, including the orange splat and the green slime. Says Banet-Weiser: "The channel thus creates a provisional unity through a field of shared symbols about the brand, and loyalty to the Nickelodeon brand is the ticket to membership" (20). Nickelodeon's appeal is effective because it doesn't seem like a "branding strategy," she says, but rather a sincere attempt to empower kids. Can branding and empowerment coexist? This is the dilemma Banet-Weiser explores throughout the book, and while she tries to maintain the tension and the complexity of consumer agency, she mainly argues that, no, this is not true empowerment: "This slipperiness, this lack of discernment within differential definitions of empowerment, assists in Nickelodeon's success as a brand, because brand loyalty does not seem so much about preference as it does about everyday cultural practice" (21).

The phrase "lack of discernment" suggests that kids are consuming Nickelodeon programming without recognizing its inherent consumerism, especially because Nick is just part of a larger context in which branding has become an everyday practice. Yet this argument does not account for the creative ways in which kids appropriate commodified texts, making them less commodified and more accessible through venues such as YouTube and Tumblr. In these cases, consumerism itself is what allows for a creative production that exists outside of, or at least to the side of, the original production. What about, though, kids' attraction to branded products within games such as *Pokémon*, *Minecraft*, and *Roblox*? While these brands are, to varying degrees, part of the gaming experience, they are never the whole experience. There are always other reasons to play the games.

"Gotta Catch 'Em All"

Pokémon dominated children's toy and game consumption worldwide for much of the 1990s; spreading across countries as well as platforms, from the original Game Boy to trading cards, a television show, a movie, toys, computers, and other gaming systems, it made Nintendo billions of dollars. Its main representative, the irresistibly cute and cuddly Pikachu, became a kind of logo that drew millions of kids around the world into a kind of community. This community was based on acquisition—the game's advertising slogan, after all, was "gotta catch 'em all"—as kids bought the trading-card packages in an effort to collect all the 100-plus characters.

While consumerism was thus a central part of the game, this consumerism was not an end in itself but rather a way to acquire the knowledge needed to be part of the *Pokémon* world—a complex and complicated world. In describing his six-year-old son Sam's obsession with the game, Julian Sefton-Green writes in an academic collection on *Pokémon* that a central component of the game is acquisition of knowledge: "it places the representation of learning and studying at the heart of its narrative drive—to become a Pokemon master." Kids strive to become masters: "For Ash [the main boy character in the television show] and the children playing the game, achieving their goal of becoming a Pokemon master seems to involve learning everything there is to know about Pokemon. I am suggesting, in effect, that Pokemon shadows the forms and status of scientific knowledge in the real world, and therefore playing the game, even enjoying participating in the culture is, to some extent, a question of learning, of becoming proficient, and of using knowledge to succeed" (2004, 142). "Success" is measured in terms of one's ability to navigate the space; as Sefton-Green observes: "The Pokemon games take place in a fictional world whose settings are connected to each other by sea or land or bridges or tunnels, as in the real world. One of the distinctive features of computer games is the way they offer players the opportunity to act within a virtual space that represents a larger, more complex physical environment than they could encounter in real life" (153). This world creates a community outside the game that is exclusive to kids: "when children gathered to talk about Pokemon, their discourse was so impenetrable (to adults) that they might as well be speaking a foreign language," what Sefton-Green calls "poke-speak." He hypothesizes that especially at first, for Sam, these conversations were not so much about sharing information as proving membership in the group and then, as he gained knowledge, to "display status and solidify group membership" (155).

Thus, although the game does emphasize acquisition, it does so in a way that also encourages social interaction and relationships not based (at least purely) on consumption and competition. To acquire all the

Pokémon on the Game Boy version, for example, kids needed to communicate with other kids. Furthermore, in their study of *Pokémon* in Israel, Dafna Lemish and Linda-Renee Bloch found that "many of the children's responses suggested that they saw the central meaning of Pokemon as revolving around relationships, including those between the trainers and their Pokemons; among Ash, Misty, and their immediate group of friends; and between the Ash team and other characters in the series. . . . Togetherness was a central theme in children's discussions" (2004, 169–70). Lemish and Bloch found that children expressed maternal feelings for their Pokémon, and that these feelings were not exclusive to girls. One nine-year-old boy told Lemish that "I'll treat him [his Pokémon] as if I'm his mother. It's important to give him food, and if he needs help, I'll help him, so he won't be upset. If he's hurt, I'll take care of him, bring him to the Pokemon center" (171).

These findings would come as no surprise to the Japanese producers of the game. As Anne Allison argues in her essay "Cuteness as Japan's Millennial Product" (2004), the company was savvy about choosing a representative character who is both cute and tough. Pikachu rides atop Ash's shoulders "like a dependent child, but is a formidable warrior under this gentle façade." Allison says that the marketers were "hoping to draw in younger children, girls, and even mothers" and thus chose for its main symbol "not a human character but a Pokemon with whom fans would not so much identify as develop feelings of attachment, nurturance, and intimacy. This was Pikachu" (38).

Attachment thus seems to be a more important feeling than identification, which is the more operative idea in gaming, especially as applied to the avatars players choose to represent themselves within the game. Allison argues that the characters become like imaginary play friends; kids described them as kind of like pets, "except mutated" (42). These "pets," carried with children in the form of cards or on their devices, serve as "transitional objects," helping children "navigate and survive the bumpy road of growing up. Functioning as personal resource, companion, possession and fantasy, imaginary creations provide an avenue for both engaging with and escaping from the real world" (42–43). Pikachu is like the Nyan Cat that six-year-old Morgan wanted to "kidnap." Creating a home for these "pets" is similar to the construction of domestic spaces in *Minecraft*—spaces, as I argued in the last chapter, where kids, in collaboration with other kids, form their own affective living spaces where they can care for each other and their creatures.

The Entrepreneurial Spirit

Roblox has exploded in popularity in the last five years; it claimed 56 million monthly players by August 2017, many of them kids under 15 years of age, on platforms including PCs, smartphones, tablets, and Xbox. The company says it has recently surpassed *Minecraft* in popularity, and one of its claims to distinction is that players themselves are constantly developing new games using in-house technology, making the *Roblox* site more like a buffet of games than a single game. The games include everything from the currently popular *Jailbreak*—after you break out of jail you can go on a crime spree—to multiple examples of the "Tycoon" genre to games where kids just hang out in various social settings, such as malls, skateboard parks, parties, and lava pits. Because the game is always multiplayer and because it features an ongoing chat session and friend requests, it functions as a huge social gathering for young kids. Each player fashions their own avatar, has their own user name, and roams around the social space seeing what and who arises. Unlike *Minecraft*, in which the avatar has less weight as a self-representative, one's avatar in *Roblox* is of utmost importance. Participants frequently change their look, and the game is played using the standard, over-the-shoulder point of view. That means the player is always watching him- or herself as they navigate the world; the visible "self" is at the center of every space, a sensation that is true to the ethos of the developers.

Many of the game developers are teenagers and former or current *Roblox* players, leading *Roblox* to describe itself as the "largest user-generated online gaming platform," with over 15 million games created by users. Because many of the games generate revenue through their integration of virtual money (which is bought with real money), some of these developers are earning considerable sums: "Roblox recently announced that it's on track to pay out $30 million to developers this year [2017], with the top earner set to rake in no less than $3 million."[9] Thus, the game's status as a grassroots entity created by anyone with access to its technology is complicated by the fact that a major component is the purchasing of Robux to advance in various ways in the different games (in most versions, Robux can also be earned within the game, it just takes a lot longer than if one buys the means to advance). A more accurate description than "community generated" might be "entrepreneurial." The creator of *Jailbreak*, for example, is an 18-year-old named Alex Balfanz who says he has made enough on the game to pay for his four-year undergraduate education at Duke University. *Business Insider* reports that "[Roblox CEO David] Baszucki says some developers are making $50,000 a month creating things within the game, at the high end. Back in 2015, too, *Business Insider* spoke to a 17-year-old who had made $100,000 in two years from Roblox" (Weinberger 2017).

While my tone here is critical, I do not mean to dismiss these young game developers. They are part of what Angela McRobbie and others have described as the creative economy—a generation of 20-somethings who are inspired to define themselves creatively in a neoliberal workforce that ostensibly values creative labor but does not provide any kind of job stability. As McRobbie (2011) says, "the dominant vocabulary for undertaking creative work under the auspices of UK neo-liberalism and its extension into EU vocabularies is one which shuns 'old' ideas such as protection and entitlement, and favours instead self reliance, ambition, competition and 'talent.'" In terms of gaming, this labor force extends to the freelance artists who are hired to do the character art, the sound design, and the user interface. The *Business Insider* article tells the story of three such freelancers—all young women—who work on various *Roblox* games. Vivian "EvilArtist" Arellano, for example, is a 17-year-old freelance artist from Texas who made about $1,000 from *Roblox* in just a few months, contributing art to projects and drawing custom portraits of in-game characters (Weinberger 2017). Her drawings are not that different from the fanart on Tumblr I discussed in chapter 6.

The games thus represent a complex combination of artistic ingenuity, gaming technology, and marketing savvy, all aimed at making one game stand out among the many *Roblox* options. For example, the first thing that happens when one begins playing *Jailbreak* is that a window pops up: "The Jailbreak Starter Pack. You'll receive $4,500 cash, a pickup truck, and a peach texture." A big "purchase" button blinks at you. Similar ads spring up on other games: on *Meep City*, there's an ad for *Roblox* figures, now available at Toys "R" Us, Target, and Walmart. "Meep City Toy! Now in Stores! Get 10,000 coins. Redeem the code included in the box, and you'll earn 10,000 coins!" The coins allow you to furnish your estate (the estate can be locked to allow only friends to enter).

Baszucki describes the game as a "platform for 'human co-experience,'" from the rather mundane experiences of attending school and playing house to more exciting adventures such as surviving a natural disaster or robbing a bank. Popular games and worlds "can get as many as 30,000 players at any one time, with players flocking to new, cool experiences," says Baszucki. He adds that "Roblox provides a world where kids can get together and socialize in hundreds of different settings at a time when many kids are either too isolated or too busy to congregate outside the virtual world." This creation of a social space is facilitated by the fact that the games are being made by other kids, albeit slightly older kids, who are close enough in age to the primary players that they understand what kinds of social experiences are appealing. As *Business Insider* reporter Matt Weinberger put it: "Besides, who better to make new hit media properties for kids than kids?" And as Baszucki put it: "We could never match the creativity and scale of the hundreds of thousands of developers on the platform" (Weinberger 2017).

For Baszucki, as well as for Weinberger, there appears to be no contradiction or even tension between calling the game "user-generated" and touting its entrepreneurial spirit. And perhaps there isn't: the fact that older kids are making considerable amounts of money off of younger kids does not negate the fact that the game is being generated by its users, and that the older kids are wise to what the younger kids want precisely because they were playing the game not so long ago. However, when the primary objective becomes making money within a social experience, one has to qualify the sociality, both in form and content. The very essence of the entrepreneur, after all, is individual advancement; the online *Business Dictionary* defines entrepreneurship as the "capacity and willingness to develop, organize and manage a business venture along with any of its risks in order to make a profit."[10] The enterprise is defined through the entrepreneur's willingness to take risks and to see the project through situations in which other people would be too nervous to persist. Unlike other forms of kids' culture that I have analyzed to this point, *Roblox* is more focused on emotional intelligence for the individual success story rather than broader concerns. Perhaps, then, it

Figure 8.2. Screenshot from a *Roblox* game, roblox.com.

is more upfront in its brand of self-management, less concerned with producing "prosocial" behavior that purports to be about the team or the nation.

This focus on the individual is reinforced by the *Roblox* emphasis on fashioning your avatar. This appeal stands in contrast to the *Minecraft* world, where changing one's "skin" happens rarely and is not integrated into the game, as previously mentioned. Again, this realm of self-fashioning should not be seen in contrast to creativity, but rather as intertwined in a complex way. In *Roblox*, you can change the expression on your face, for example, from happy to grumpy, or you can simply add a mustache or change your hair style (see figure 8.2). Also, the game doesn't care what gender your character is, and anyone can wear anything.

Some games are explicitly about fashion, yet the fashions are often quite eclectic and imaginative. In the game *Fashion Frenzy*, for example, players are encouraged to transform themselves into pirates and unicorns—to create the best theme outfit, then "strut your stuff on the runway against other models." It is a competition, however, and thus introduces the idea to young gamers that there is a hierarchy of appearances, and that you will be judged in comparison to other people. This self-awareness is likely just setting in at the ages on which I'm focused—the kids beginning school, interacting more with peers, becoming aware of differences and the desire to belong. *Fashion Frenzy* appeals to this interest in appearances, though it does so in nonconventional and whimsical ways (see figure 8.3).

The YouTuber Zaira, for example, narrates a runway contest in which her avatar competes under the category "Darkside." She decides to go for a goth look, more specifically, to become a "cute goth chick," and dons ripped jeans, a pink shirt, pink hair, glasses, and a pair of black wings. The runway competition begins, with anyone playing the game allowed to vote for one of the ten contestants, giving them a ranking of one to five stars. Zaira's goth girl comes in sixth, and although she's disappointed, she doesn't berate the winners but just moves on to the next contest. *Fashion Frenzy* is not inevitably linked to consumerism, but it does point in that direction, both temporally and spatially. Players have only a few minutes to figure out their look, to race around and find the

Figure 8.3. The homepage for the *Roblox* game *Fashion Frenzy*, roblox.com.

Figure 8.4. Screenshot from a *Roblox* game, roblox.com.

right clothing, hairstyle, and accessories; then the only place to go next is the runway. There is some surprise in the question of who will win, but there's no random movement or unexpected developments beyond the announcement of the winner. It thus limits the affective potential that comes with the kind of roaming embedded in *Minecraft*.

At any time, in any game, a player may decide to change his or her look, which includes the possibility of buying branded clothing from companies such as Adidas and Nike. These articles of clothing then become part of one's repertoire, which means that the player's movement is back and forth to what amounts to a closet of new looks (see figure 8.4).

Affective Detours

Rather than seeing this consumerism as a kind of internalization of capitalism, a false consciousness, I propose that it functions as an affective detour, compelling the player to stop and consider a purchase, or to be frustrated by their lack of Robux, or to beg their parent to buy them some Robux, or memorize their parent's account password so they can buy some Robux. All of these activities are interruptions to the sort of affective flow that characterizes *Minecraft*. It's impossible to say whether the players are internalizing this sense of themselves as consumers—which is Banet-Weiser's suggestion—or whether the act of stopping is making them more aware of the frustrations that consumerism generates. It is definitely, however, a different world than that of *Minecraft*, which relies on a barter economy rather than cash and which does not emphasize the look of the avatar.

Many of the *Roblox* teen developers make games that reproduce this sense of money-making adventure, although this emphasis is much more explicit in some games than others. Many games are "Tycoon" games, in which the goal is to make as much money as possible, through tasks such as clicking buttons or through fighting with lasers and swords. This feature doesn't negate the possibility that kids will gather together in social spaces, but it does mean the social experience will be more frequently defined and interrupted by the imperative to buy something in order to fit in and/or become successful. In *Meep City*, for example, we see kids just hanging out, at a big party, dancing to 21 Pilots' hit song "Stressed Out" (see figure 8.5); this social scene is quickly interrupted, however, by purchasing options, as I describe below.

Figure 8.5. Screenshot from the *Roblox* game *Meep City*, roblox.com.

Figure 8.6. Screenshot from *Meep City*, a game that foregrounds a fidget spinner.

The games together constitute a huge archive of kids' popular culture, producing a common vernacular. The lineup of most frequently played *Roblox* games references popular texts: *Stop Professor Poopypants!!* (from the popular book series *Captain Underpants*); *Mario Adventure Obby!* (from the video game *Mario and Luigi*); *Escape the Minions* (from the *Despicable Me* film series); *Escape Emoji Movie Obby* (from the 2017 *Emoji* film); *The SpongeBob Movie Adventure Obby*; *Pokemon Brick Bronze-Beta*; *Fidget Spinner TYC* (referencing the popular toy); *Escape Pacman Tycoon*; *Escape Mineblox Obby!*; *Sonic World Adventure* (referencing the cartoon character Sonic); and many more. Games foreground the most recent toy or gadget, for example, such as the Meep City game, which foregrounds a fidget spinner, the handheld spinning device that gained popularity in 2017 (see figure 8.6).

In *Meep City*, players are looking to create their homes and neighborhoods as well as their social spaces. This requires money, and the amount of money you spend establishes your class status. For 500 coins, you get the trailer estate; for 2,500, you acquire "estate tier 3." Some games do not require a purchase but are heavily adorned with consumer logos that kids find appealing and familiar. This familiarity builds a sense of community, but it does so with an already established vocabulary of consumerism.

However, it's crucial to note that this vocabulary does not replace the kids' means of communicating with more organic expressions; rather, the consumerist and the organic coexist, as is illustrated in this example of an 18-minute YouTube video in which Ethan of EthanGamerTV (see previous chapter) narrates his experience playing the *Roblox* game *Food Fight* (which had received 3.7 million views as of April 2018).[11]

Ethan begins the video with his signature greeting: "Hey guys!" He then immediately immerses himself in the scenario: "Here we go. Whoa!" It looks like he's walking through a giant food court and amusement park, with enormous floating burgers, pizza slices, and fast-food signs. His avatar looks around, confused, trying to get his bearings, and Ethan observes: "There's taco slices, cake grenades, peaches, ice cream." He wanders around a bit more, and then reads the list of "food weapons" that pops up in a side box: "Apple assault, orange shotgun, banana assault, melon grenade, carrot sniper, ice cream assault, burger shot gun, pizza assault, cake grenade, taco sniper."

Ethan's enthusiasm is infectious: "Oh my gosh, this is so cool. Look at that! It's literally a pepperoni pizza. It's a taco! I just heard a laugh, heh heh heh." (In the background, we also hear the laugh.) He sees the golden arches of McDonald's, exclaims, "McDonald's pizza!" then chants, "McDonald's pizza, McDonald's and some pizza." The connections derive their appeal from their seeming incongruity—McDonald's doesn't serve pizza—yet Ethan's narration connects these items within the space of the game in a whimsical manner.

As the camera shifts from Ethan's face to the game, we see them as integrated, and Ethan's experiencing of the game merges with his avatar's and with ours as consumers/fellow players. We experience his satisfaction when he hits someone: "Ooo ooo ooo! I nearly nailed someone in the face with a pizza!" Then his weapon turns into an ice cream cone. "It is literally an ice cream, with a cone in the back!" Our feelings are enhanced by the sounds Ethan makes; when inexplicably his avatar's neck gets stuck in the elevator floor, Ethan makes the sounds of being choked: "Eeeh. Ahh. Eeeh. Ahh. Getting crushed. Eeeh. Ahhh. Finally free." He draws the viewer into his battle against various opponents: "This is so cool. Prepare to get food in your face! Skittles, pizza, tacos, Taco Bell" (all represented with their brand logos). He's having some success with his ice cream missiles, and his score goes up on the sidebar chart.

While the camera usually stays focused on his avatar, with Ethan's face in the corner, occasionally it switches to Ethan sitting in front of his computer, as when he says, dancing a bit, "We're going to Fun Town, with a pizza, ice cream, cake, uhh, tacos, pizza. I already mentioned pizza. [gasps] Juicy Fruit. Fruit Loops, KFC." (These logos float across the screen.)

Because we are taken through the game with Ethan, we also anticipate retaliation: "Where's that MLGwaffle?" he says, referring to another player. Ethan gets hit by some ice cream. "Oh my gosh, my face, I can't see! LOL! Whoa! Those are real ice creams, man. MLG shot! What! I'm doing so good all because I camp in my house. I'll give you one. Banana assault! It's not fun. Back from behind, sir. Hungry, no, I'm shooting everybody in the face. No, I don't want pizza, I don't want tacos. I want bananas. No, sanity forever! Curse you! You tomato, me banana, you taco! He got me with a taco!" (referring to MLGwaffle). In this sequence and the following, Ethan's excitement manifests itself through his abbreviated sentences and expressions, all of which constitute a kind of common vernacular that other players replicate. It is more stream of consciousness than narration, a constant flow of exclamations and observations.

Ethan ponders at times, deliberating or unsure what to do. "Hmmm. A grape shotgun. Not tried that one. But it's a shotgun of grapes. And it looks cool. Taste my screaming grapes. Ackk! Yep yep yep. LOL. My grapes went a little wide of you. They want to say ahh ahh ahh! Literally, that's exactly what they say. Take my grape. Hashtag take my grape. Ethan says hi, hihi. Idk, idk. Oh wait, lol. Ding! It's like a ding dong, ding dong." Here, we go from Ethan talking to Ethan's grapes talking, to the expression "idk" (short for "I don't know"), to the sound "ding dong." Language gradually dissolves, from sentences to abbreviations to sounds.

While Ethan is the leader, the potential sense of hierarchy is undermined by the fact that he cannot control what happens. Unexpectedly, Ethan's avatar's body changes into a tomato and he exclaims, "I'm a tomato. Why am I a tomato? I don't want to be a tomato." And then: "Ahh—you just killed me with a cheeseburger. I'm not actually happy about that."

The comments below this video are almost unanimously glowing, most often referring to Ethan himself, such as Reza Gamer's "I Love Yooouuu ETHAN!!!!!!!!!!!!! And Alex Walcott's "i love you ethan your the best YouTuber EVER! im so glad you were BORN ps. you will be a great YouTuber ever when you grow up :}" And from Barcelona boy: "Bro u r cool as hell."

Fans identify with Ethan, as when Christy says, "I wear glasis too," and Adam says, "I'm 11 and u Ethan?" There's also a desire for recognition from Ethan; from Marvin Martinez comes this comment: "Ethan please reply this I never said this but when I just started watching your videos I started to like it and your videos are so good I thank you for making them keep on the good work! And also accept my friend request please I'm pikachulover728."

Other kids are less adoring of Ethan, and sometimes not even fully engaged in the game itself but rather in the conversation, which is marked by references to other games and memes. A player going by the name Minecraft Master, responding to MLGWaffle, refers to a popular meme about waffles when he asks: "MLGWAFFEL do u like waffles yes we like waffles do u like pancakes yes we like pancakes do u like French toast yes we like French toast do do do do waffles!" Minecraft Master seems to know from where MLGWaffle took his name, and by acknowledging the meme, he affirms the choice.

Performing Gender

In the introduction, I argued that a valorization of emotional intelligence has considerable potential to diminish the essentialist belief that girls are more emotional than boys. Within the parameters of emotional intelligence, it's important for all kids, no matter their gender, to be able to express and manage all of their emotions. The relative insignificance of gender is demonstrated in my earlier chapters on spaces (immigration, education) as well as in television programing with animated bodies of different shapes and sizes, and explicitly gender nonconforming shows such as *Steven Universe*. In the shift from emotions to affect, we see an even greater potential to dissolve the gendered binary and to embrace instead the affective intensities of different bodies, with difference not defined through categories.

Many of the *Roblox* games also support this move away from gender essentialisms; in the EthanGamer videos, it appears that equal numbers of girls and boys (judging from their avatars, their screen names, and their comments) are playing. The company says that 40 percent of *Roblox* players are now girls, up from just 10 percent a few years ago.[12] One can also find many girl gamers on YouTube, such as Zaira (above) and Gamergirl (below). I am not claiming that gendered assumptions have disappeared completely, but even in the games that seem directed at one or the other gender, there are multiple opportunities for gender-bending performances.

For example, one popular *Roblox* series features variations on the idea of "adopt a cute kid," or "adopt a bad baby." A ten-year-old girl named Karina, who goes by Gamergirl, narrates many of these games: *My Kids Run Away*, *My Kids Won't Go to Sleep*, *Crying Babies*, *Being a Mom to My Bad Kid*, and *Baby Eats Cat Poop*. Gamergirl is almost as popular as EthanGamer, with about 700,000 followers and the same kind of fan accolades as Ethan gets ("I love you, Karina.") While it initially seems that Karina is reproducing stereotypes about girls-becoming-mothers, upon watching her videos, it's clear that she is just as likely making fun of these roles and definitely not assuming their inevitability. In some games, Karina is the baby waiting to be adopted; in other games, she is the mother doing the adopting. In one game, she is waiting to be adopted by Ronald, her fellow YouTuber (seated right next to her), who is in the game playing her want-to-be father. Another player, Ashley, adopts Karina, beating Ronald to the punch and ignoring Ronald's marriage proposal. Ashley seems more interested in Max, "a rich professional football player." Karina and siblings follow Ashley to her new home, with Ashley still ignoring Ronald. "Everyone's ignoring me," he whines. Ronald finally gives up and becomes the pet dog instead. Along the way, Ashley leaves, and Karina and a bevy of siblings acquire several new moms.

In another variation, Ronald, who also has his own channel, with 582,000 subscribers, plays the baby games. As a baby waiting in a crib at the Adoption Center, Ronald says, "This baby right here is going to get adopt [*sic*]. Which is really me. . . . I want a mommy!" Karina enters and says, "I'm going to adopt a kid, because I'm lonely. My life is lonely." She checks him out and says, "Let me see if you're good or not. You're not cute there, but you're pretty cute here, so I guess yes. Come on, let's go." Other kids start bopping around, asking to be adopted. Ronald types in baby talk: "goo goo ga ga." Karina leaves, and Ronald worries that she is not coming back. "We need to be surviving now. We have no mommy." He and his adopted sibling Jada, also two, go to the park together. Feeling hungry, they decide to eat the grass. "We have no mommy, no food." They find their way to a convenience store and try to buy a candy bar, but the game won't let them. He starts wandering down the street, saying, "Adopt me, I'm a lonely kid." We see his avatar, in juxtaposition with Ronald at his computer in the lower-left corner of the screen, typing with a painstaking hunt-and-peck motion. Another avatar gives him a slice of pizza, and he says, "Yay," while writing, "yah. I don't know how to spell yah." Two other avatars give him some food, and one types, "Give the child some food." One, named JadaC, leads him in the direction of a McDonald's, and when it is visible off in the distance, Ronald exclaims, "McDonald's! Yes! Yes!" His avatar runs toward the restaurant, but when he arrives, he decides, "This McDonalds is garbage! Garbage! This is absolutely garbage." He starts looking around again for his mommy. "Mommy. Mommy. I am surviving. I have no mommy. I don't need clothes, or do I. Pretty naked. I need food. I should go to Adopt Center." He finds a car to drive: "Baby driving a car!" He starts pleading, writing, "Adopt me! Plz I have no food what so ever. Adopt meeeeeeeeeeeeeeeeeeeeeeeeeeeeeeeeeeeeeeeeee eeeeeeeeeeeeeeeeeeeeeeeeee." He looks for a house, but several won't let him in, then he finds one that lets him in, with food in the kitchen. He eats it, goes upstairs, and finds a baby bed. The video ends with him saying, "I literally survived with no mom!"[13]

While Ronald maintains his equanimity through the video and does not appear to be panicking, his expressions of loneliness, anxiety, and insecurity come across quite powerfully. Even though typing is a chore for him (several people comment about his slow typing), he repeatedly conveys his desire to be adopted, especially with the long drawn out plea, "meeee." He has a sense that he can take care of himself if he has to ("I survived"), but he would rather not.

Looking for Belonging

The theme of adoption runs throughout other games, such as *Meep City*, where the avatars roam throughout the streets, running into other players. In my many hours of playing and observing *Roblox* games, I was struck by how many times I saw avatars typing into the chat box variations on "Will someone please adopt me?" and "Be my mom! Plz." Quite often, these requests were met with affirmatives, but sometimes no one answered, and I waited, staring at the screen, hoping that someone would respond, tempted to respond, "Yes, I'll adopt you!"

Despite the frequent exhortations to buy something, *Roblox* functions as an intensely social space, where kids turn to each other to constitute a kind of family. The multiplayer games—with their built-in sociality—offer kids this opportunity in a way that the other texts I've discussed in this book often don't. Still, even these other media illustrate kids' desires for community and belonging. *Steven Universe*, both the show and the fanart, speak to the desire for acceptance when one belongs to a different kind of family. And kids commenting on each other's YouTube channels provide each other with a (usually) supportive community. Many of these videos actually invite viewers into their bedrooms, as did EthanGamer and Shawn Carter (last chapter), making them part of the domestic. Even if there is disagreement, it is still a place where kids connect with each other, outside the mediating influence of adults. Kids are making their own home spaces, expressing their feelings regardless of whether adults understand.

Conclusion

"Shame on You Killers, Shame on You"

On April 4, 2017, Bana al-Abed, the seven-year-old Syrian girl I discussed in part I, posted several graphic pictures of dead children and tweeted the following: "Dear world, today these children were murdered with chemical in Idlib. Shame on you killers, shame on you. Shame on you, shame on you."

A child shaming adults seems to reverse the usual positions of power and moral authority. When accompanied by an image of half-clothed children laying in the streets, being sprayed with hoses in an attempt to remove the chemicals, there is little doubt that Bana is in a position to shame anyone who is following her. Indeed, it is hard to imagine someone who will not be affected by the tweet, both because of the picture and because shame is such a powerful affect. Even if we don't identify as the "killers," we feel the shame of complicity. The sensation of heat rushing to one's cheeks. A racing heart. A faint shimmer of sweat across one's lips. Clammy palms. I know that as I scroll through Bana's Twitter feed, reading her tweets and viewing the gruesome videos and photos, I feel sick to my stomach. I have to turn away because I am doing so little to address the situation. Just this week (April 6, 2018), there are more accounts of Bashar al-Assad using chemicals in the rebel stronghold of Douma. Yet Bana calls me back, with this tweet quickly following the first one: "More than 100 people were just killed in #Idlib. Get up, come out, demand justice for the people of Syria wherever you are. Justice. justice." And then, with a horrifying image of dead children sprawled in the back of a pickup truck, she says, "This is today in Syria in #Idlib. Hi @realdonaldtrump do you love this?"

It's a powerful combination: Twitter and shame. The capacity to feel shame is innate to all humans, argues Elspeth Probyn: "Affects are innate and compel us to see the human body as a baseline in all human activity" (2005, 8). Specifically, she says, "Shame goes to the heart of who we think we are" because its presence indicates a desire for belonging and connection (ix). At a fundamental level, we feel shame because we have done something to endanger this connection, a connection that makes us feel human—and that can be produced through Twitter, which has the potential to reach millions. Bana has 352,000 followers, and the media coverage has further disseminated her message, leading as well to the publication of a book, *Dear World*, that tells her story.

While, throughout this book, I have emphasized the differences between adults and children, in this conclusion, I would like to consider what we have in common, at least in moments, within the realm of affect, embodiment, and vulnerability. I am following Judith Butler here, who says: "I propose to start and to end with the question of the human"—not, she says, "because there is a human condition that is universally shared—this is surely not yet the case." Rather, what we all share is the condition of vulnerability: "each of us is constituted politically in part by virtue of the social vulnerability of our bodies—as a site of desire and physical vulnerability." This vulnerability is differentially allocated—some bodies, such as those of Syrians, are very vulnerable at this time given the political and social conditions there. Yet everyone is, at some time or other, vulnerable to pain, loss, and death by virtue of the fact that we are all "socially constituted bodies, attached to others, at risk of losing those attachments, exposed to others, at risk of violence by virtue of that exposure." This potential for vulnerability makes a "tenuous 'we' of us all" (20).

It is this "tenuous we" to which Bana appeals. We can trace this appeal through three levels of address in her tweets. One, children—her most frequent concern—are especially vulnerable. Second, everyone in Syria is suffering, not just children. Third, this suffering is experienced throughout the world, in places where violence and war rage. Throughout her tweets, Bana both informs us of these levels of vulnerability and expresses a range of affects, from sorrow to fear to anger to hope.

Bana's most frequent self-identification is as a child, speaking for other children: "I am a child with something to say, And that's let's help every child in war zone" (December 25, 2016). However, her messages illustrate that vulnerability is not inherent to being a child, countering stereotypes of the passive victim waiting to be rescued. She demonstrates this by constantly documenting the bombing, both while she was in Aleppo and afterward, and assigning blame to individual leaders. Furthermore, we see through Bana's comments that she and other kids continue being active kids as she intersperses images and messages of the violence with everyday life. For example, next to a picture of her bombed-out house, she writes, "This is my reading place where I wanted to start reading Harry Potter but it's bombed. I will never forget" (November 29, 2016). And above a picture of her with a gap-toothed smile: "Good evening my friends. What are you doing today? I am happy I lost two more teeth.—Bana" (December 8, 2016).

While she emphasizes the violence done to children, Bana does not ignore adults; she demands attention for everyone, thus demonstrating the shared vulnerability of all people, no matter their age. "Dear world. my name is Bana, I am 7 years old Syrian girl. My people are dying everyday as you watch. This is the end of humanity" (April 4, 2017). Bana does not deny the differential allocation of power, as indicated by the phrase "as you watch." However, this recognition does not keep her from recognizing a common humanity. She does not insist on distinguishing between self and other and thus invites us to consider our common vulnerabilities. At one moment, she is one of those targeted; at another, she is one of those acting on behalf of those targeted, part of the "we" that could help: "The world must help the refugees. We cannot just watch. We cannot be silent. We are all the same & must help each other in their pain. (August 17, 2017). She says later, "Everyday I wake up angry because people are suffering & dying. We should be angry, we should speak up, we must fight for each other. It's time to be united. we the peace loving people, we have the power & can do anything. WE JUST NEED TO WAKE UP." And on November 24, 2017: "We should be angry."

Bana invites us into her world in order to shame us into action, illustrating an aspect of shame that Probyn describes: "shame [is] the fine line or border between moving forward into more interest or falling back into humiliation" (xii). She establishes connections based on our humanity, threatening to humiliate us as we contemplate the sheer horror of chemical attacks and bombings as we sip our morning coffee. Yet she does not remain within the realm of humiliation; rather, she invites us back into her world, rejecting any kind of static identity category that would keep her separate and othered. This maneuver happens on Twitter, a technology that speaks to both kids and adults.

Throughout this book, I have been arguing that the manner in which kids express their feelings is better captured through an affective lens, rather than through the naming of emotions embedded in a linear narrative. Because of its reliance on short messages and visuals, Twitter lends itself to the production of affect, even by a child with limited access to technology. Yet there is no reason to exclude adults from this realm of affective intensity; in fact, Twitter could function as a shared space of communication.

There is, of course, no guarantee that the affect being expressed will increase communication, as evidenced in the tweets of the current U.S. president, who is clearly not interested in communication. Even in that situation, however, we see Bana directly addressing Trump, shaming him, in the very medium he presumes to dominate. In his lack of response, in his arrogance, Trump shows his imperviousness to shame, his refusal to recognize connections and common vulnerabilities.

Many other adults did enter into Bana's Twitter space—celebrities ranging from author J. K. Rowling to comedian Dave Chappelle, and many "ordinary" people as well. This space becomes one of mutual affective exchanges—countering the normative developmental model that argues for the gradual suppression of affect in the interest of "rational" communication. The concept of "growing sideways" reminds us that the brain is malleable—in fact, it is possible to grow backward before growing sideways, in the interest of rediscovering one's neurodiversity.

While it's hard to make a direct connection to these interactions and material change, such as an end to the war in Syria, we can say without a doubt that Bana has used Twitter to increase awareness of the situation in her home country as well as demonstrate that kids can use technology to express themselves. Thus, while my book does not argue that increasing opportunities for kids' affective expressions will necessarily lead to structural change, that is in fact my hope, and, I believe, as good a way to proceed as any other. If we lived in a world in which kids' expressions were valorized, refugee children in U.S. immigration court could tell their stories in a variety of ways, all of which would be taken seriously. Kids who are scared and angry about Trump's election would be encouraged to be ardent activists, rather than being patronized and told to write polite letters. Young children in school settings would be allowed to cavort, dance, and sing loudly rather than being told to sit cross-cross applesauce or go to the thinking chair.

To contemplate kids' media consumption and production almost seems like a luxury in the context of these global and national injustices. Yet despite the differences in privilege between a child in immigration court and a child narrating a *Roblox* game, the basic question remains the same: how can adults avoid imposing our sense of the world on children, while simultaneously providing the structures they need to feel creative, safe, and loved? By reproducing something of an archive of feelings here, I hope to contribute to the broader conditions in which such an archive would accumulate power, in turn giving each individual child an opportunity for fuller expression, and, perhaps, shifting the larger power structures. The fact that young kids have figured out how to form communities on the internet should reverberate into the policy arenas I critique, giving policy makers some clue as to how kids express themselves.

The expressions allowed in the world of kids' pleasure—television, internet surfing, gaming—need to remain within that realm. They need spaces of collaboration and communication that do not necessarily involve adults. I maintain my initial argument as stated in the second paragraph of this book: the gap between kids and adults should remain. Adults can, however, enter briefly, engage, and depart. They must enter on kids' terms, however, which means no judgment, no invocations of proper behavior, and no rules about what can and cannot be said. Perhaps we should all aspire to be more like Cartoon Network's Uncle Grandpa, who freely admitted his fear of the dark to Susie, whose mother had told her to "just hang in there." Rather than waiting for the fear to dissipate, Uncle Grandpa encourages Susie to embrace and explore their fears together, exclaiming, "I didn't know our imaginations were so terrifying!"

ACKNOWLEDGMENTS

It would be impossible to identify when I began writing this book. It might have been quite some time ago, while watching *Sesame Street* with my older son, Alex. Or perhaps I didn't really start "in earnest" until a few years ago, while jotting down observations of my younger son, Ezra, playing *Minecraft*. More likely, it has been gradually accumulating over the years of parenting, volunteering in elementary school classrooms, and teaching kids' media studies to young adults for whom childhood is not a distant memory. To all these students, I offer my sincere gratitude, especially to the students in my children's popular culture class at Cornell in spring 2017—a class that helped me deepen and broaden my analysis of kids' texts. Thanks to the following for teaching me about memes and GIFs, for listening to each other as well as to me, for laughing at my stories even if you had heard them before, and for countless smart comments in class and in your papers: Clare Boland, Isabel Bosque, Anna Elling, Salvador Herrera, Hannah Kaiser, Anna Ravenelle, Shaneese Sicora, Jay Yang, Amelia Bracket, James Burke, Lauren Charpentier, Eisha Conrad, Samuel Evans, Becket Harney, Zaria Holcomb, Simran Khosla, Jami Nicholson, Christine Sea, Gabrielle Villafana, and Yujue Wang.

Alexandra Burton and Samuel Evans were stellar research assistants, not only tracking down valuable information but also taking time to process it within the context of the overall argument. I also had the privilege of working with Nicolette Bragg on her dissertation; our coffeeshop conversations stayed with me through my own writing.

I was fortunate to have several key interlocutors shaping my chapter on the Central American refugee children. I owe much to Virginia Raymond, a passionate and brilliant social justice advocate, for her inspiration and friendship these many years. Thanks also to Rachel Lewis for organizing a stimulating symposium for three consecutive years; conversations there with Rachel, Eithne Luibheid, Wendy Hesford, and Amy Schuman were very helpful. I'm grateful to the journal *Feminist*

Formations for granting me permission to use a revised version of the essay that grew out of these seminars and that was published as part of a special issue on migration and vulnerability (28 [1], Spring 2016). Thanks to Gregory Cuellar for organizing the *Arte de Lagrimas* exhibit and letting me reprint some of the artwork in the journal and here.

Two readers for NYU Press gave me a much-needed new perspective on the manuscript; thanks to Sara Projanky and one anonymous reader for their valuable suggestions. My gratitude goes to Dolma Ombadykow for her valuable editorial wisdom and patience answering my many questions. Thanks to Dan Geist for his meticulous copyediting. I owe a huge debt of gratitude to Eric Zinner, who with this book and two previous ones has been able to locate my work within a recognizable field that still allows me considerable leeway.

The teachers and staff at Elizabeth Ann Clune Montessori School in Ithaca have consistently demonstrated the importance of seeing each child both as an individual and as a member of a larger community, local and global. Laura Gottfried inspires this community through her strength and open-mindedness, through her convictions as well as her willingness to rethink her beliefs. Thanks to the teachers—Leah, Meridith, Liz, Sarah, Donyan, Virginia, Dawn, Katri, and Rebecca—for their generous pedagogy, day in and day out.

In Minneapolis, thanks to Steve and Mary for helping us redefine family and to Anton, for being a kind and thoughtful big brother (and one cannot forget Rudy, Charlie, Leo, and Mavis). To my mom, Peg, whose sense of humor and forthrightness continue to impress. To my dad, Ron, for your constant encouragement and open-mindedness, and for believing in my girl power before either of us knew about feminism.

To Grant, mi amor, for supporting this project even though I know you really believe in "proper expression" and good manners. To my kids: Alex, who sees the world with such clarity and humor. I look to him for insights whenever I can. Ezra's ability to express the complexity of his feelings inspires me. Together, you brothers are formidable.

NOTES

INTRODUCTION

1 I am drawing on the concept as articulated by Ann Cvetkovich in her 2003 *An Archive of Feelings: Trauma, Sexuality, and Lesbian Public Cultures*.
2 In asking this question, I recognize the potential to homogenize and generalize "kids." There is clearly great variation in the category, as I demonstrate throughout the book, addressing kids in different situations. I would argue that there is also a need to invoke the category of kids, for strategic reasons, in order to understand the way they are often treated as a category and the way they can redefine that category as a group.
3 Hall defined an articulation as "the form of the connection that can make a unity of two different elements, under certain conditions. It is a linkage which is not necessary, determined, absolute and essential for all time. You have to ask under what circumstances can a connection be forged or made? The so-called 'unity' of a discourse is really the articulation of different, distinct elements which can be rearticulated in different ways because they have no necessary 'belongingness.' The 'unity' which matters is a linkage between the articulated discourse and the social forces with which it can, under certain historical conditions, but need not necessarily, be connected" (1996, 115).
4 Historians of childhood have found considerable archival evidence. Two notable examples are Karen Sánchez-Eppler's *Dependent States: The Child's Part in Nineteenth-Century American Culture* (2005) and Robin Bernstein's *Racial Innocence: Performing American Childhood from Slavery to Civil Rights* (2011).
5 The Centre for Contemporary Cultural Studies, located at the University of Birmingham in England, was founded in 1964 by Richard Hoggart. It became the site for what has become known as Birmingham cultural studies, defined through the work of scholars including Stuart Hall, Angela McRobbie, and David Morley.
6 An especially promising subfield of childhood studies is girlhood studies, where several recent books have analyzed the growth of "girl power" across media. See, for example, Emilie Zaslow's *Feminism, Inc.: Coming of Age in Girl Power Media Culture* (2009) and Sarah Projansky's *Spectacular Girls: Media Fascination and Celebrity Culture* (2014).

PART I. POLITICAL SUBJECTS

1 All of these tweets can be found at Bana al-Abed, Twitter, https://twitter.com/AlabedBana.

2 "President al-Assad to Denmark's TV 2: Moderate Opposition Is a Myth . . . We Won't Accept That Terrorists Will Take Control of Any Part of Syria." Syrian Arab News Agency, October 16, 2016, https://sana.sy.

CHAPTER 2. THE PRODUCTION OF FEAR

1 The quotes and information about this case came from a brief written by Stephen Manning and Andres Benach. The details were gathered and recorded by members of the AILA-AIC Artesia Pro Bono Project while they were volunteering at the Artesia, New Mexico, family detention center in 2014. See Stephen Manning, *Ending Artesia*, chap. 2 (Jan. 25, 2015), available at https://innovationlawlab.org. "Juan Felipe" is not the child's real name.
2 Throughout the book, I make a distinction between "emotions" and "feelings," whereas Ahmed uses them interchangeably.
3 "Human Rights Situation of Refugee and Migrant Families and Unaccompanied Children in the United States of America." Inter-American Commission on Human Rights, July 24, 2015, www.oas.org.
4 Prior to 2003, unaccompanied children were not transferred to DHS but rather held by the same agency that apprehended them—what was then the Immigration and Naturalization Service. As part of the 2002 Homeland Security Act, Congress acknowledged that children should be cared for by a child welfare agency. The Trafficking Victims Protection Reauthorization Act of 2008 (TVPRA) was a further attempt to attend to the specific needs of children; as many critics argue, however, it does not sufficiently "adopt the best interests of the child as a substantive standard for all policies and decisions affecting immigrant children" (Musalo, Frydman, and Cernadas 2015).
5 "Immigration Court Backlog Reaches Almost Half a Million Pending Cases." *Numbers USA*, July 22, 2016, www.numbersusa.com.
6 It is important to note that there are other ways for children to seek legal status in the U.S., including withholding of deportation and application under the Convention against Torture. However, neither of these approaches attends to the specific experiences of children. The most promising approach in this regard—the only one to really consider children as children—is the application for Special Immigrant Juvenile status, a form of deportation relief available to children who have been abused or abandoned and for whom reunification with parents is not possible.
7 One improvement in this situation was made in 2008, when Congress, acting in response to advocates who argued that the adversarial climate of an immigration courtroom was inappropriate for children, changed the law to give United States Citizen and Immigration Services (USCIS) initial jurisdiction over unaccompanied children's claims; the hearing thus proceeds in a much less adversarial atmosphere. If USCIS grants the claim, it is a final decision; if they do not, the case goes to an immigration judge to consider.

8 Dr. Zayas presented his affidavit to a group of U.S congressmen who objected to the detention of families; Congresswoman Zoe Lofgren posted the statement on her website. "Declaration of Luis H. Zayas," December 10, 2014, https://lofgren.house.gov.

CHAPTER 3. "I HATE YOU, DUNEL TRUMP"
1 "Children Speak Out about Donald Trump." *Jimmy Kimmel Live*, November 11, 2016, www.YouTube.com/watch?v=TycvgoeyA3s.
2 Noah Fish, "Hey Jimmy Kimmel! I Told My Kids the 2016 Election Results." YouTube video, November 14, 2016, www.YouTube.com/watch?v=_VYd22M7Z4s.
3 Fernando Ramirez, "Trump-Themed Art Show Receives Dozens of Submissions from Anonymous School Children." *Houston Chronicle*, May 12, 2017, www.chron.com. All of the artwork from the Houston show discussed herein can be seen at www.chron.com/news/houston-texas/houston/article/Anti-Trump-Houston-art-show-receives-dozens-of-11142470.php.
4 Carla Herreria, "Kids Are Writing Letters to Donald Trump to Ask Him to Be Kind." *Huffington Post*, November 22, 2016, www.huffingtonpost.com.
5 "The Trump Effect: The Impact of the Presidential Campaign on Our Nation's Schools." Southern Poverty Law Center, April 23, 2016, www.splcenter.org.
6 "The Trump Effect: The Impact of the 2016 Presidential Election on Our Nation's Schools." Southern Poverty Law Center, November 28, 2016, www.splcenter.org.
7 "Read Letters Written by First-Grade Students to Donald Trump." *The Cut*, November 11, 2016, www.thecut.com.
8 Roque Planas and Jessica Carro, "This Is What Trump's Immigration Crackdown is Doing to Schoolkids." *Huffington Post*, February 27, 2017, www.huffingtonpost.com.
9 Erica Palan, "'I Wish I Could Open Your Heart': Philly Kids Draw on Their Anxiety to Express What They Think about Trump and His Immigration Plans." *Philly.com*, June 12, 2017, www.philly.com.

CHAPTER 4. "CRISS-CROSS APPLESAUCE"
1 The children's names (except Ezra's) have been changed.
2 By contrast, the Trump administration has not proposed any kind of educational accountability program. Instead, Education Secretary Betsy DeVos has argued for more parental choice, such as in the form of charter schools and vouchers that allow parents to send their kids to private schools.
3 In addition to quoting Fuchs and Craft's book, I interviewed Melani Fuchs on May 27, 2015.

CHAPTER 5. TV'S NARRATIVES FOR EMOTIONAL MANAGEMENT
1 Elizabeth Jensen, "A Coming of Age at Nickelodeon: Noggin and the N Will Get Their Own Channels." *New York Times*, August 13, 2007, www.nytimes.com.

2. In 1998, *Sesame Street* decided to add a narrative segment at the end, the 15-minute "Elmo's World," acknowledging a need to move away from a strictly magazine-style format.
3. Emily Ashby, "What Parents Need to Know," Common Sense Media, accessed September 24, 2018, www.commonsensemedia.org.
4. Ashby, "What Parents Need to Know."

CHAPTER 6. THE STEVEN UNIVERSE, WHERE YOU ARE AN EXPERIENCE

1. Tracy Brown, "Steven Universe's Rebecca Sugar Confirms Fluorite Is a Representation of a Polyamorous Relationship," *Los Angeles Times*, July 21, 2017, www.latimes.com.
2. Nia Howie Smith, "'Steven Universe' Creator on Growing Up, Gender Politics, Her Brother," *Entertainment Weekly*, June 15, 2015, www.ew.com.
3. Ashby, "What Parents Need to Know."
4. "Stronger than You," *Steven Universe*, December 4, 2015, www.YouTube.com/watch?v=6OWq38TikzU.
5. The strength of all the female characters appeals to many young fans: "Steven Universe shows you that women can do anything men can do" (11 years old); "I really enjoy this show, it has legitimately strong female characters, not just the stereotypical 'strong female character' who doesn't do much and needs to be saved anyway. The three Crystal Gems have very different personalities and show that you can be strong in different ways" (12 years old); "Also, Common Sense Media, in your blog, you keep saying there needs to be more TV with good role models for girls. This is the show you need to look at a little closer, as it is a brilliant show, and although I admit I may be a tiny bit biased due to Rebecca Sugar's amazing music, it still is a very well done show" (nine years old).
6. The *Steven Universe* fandom erupted in controversy in 2015 when Paige Paz—Tumblr name Zamii070—a member of the fandom, was targeted by her online community for her "problematic" representations of some *Steven Universe* characters. One of the primary examples of Zamii's artwork with which people took issue was her depiction of Rose Quartz, Steven's mother in the show. People accused her of fat-shaming by drawing the rather large woman as skinnier. People also accused her of white-washing some of the black characters in the show, citing her depiction of Gem-fusion Sardonyx: Sardonyx is voiced and inspired by black women, yet Zamii's drawing seems to show her as having blonde hair. People began responding to her work with abusive comments, and their insults extended beyond critiques of the work itself, escalating to insulting her character in some cases. More than 40 temporary blog pages were created to discuss the issue, and people criticized her work in ways that could be described as bullying. After the targeted attacks continued, Zamii posted on her Tumblr page, "I'm going to sleep forever. I'm sorry everyone I'm just super tired. This will be the last you'll hear from me. I'm going to be at peace now. I'm sorry." A few days later, she

posted a video of herself having recently been discharged from the hospital. See Aja Romano, "Steven Universe Fandom Is Melting Down after Bullied Fanartist Attempts Suicide." *Daily Dot*, October 27, 2015, www.dailydot.com.

7 It is difficult to ascertain the age of the Tumblr users. While some of them do include their ages, it is hard to know if they are accurate. Tumblr requires users to be 13, but nothing prohibits users from lying about their age to get an account, or from using someone else's account. For example, a user named going by the name "Notice me Senpai" and with the address stevenkunchan.tumblr.com admits to using her brother's account in order to post art made by her brother: "Alright a lot of u guys want to know why I not doing requests because it's not really my art it's my brothers I really want them to draw there fusions again he has been depressed and really trying to draw good I just want him to get better."

8 Nyong-Choi, "Baby Steven and Child Crystal Gems." Tumblr, accessed January 20, 2018, http://nyong-choi.tumblr.com/post/142409751327/baby-steven-child-crystal-gems.

9 Three academics who studied Tumblr and its users describe the site this way: "Tumblr is described as a blogging site where users can post small messages in the form of text, photos, quotes, links, audio, and video. These posts can be tagged for key terms, and other users can then search for tagged key terms to find posts to re-blog, like, share, and/or follow the other user. Once users follow an individual, their posts are displayed on their dashboard. Within the Tumblr site, fandoms (the community that surrounds a television show, movie or book) have become key contributors. These users write stories about the characters in the show; they also analyze particular scenes in a show through posts" (Hillman, Procyk, and Neustaedter 2014, 286).

10 Tumblr. "Community Guidelines." April 2018, www.tumblr.com/policy/en/community.

PART III. THE LIMITS OF DIGITAL LITERACY

1 A search on Google Scholar for "Minecraft" yields articles on the game as a site for learning a variety of skills, including how to how to teach mathematics through *Minecraft*, how to promote interest in computer programming. and how to use dialogue as a way to self-regulate.

CHAPTER 7. *MINECRAFT*'S AFFECTIVE WORLD BUILDING

1 Thompson's article, published in April 2016, reported that *Minecraft* then had "over 100 million registered players" and was "the third-best-selling video game in history, after Tetris and Wii Sport" (50).

2 EthanGamer, EthanGamerTV YouTube channel. Accessed June 21, 2018, www.youtube.com/user/EthanGamerTV.

3 EthanGamer, "It's the Grand Opening!!! Ethan's Minecraft Server!!" YouTube video, July 25, 2016, www.YouTube.com/watch?v=68JBI1creSg&t=438s.

4   EthanGamer, "It's My Room in Minecraft!!" YouTube video, July 21, 2016, www.YouTube.com/watch?v=n-uHqXLmQPo.
5   See, for example, Jim Pike and John Stuppy, "Use Minecraft to Teach Math." ISTE, September 25, 2015, www.iste.org.
6   Stephanie Mundt, "Minecraft Monster Gallery." Artsonia, accessed November 15, 2017, www.artsonia.com/museum/gallery.asp?project=1355264.

CHAPTER 8. FROM MEMES TO LOGOS

1   According to Wikipedia, "The Nyan Cat music video reached ninth place in *Business Insider*'s top ten viral videos of April 2011, with 7.2 million total views. The original YouTube video has received over 146 million views as of 30 May 2017. Due to its popularity, many new remixes and cover versions have been made, some several hours long. There are also ringtones, wallpapers and applications created for operating systems and devices. . . . 'Nyan Cat Adventure,' by 21st Street Games, is an officially licensed game. An officially licensed cryptocurrency entitled 'Nyancoin' with the domain name nyanco.in (later nyan-coin.org) was launched in January 2014." "Nyan Cat." Wikipedia, accessed August 25, 2018, https://en.wikipedia.org.
2   According to Wikipedia (ibid.), the cat was originally posted in 2011 as a GIF animation by 25-year-old Christopher Torres of Dallas; he came up with the idea for a hybrid Pop-Tart/cat, based in part on his own cat. The song comes from a Japanese pop song drawing on the Japanese word "nya," which imitates the sound of a cat. A YouTube user going by "sarajoon" combined the cat animation with the "Momo Momo" version of the song "Nyanyanyanyanyanya!" and uploaded it to YouTube on April 5, 2011, three days after Torres had uploaded his animation, giving it the title "Nyan Cat."
3   Ira Shifman defines memes as "small cultural units of transmission, analogous to genes, which are spread by copying or imitation" (2011, 189).
4   "Nae Nae." Wikipedia, accessed June 21, 2018, https://en.wikipedia.org.
5   Jared Paschall, "Whip/Nae Nae Elementary Cardio Workout." YouTube video, August 20, 2015, www.YouTube.com/watch?v=6b-2wEkhOnk.
6   Modern Street Dance, "Modern Street Dance—Silento Watch Me (Whip/Nae Nae) by Yak Films." YouTube video, September 15, 2015, www.YouTube.com/watch?v=Jeo2Gp6FQ10.
7   "Dab (dance)." Wikipedia, accessed June 21, 2018, https://en.wikipedia.org.
8   CNN, "Paul Ryan Stops Kids from Dabbing." YouTube video, January 4, 2017, www.YouTube.com/watch?v=Mb6d9K9ygag.
9   Matt Weinberger, "An 11-Year-Old and a 7-Year-Old Teach Me about *Roblox*, the Video Game That's Turning Teens into Millionaires." *Business Insider*, August 19, 2017, www.businessinsider.com.
10 "Entrepreneurship." *Business Dictionary*, accessed August 25, 2018, www.businessdictionary.com.

11 EthanGamer, "Food Fight!!! *Roblox*/Kid Gaming." YouTube video, January 27, 2016, www.YouTube.com/watch?v=-RgOCT82F5M.
12 Dean Takahashi, "The DeanBeat: *Roblox*'s Kid Developers Make Enough 'Robux' to Pay for College." *Venture Beat*, July 21, 2017, https://venturebeat.com.
13 RonaldOMG, "Baby Survives with No Mommy/*Roblox*." YouTube video, September 21, 2016, www.YouTube.com/watch?v=bfCj8SpubyA.

BIBLIOGRAPHY

"Afraid of the Dark." 2013. *Uncle Grandpa*. Cartoon Network, 21 October.
Ahmed, Sara. 2004. *A Cultural Politics of Emotion*. New York: Routledge.
Allison, Anne. 2004. "Cuteness as Japan's Millennial Product." In Tobin 2004, 34–52.
"Alone Together." 2015. *Steven Universe*. Cartoon Network, 15 January.
Anderson, Daniel R. 2004. "Watching Children Watch Television and the Creation of Blue's Clues." In *Nickelodeon Nation: The History, Politics, and Economics of America's Only TV Channel for Kids*, edited by Heather Hendershot, 241–68. New York: New York University Press.
"Apple Investors Call for Action over iPhone 'Addiction' among Children." 2018. *Guardian*, 8 January. www.theguardian.com.
Appleseed. 2011. "Children at the Border: The Screening, Protection, and Repatriation of Unaccompanied Mexican Minors." www.appleseednetwork.org.
Atkins, Rebecca. 2016. "10-Year-Old Albuquerque Boy and Sister Write to Child in Aleppo." KRQE Radio, 12 December.
Banet-Weiser, Sarah. 2007. *Kids Rule! Nickelodeon and Consumer Citizenship*. Durham, NC: Duke University Press.
Barnes, Brooks, and Amy Chozick. 2013. "New Disney Characters Make It Big in TV's Preschool Playground." *New York Times*, 31 March. www.nytimes.com.
Bernstein, Robin. 2011. *Racial Innocence: Performing American Childhood from Slavery to Civil Rights*. New York: New York University Press.
Bhabha, Jacqueline. 2014. *Child Migration and Human Rights in a Global Age*. Princeton, NJ: Princeton University Press.
"Body Language." 2003. *Blue's Clues*. Nick Jr., 19 September.
Boler, Megan. 1997. "The Risks of Empathy: Interrogating Multiculturalism's Gaze." *Journal of Cultural Studies* 11 (2): 253–73.
"A Brand New Game." 2002. *Blue's Clues*. Nick Jr., 21 October.
Brenner, Eliot M., and Peter Salovey. 1997. "Emotional Regulation during Childhood: Developmental, Interpersonal, and Individual Considerations." In *Emotional Development and Emotional Intelligence: Educational Implications*, edited by Peter Salovey and and David J. Sluyter, 168–92. New York: Basic Books.
Brysk, Alison. 2005. *Human Rights and Private Wrongs: Constructing Global Civil Society*. New York: Routledge.
Buckingham, David. 2008. "Children and Media: A Cultural Studies Approach." In *The International Handbook of Children, Media, and Culture*, edited by Kirsten Drotner and Sonia Livingstone, 219–36. London: Sage.

Butler, Judith. 2004. *Precarious Life: The Powers of Mourning and Violence*. London: Verso.
Carlsson-Paige, Nancy, Geralyn Bywater McLaughlin, and Joan Wolfsheimer Almon. 2015. "Reading Instruction in Kindergarten: Little to Gain and Much to Lose." Defending the Early Years Alliance for Childhood. www.deyproject.org.
Carro, Jessica, and Roque Planas. 2017. "This Is What Trump's Immigration Crackdown Is Doing to School Kids." *Huffington Post*, 2 February. www.huffingtonpost.com.
Chacko, Anil, Lauren Wakschlag, Carri Hill, Barbara Danis, and Kimberly Andrews Espy. 2009. "Viewing Preschool Disruptive Behavior Disorders and Attention-Deficit/Hyperactivity Disorder through a Developmental Lens: What We Know and What We Need to Know." *Child and Adolescent Psychiatric Clinics* 18 (3): 627–43.
Christensen, Claire, and Kate Zinsser. 2014. "Can TV Promote Kids' Social-Emotional Skills?" *Psychology Today*, 26 February. www.psychologytoday.com.
Cvetkovich, Ann. 2003. *An Archive of Feelings: Trauma, Sexuality, and Lesbian Public Cultures*. Durham, NC: Duke University Press.
Deleuze, Gilles. 1997. "What Children Say." In *Essays Critical and Clinical*. Translated by Daniel W. Smith and Michael A. Greco, 61–67. Minneapolis: University of Minnesota Press.
Deruy, Emily, Alia Wong, and Hayley Glatter. 2016. "Learning in the Aftermath of a Divisive Election." *Atlantic*, 15 November. www.theatlantic.com.
Dezuanni, Michael, Joanne O'Mara, and Catherine Beavis. 2015. "'Redstone Is like Electricity': Children's Performative Representations in and around *Minecraft*." *E-Learning and Digital Media* 12 (2): 147–63.
Driver, Saige. 2018. "Tumblr for Business: Everything You Need to Know." Business News Daily, 24 August. www.businessnewsdaily.com.
Duane, Anna Mae. 2013. "The Children's Table: Childhood Studies and the Humanities." In *The Children's Table: Childhood Studies and the Humanities*, edited by Anna Mae Duane, 1–14. Athens: University of Georgia Press.
"Earthlings." 2016. *Steven Universe*. Cartoon Network, 8 August.
Ehrenreich, Barbara. 2009. *Bright-Sided: How the Relentless Promotion of Positive Thinking Has Undermined America*. New York: Metropolitan Books.
"The Elephant Sprinkler." 2010. *Team Umizoomi*. Nick Jr., 15 April.
"Extreme Spots." 2012. *SpongeBob SquarePants*. Nickelodeon, 21 July.
"Fartwerk." 2014. *Sanjay and Craig*. Nickelodeon, 22 November.
Fausto-Sterling, Anne. 2000. *Sexing the Body: Gender Politics and the Politics of Sexuality*. New York: Basic Books.
Firestone, Lisa. 2016. "Why We Need to Teach Kids Emotional Intelligence: The Most Important Thing We Can Teach Our Children." *Psychology Today*, 16 March. www.psychologytoday.com.
Fuchs, Melani Alexander, and Diane H. Craft. 2012. *Movement Matters: A Movement Album for Montessori Early Childhood Programs*. Cortland, NY: Active Play Books.
"Fusion Cuisine." 2014. *Steven Universe*. Cartoon Network, 6 November.

Gagen, Elizabeth A. 2010. "Commentary: Disciplining Bodies." In *Contested Bodies of Childhood and Youth*, edited by Kathrin Horschelmann and Rachel Collis, 178–85. New York: Palgrave Macmillan.

Gopnik, Allison. 2009. *The Philosophical Baby: What Children's Minds Tell Us about Truth, Love, and the Meaning of Life*. New York: Farrar, Straus & Giroux.

Grace, Donna J., and Joseph Tobin. 1997. "Carnival in the Classroom: Elementary Students Making Videos." In *Making a Place for Pleasure in Early Childhood Education*, edited by Joseph J. Tobin, 159–87. New Haven, CT, and London: Yale University Press.

Greenberg, Mark T., and Jennie L. Snell. 1997. "Brain Development and Emotional Development: The Role of Teaching in Organizing the Frontal Lobe." In *Emotional Development and Emotional Intelligence: Educational Implications*, edited by Peter Salovey and David J. Sluyter, 93–119. New York: Basic Books.

Grossberg, Lawrence. 1997. *Dancing in spite of Myself: Essays on Popular Culture*. Durham, NC: Duke University Press.

Guerrero, Nina, David Marcus, and Alan Turry. 2015. "Poised in the Creative Now: Principles of Nordoff-Robbins Music Therapy." In *The Oxford Handbook of Music Therapy*, edited by Jane Edwards. Oxford: Oxford University Press. www.oxfordhandbooks.com.

Hall, Stuart. 1996. "On Postmodernism and Articulation" [interview with Lawrence Grossberg]. In *Stuart Hall: Critical Dialogues in Cultural Studies*, edited by Kuan Hsing Chen and David Morley, 131–50. New York and London: Routledge.

Harding, Jennifer, and E. Deidre Pribram. 2009. *Emotions: A Cultural Studies Reader*. New York: Routledge.

Harmon, Amy. 2004. "Neurodiversity Forever: The Disability Movement Turns to Brains." *New York Times*, 9 May. www.nytimes.com.

Hayes, Dade. 2008. *Anytime Playdate: Inside the Preschool Entertainment Boom, or How Television Became My Baby's Best Friend*. New York: Free Press.

Hendershot, Heather. 2004. "Nickelodeon's Nautical Nonsense: The Intergenerational Appeal of SpongeBob SquarePants." In *Nickelodeon Nation: The History, Politics, and Economics of America's Only TV Channel for Kids*, edited by Heather Hendershot, 182–208. New York: New York University Press.

Hennessy-Fiske, Molly. 2018. "U.S. Is Separating Immigrant Parents and Children to Discourage Others, Activists Say." *Los Angeles Times*, 20 February. www.latimes.com.

Herreria, Carla. 2016. "Kids Are Writing Letters to Donald Trump to Ask Him to Be Kind." *Huffington Post*, 22 November. www.huffingtonpost.com.

Hesford, Wendy. 2011. *Spectacular Rhetorics: Human Rights Visions, Recognitions, Feminisms*. Durham, NC: Duke University Press.

Hillman, Serena, Jason Procyk, and Carmen Neustaedter. 2014. "Tumblr Fandoms, Community, and Culture." In *CSCW Companion '14*, 285–88. Proceedings of the 17th ACM Conference on Computer Supported Cooperative Work and Social Computing (Baltimore, 15–19 February).

Hinshaw, Stephen P., and Katherine Ellison. 2016. *ADHD: What Everyone Needs to Know*. New York: Oxford University Press.

Hinshaw, Stephen P., and Richard Scheffler. 2014. *The ADHD Explosion: Myths, Medication, Money and Today's Push for Performance*. New York: Oxford University Press.

Holland, Patricia. 2004. *Picturing Childhood: The Myth of the Child in Popular Imagery*. New York: I.B. Tauris.

Holloway, Donell, Lelia Green, and Sonia Livingstone. 2013. "Zero to Eight. Young Children and Their Internet Use." London: EU Kids Online/London School of Economics. http://eprints.lse.ac.uk.

Holt, Louise. 2010. "Embodying and Destabilising (Dis)ability and Childhood." In *Contested Bodies of Childhood and Youth*, edited by Kathrin Horschelmann and Rachel Collis, 203–14. New York: Palgrave Macmillan.

Hussey, David L. 2003. "Music Therapy with Emotionally Disturbed Children." *Psychiatric Times* 20 (6). www.psychiatrictimes.com.

"Jail Break." 2015. *Steven Universe*. Cartoon Network, 12 March.

James, Allison. 1994. *Childhood Identities: Social Relations and the Self in the Experience of the Child*. Edinburgh: Edinburgh University Press.

———. 2007. "Giving Voice to Children's Voices: Practices and Problems, Pitfalls and Potentials." *American Anthropologist* 109: 261–72.

James, Allison, Chris Jenks, and Alan Prout. 1998. *Theorizing Childhood*. Oxford: Blackwell.

"Jeff's Secret." 2016. *Clarence*. Cartoon Network, 2 June.

Jenkins, Henry, and Sam Ford. 2013. *Spreadable Media: Creating Value and Meaning in a Networked Culture*. New York: New York University Press.

Jenks, Chris. 2005. *Childhood*. London: Routledge.

Kahn, Jennifer. 2013. "Can Emotional Intelligence Be Taught?" *New York Times Magazine*, 11 September. https://archive.nytimes.com.

Kinder, Marsha. 1991. *Playing with Power in Movies, Television, and Video Games: From Muppet Babies to Teenage Mutant Ninja Turtles*. Berkeley and Los Angeles: University of California Press.

Koh, Adeline. 2014. "Niceness, Building, and Opening the Genealogy of the Digital Humanities: Beyond the Social Contract of Humanities Computing." *Differences: A Journal of Feminist Cultural Studies* 25 (1): 93–106.

Krogstad, Jens Manuel. 2014. "5 Facts about the Modern American Family." Pew Research Center, 30 April. www.pewresearch.org.

Lange, Patricia. 2014. *Kids on YouTube: Technical Identities and Digital Literacies*. New York: Routledge.

Leavitt, Robin L., and Martha Bauman Power. 1997. "Civilizing Bodies: Children in Day Care." In *Making a Place for Pleasure in Early Childhood Education*, edited by Joseph Tobin, 39–75. New Haven, CT: Yale University Press.

Lemish, Dafna. 2008. "The Mediated Playground: Media in Early Childhood." In *The International Handbook of Children, Media, and Culture*, edited by Kirsten Drotner and Sonia Livingstone, 152–67. London: Sage.

Lemish, Dafna, and Linda-Renee Bloch. 2004. "Pokemon in Israel." In Tobin 2004, 165–86.

"Lion 3: Straight to Video." 2014. *Steven Universe*. Cartoon Network, 4 December.

Livingstone, Sonia, and Kirsten Drotner. 2008. "Editors' Introduction." In *The International Handbook of Children, Media, and Culture*, edited by Kirsten Drotner and Sonia Livingstone, 1–16. London: Sage.

Long, Clara. 2014. "'You Don't Have Rights Here': U.S. Border Screening and Returns of Central Americans to Risks of Serious Harm." Human Rights Watch, 16 October. www.hrw.org.

"Mad Feelings." 1995. *Mr. Roger's Neighborhood*. PBS, 20 October.

Massumi, Brian. 1995. "The Autonomy of Affect." *Cultural Critique* 31 (Autumn): 83–109.

"Max Misses the Bus." 2003. *Max and Ruby*. Nick Jr., 6 January.

"Max's Rainy Day." 2003. *Max and Ruby*. Nick Jr., 8 January.

McRobbie, Angela. 2011. "Rethinking Creative Economy as Radical Social Enterprise." *Variant*, Spring. www.variant.org.uk.

Messenger Davies, Máire. 2008. "Reality and Fantasy in Media: Can Children Tell the Difference and How Do We Know?" In *The International Handbook of Children, Media, and Culture*, edited by Kirsten Drotner and Sonia Livingstone, 121–36. London: Sage.

Michael, Ali. 2016. "What Do We Tell the Children?" *Huffington Post*, 9 November. www.huffingtonpost.com.

Milrod, Barbara. 2017. "Why Children Bear the Brunt of Trump's America: The Stress Test." *Newsweek*, 19 May. www.newsweek.com.

Musalo, Karen, Lisa Frydman, and Pablo Ceriani Cernadas, eds. 2015. *Childhood and Migration in Central and North America: Causes, Practices, and Challenges*. Center for Gender & Refugee Studies at the University of California Hastings College of the Law and the Migration and Asylum Program, Center for Justice and Human Rights at the National University of Lanús, Argentina.

O'Connell Davidson, Julia. 2011. "Moving Children? Child Trafficking, Child Migration, and Child Rights." *Critical Social Policy* 31 (3): 454–77.

Olsson, Liselott Mariett. 2009. *Movement and Experimentation in Young Children's Learning*. New York: Routledge.

Palan, Erica. 2017. "'I Wish I Could Open Your Heart': Philly Kids Draw on Their Anxiety to Express What They Think about Trump and His Immigration Plans." *Philly.com*, 12 June. www.philly.com.

Passel, Jeffrey S., and Paul Taylor. 2010. "Household Structure; Mixed Families." Pew Research Center: Hispanic Trends, 11 August. www.pewhispanic.org.

Probyn, Elspeth. 2005. *Blush: Faces of Shame*. Minneapolis: University of Minnesota Press.

Projansky, Sarah. 2014. *Spectacular Girls: Media Fascination and Celebrity*. New York: New York University Press.

Ramirez, Fernando. 2017. "Trump-Themed Houston Art Show Receives Dozens of Submissions from Anonymous School Children." *Houston Chronicle*, 12 May. www.chron.com.

Raver, C. Cybele. 2003. "Young Children's Emotional Development and Social Readiness." ERIC Clearinghouse on Elementary and Early Childhood Education, Champaign, IL, July. www.eric.ed.gov.
Ravitch, Diane. 2010. *The Death and Life of the Great American School System*. New York: Basic Books.
Richmond, Emily. 2016. "Why Are Third-Graders Afraid of Donald Trump?" *Atlantic*, 18 July. www.theatlantic.com.
Ringland, Kathryn E., Christine T. Wolf, Heather Faucett, Lynn Dombrowski, and Gillian R. Hayes. 2016. "'Will I Always Be Not Social?': Re-Conceptualizing Sociality in the Context of a Minecraft Community for Autism." In *Proceedings of the 2016 CHI Conference on Human Factors in Computing Systems* (San Jose, 7–12 May), 1256–69.
Rose, Jacqueline. 1984. *The Case of Peter Pan, or, The Impossibility of Children's Fiction*. London: Macmillan.
Rose, Nikolas. 1999. *Governing the Soul: The Shaping of the Private Self*. London: Routledge.
Rutkin, Aviva. 2016. "How *Minecraft* Is Helping Children with Autism Make New Friends." *New Scientist*, 27 April. www.newscientist.com.
Saarni, Carolyn. 1997. "Emotional Competence and Self-Regulation in Childhood." In *Emotional Development and Emotional Intelligence*, edited by Peter Salovey and David J. Sluyter, 35–66. New York: Basic Books.
Sanchez-Eppler, Karen. 2005. *Dependent States: The Child's Part in Nineteenth-Century American Culture*. Chicago: University of Chicago Press.
Saulny, Susan. 2011. "Census Data Presents Rise in Multiracial Population of Youths." *New York Times*, 24 March. www.nytimes.com.
Schoenholtz, Andrew. 2013. "Developing the Substantive Best Interests of Child Migrants: A Call for Action." Symposium: Children and Immigration: A Lost Generation. *Valparaiso University Law Review* 46: 991–1018.
"Secret Garden." 2016. *Teen Titans Go*. Cartoon Network, 21 January.
Sefton-Green, Julian. 2004. "Initiation Rites: A Small Boy in a Poke-World." In Tobin 2004, 141–64.
Shore, Amy. 2009. "Convergence Citizens: The New Media Literacy of Pre-School Television." *Afterimage* 37 (2): 29–32.
Shifman, Limor. 2011. "An Anatomy of a YouTube Meme." *New Media & Society* 14 (2): 187–203.
"Steven vs. Amethyst." 2016. *Steven Universe*. Cartoon Network, 3 August.
Stockton, Kathryn. 2009. *The Queer Child, or Growing Sideways in the 20th Century*. Durham, NC: Duke University Press.
"Story for Steven." 2015. *Steven Universe*. Cartoon Network, 9 April.
Strauss, Valerie. 2014. "Everything You Need to Know about Common Core—Ravitch." *Washington Post*, 18 January. www.washingtonpost.com.
Taylor, Adam. 2016. "In Aleppo's Misinformation War, a 7-Year-Old Girl Prompts a Fact Check." *Washington Post*, 14 December. www.washingtonpost.com.

Thompson, Clive. 2016. "The *Minecraft* Generation." *New York Times Magazine*, 14 April. www.nytimes.com.
Tisdall, E. Kay M. 2012. "The Challenge and Challenging of Childhood Studies? Learning from Disability Studies and Research with Disabled Children." *Children & Society* 26: 181–91.
Tobin, Joseph, ed. 2004. *Pikachu's Global Adventure: The Rise and Fall of Pokemon*. Durham, NC, and London: Duke University Press.
Toshalis, Eric, and Michael J. Nakkula. 2012. "Motivation, Engagement, and Student Voice." Jobs for the Future. www.studentsatthecenter.org.
"Unbarfable." 2013. *Sanjay and Craig*. Nickelodeon, 21 September.
UNHCR (United Nations High Commissioner for Refugees). 2014. *Children on the Run: Unaccompanied Children Leaving Central America and Mexico and the Need for International Protection*. 13 March. www.refworld.org.
"We Need to Talk." 2015. *Steven Universe*. Cartoon Network, 18 June.
Weinberger, Matt. 2017. "A Video Game That Has Turned Players into $50,000-a-Month Entrepreneurs Just Raised $92 Million to Turn Them into Media Moguls." *Business Insider*, 14 March. www.businessinsider.com.
Werner, Erica. 2011. "Obama Says Too Much Testing Makes Education Boring." Associated Press, 28 March. http://archive.boston.com.
Williams, Raymond. 1977. *Marxism and Literature*. Oxford: Oxford University Press.
Zolyomi, Annuska, and Marc Schmalz. 2017. "Mining for Social Skills: *Minecraft* in Home and Therapy for Neurodiverse Youth." In *Proceedings of the 50th Hawaii International Conference on System Sciences* (Waikoloa, 4–7 January), 3391–400.

INDEX

ABCmouse.com, 110–11
Adoption, 252–254
Affect, 6, 33; as alternative to identity categories, 173–200, 251–253; as distinct from emotions, 34, 45, 196; as a form of intensity, 43–47, 167, 181, 196, 217; in the form of shame, 255–258; media studies, 42–49; as nonlinguistic form of expression, 49–51, 172, 192; pets, 233, 240–241; in play, 52; produced through children's television, 144, 161–172; in relation to fear, 78; in relation to physiology, 38–42; in Tumblr art, 196; as theorized by Deleuze, 217; on Twitter, 258; within consumerism, 246–247
Agency, of children, 21–23, 153; gained through gaming, 206; via consumerism, 238; in relation to media consumption, 47–49, 140; as political subjects, 55–60; in relation to YouTube, 86–89
Ahmed, Sara, 35, 37, 63–64, 78–79, 92–93
al-Abed, Bana, 28–29, 55–60, 255–258
Alliance for Childhood's *Defending the Early Years* report, 114–115, 121–122
Allison, Anne, 240
Amazing World of Gumball, The, 152–153
Anderson, Daniel, 43–44, 46, 144–145
Anger: in kids' responses to Trump's election, 99, 101–104; as physiological response, 124–125, 165–67; as response to lack of power, 125–126, 257

Appleseed immigrant rights' group, 68–72
Archive of feelings, 2, 11–12, 15, 65, 259; composed of Minecraft videos, 224; in the form of Central American children's art, 76–82; in the form of children's art as a response to Trump's election, 99–106; in Tumblr fanart, 194–195
Arte de Lagrimas, 64–65, 76–82
Attachment, 240
Attention deficit hyperactivity disorder, 3, 40–42
Autism, 208

Banet-Weiser, Sarah, 48–49, 144–145, 161–162, 237–238
Baszucki, David, 242–243
Beavis, Catherine, 205–206
Becoming, through mapping in gaming, 207–208
Bernstein, Robin, 263n4
Best interests of the child standard, 67, 71
Biden, Joe, 63
Bloch, Linda-Renee, 240
Blue's Clues, 2, 43, 144, 147–148
Bhabha, Jacqueline, 59–60
Bodily differences: in children's television programming, 152–156; in Tumblr fanart, 194–195
Bodily pleasure, 157–158; in *SpongeBob SquarePants*, 162–165; in Tumblr fanart, 194–195
Brain development in children, 39–42, 127

279

Branding, 233–235, 242, 249–250
Breadwinners, 158
Brenner, Eliot M., 124–125
Brown, Laura G., 2, 5
Brysk, Alison, 59
Buckingham, David, 21, 28, 140–141
Butler, Judith, 14, 51, 117, 192, 256

Candid Camera, 86
Cartoon Network, 144, 152–154, 174; as distinct from Nick Jr. and Disney Jr., 165
Center for Gender and Refugee Studies, 72, 75–76
Central America, violence in, 66, 75–77
Centre for Contemporary Cultural Studies, 21, 263n5
Chappelle, Dave, 258
Childhood, as a constructed category, 20, 38, 122, 140, 263n1
Childhood studies, 21–28
Christensen, Claire, 3
Civility, discourse of: in children's education: 84–98; as a form of "niceness," 84, 91–95; in democracy, 91–98; through letter writing, 93–95, 98
Clarence, 152–156, 165
Common Core, 108–109, 111, 114–116, 119–123, 149, 202. See also Obama administration
Common Sense Media, 158–159, 168, 178–179
Community: blogging, 194–200; dance remixes, 236–237; as families formed through Roblox games, 253–254; online gaming, 205–208, 219–228; YouTube, 233. See also Fandom
Consumerism, 233–234, 237–239, 246, 248–249. See also Branding
Convention on the Rights of the Child, 59–60, 67
Craft, Diane, 132–134
Creative economy, 242

Cuellar, Gregory, 64, 80, 82
Cvetkovich, Ann, 11–15, 37, 82

Dabbing, 237
Damasio, Antonio 40
Daniel Tiger's Neighborhood, 138
DanTDM, 221
Davidson, Jessica O'Connell, 66–67
Davis, Maire Messenger, 44–45
Deleuze, Gilles, 169, 206, 207–208, 217, 223. *See also* Becoming
Detention, of families, 61, 63; of unaccompanied minors, 68, 71, 73, 76
Dezuanni, Michael 205–206
Digital literacy, 201–204
Disability studies, 10, 23
Disney Jr. channel, 3, 142, 146, 149, 151
Diversity management, 142
Doc McStuffins, 146
Dora the Explorer, 145
Drotner, Kirsten, 47–48

Ehrenreich, Barbara, 7
Elizabeth Ann Clune Montessori School, 129–135
Emotional intelligence, 2, 5; in civility discourse, 84, 91; digital literacy, 201–202; as distinct from affect, 34; in political discourse, 58–59; in public school settings, 111–12, 127–129; in technology business practices, 138; as a set of skills and competencies, 7–8, 123; in television narratives, 145–146, 150; within Roblox, 243
Entrepreneurs, 235, 241–244
EthanGamerTV YouTube channel, 220–224, 249–251
Everyday life, 228–231, 257

Family, alternative forms, 181–187, 194, 254
Fandom, 192–200; online bullying within, 266n6

Farts, 159–161, 168–169, 232
Fashion, 244–246
Fausto-Sterling, Anne, 38
Fear: as an affective response, 167; in children migrating to the U.S., 76–82, 96; of the dark, 167–172; of Donald Trump, 83–85, 89–91, 96; in political asylum claims, 61, 72, 74–76
Ford, Sam, 6
Fuchs, Melani, 132–134
Fusion of bodies, 173–200. See also *Steven Universe*

Gagen, Elizabeth A., 116
Gamergirl, 252–253
Gaming, 202–254. See also *Minecraft*; *Roblox*
Gender categories, 162–164, 174, 176, 179, 185, 197, 206, 251–253
Gopnik, Alison, 39–40
Grace, Donna G., 157–158
Greenberg, Mark T., 127–128
Grossberg, Lawrence, 37–38
"Growing sideways," 16–17, 156–157, 171–172, 258. See also Stockton, Kathryn

Hall, Stuart, 2, 263n3
Happiness, 5, 7
Harding, Jennifer, 36–37
Hendershot, Heather, 161–162
Hesford, Wendy, 57–58
Hinshaw, Stephen, 41–42
Holland, Patricia, 118
Holt, Louise, 117–118
Hussy, David, 17–18

Identification, through avatars, 209, 216, 240–241, 251
Identity categories, critique of, 173–200; 207
Inside Out, 4–5

Internet usage: by children, 201–204; as a site for gaming, 219. See also YouTube
Interpellation, 147, 151

Jake and the Neverland Pirates, 151
James, Allison, 21–22, 122–123
Jenkins, Henry, 6, 139
Jenks, Chris, 20, 21, 122
Jimmy Kimmel (talk show moment), 87–89

Kinder, Marsha, 25–26
Kindergarten, 107–109, 114–123
Koh, Adeline, 91–92

Lange, Patricia, 86–87, 219–220
Leavitt and Power, 157
Legal status, 188
Lemish, Dafna, 139–140, 143, 240
Lesbian identity, 190–191
Livingstone, Sonia, 47–48

Manning, Stephen, 61–62, 264n1
Massumi, Brian, 6, 33, 42–52, 78, 143; and lack of attention to children, 34. See also Affect
Max and Ruby, 149–150
Mayer, John 7
McRobbie, Angela, 242
Memes, 233–238, 251
Mental health, 196–197, 199
Michael, Ali, 83–84
Mighty Writers' Workshop, 99
Milrod, Barbara, 85, 89–90
Minecraft, 30, 201–231; community building, 206, 219–224; in contrast to *Roblox*, 246–247; as Deleuzian space, 207, 217, 223; everyday life, 228–231; neurodiversity, 202–203; as site of domesticity, 206, 214, 224
Montessori, Maria, 131, 133–134
Mothering, 183–186, 240, 252–254

Movement: as part of learning process, 132–133; in children's music, 236
Music therapy, 17–20

Narrative, 23–27; on children's television, 44–45, 139, 143–167; in contrast to intensity, 47; in political asylum application process, 69; as site for the production of meaning, 35–36
Neurodiversity, 10, 30, 40, 135, 187, 202–203, 231, 258
Ni Hao, Kai-Lan, 2, 142
Nickelodeon, 2, 48–49, 144–146, 159, 237
Nick Jr., 43, 142, 145–146, 150
Nicktoons, 158
No Child Left Behind, 111, 112–114
Nonsense, 169–172
Nordoff Robbins method, 19–20
Nyan Cat, 232–233, 268n1, 268n2

Obama administration: immigration policies, 63, 65, 73; Race to the Top and Common Core education initiatives, 114–116
Office of Refugee Resettlement, 73
Olsson, Liselott Mariett, 15–16, 123, 169, 217
O'Mara, 203, 205–206

PBS, 3, 142, 144, 146
Persson, Markus, 219
Pets, 232, 240
Phineas and Ferb, 153
Piaget, Jean, 21, 25, 85, 122–123
Plug-In Drug, The, 3. *See also* Winn, Marie
Pokemon, 233, 238–241
Political asylum process for Central American children, 73–76, 264n7
Pribram, Deirdre, 36–37
Problem-solving skills, 127; taught through television narratives, 145–152; as a way to learn how to name one's emotions, 148–151

Probyn, Elspeth, 36, 255–257
Projansky, Sarah, 26–27, 263n6
Prout, Alan, 21

Racial identity, 142, 174, 179, 187–188
Ravitch, Diane, 109, 112–114
Ringland, Kate, 219
Roblox, 31, 203, 233–235, 241–254; common vernacular, 233–34, 248; entrepreneurial game developers, 241–244; fashion games, 244–246; gender of players, 251–252; monetization, 235; social space for kids, 235, 247; use of logos and brands, 234, 247, 250; YouTube videos, 249–254
Rogers, Fred, 137–138
Rose, Jacqueline, 24, 50
Rose, Nikolas, 8
Rowling, J. K., 55, 258

Saarni, Carolyn, 128–129
Sadness, 4, 180–181, 199
Salovey, Peter, 7, 124–125
Sanjay and Craig, 159–161
Sanchez-Eppler, Karen, 263n4
Scheffler, Richard, 41–42
Schoenholtz, Andrew, 67
Schmalz, Marc, 202
Sefton-Green, Julian, 239
Self-management: of children's bodies, 111. 151; of emotions, 111, 117, 125–128, 151; of learning process, 116, 149, 152; through technology, 139, 203–204
Sesame Street, 3, 144–145, 266n2 ch. 5
Sexual identity, 177, 179, 190–191, 197
Shame, 255–257
Shifman, Limor, 233, 235–236
Shore, Amy 139, 145
"Sideways growth," 16–17, 156–158. *See also* Stockton, Kathryn
Silento, 236
Snell, 127–128
Sofia the First, 146

Southern Poverty Law Center, 96–97
SpongeBob SquarePants, 161–165
Steven Universe, 30, 49, 140, 165, 173–200; feelings, 177, 179–180, 191; gender and sexual fluidity, 176–177; LGBTQ positivity, 190–191; mixed legal status, 177; nuclear family critique, 181–187; refusal of identity categories, 187–190; reviewed on Common Sense Media, 178–179; Tumblr fanart, 192–200
Stockton, Kathryn, 16–17, 156–157
"Structure of feeling," 12–13, 85, 90–91, 98, 206
Stuart, Keith, 208–209, 217
Sugar, Rebecca, 174, 176
Syrian crisis, 55–60, 255–258

Team Umizoomi, 150–151
Teen Titans Go!, 153–154, 165–167
Thompson, Clive, 210–211, 219
Tisdall, E. Kay M., 10, 23
Tobin, Joseph, 157–158
Trafficking Victims Prevention and Reauthorization Act of 2008 (TVPRA), 69, 264n4
Transgression, 158–159
Trauma, 13–14
Trump, Donald: educational policy, 265n2 Ch. 4; immigration policies, 63, 85; kids' responses to election of, 83–106; use of Twitter, 258
Tumblr, 192–200; age of users, 267n7; community orientation, 194–199, 267n9; diversity of bodies in fanart, 194–195; focus on feelings, 196–197; mental health emphasis, 197; sexual fluidity, 197–198
Twitch, 208
Twitter, 55–60, 84, 255–258

Unaccompanied minors, 66
Uncle Grandpa, 165, 168–172, 259
United Nations High Commission on Refugees, 65, 68–69, 74
U.S. Customs and Border Patrol, 61–65, 67–71

Vernacular, common, as developed by children online, 203, 221–224, 228, 233; through *Pokemon*, 239; in *Roblox* game, 248–251
Vulnerability, 192–194, 199, 204, 256

Williams, Raymond, 12–13, 98, 100, 206. See also "Structure of feeling"
Winn, Marie, 3. See also *Plug-In Drug, The*
Wonder Pets, 2
World building, 206, 211–212, 217. See also *Minecraft*

YouTube, 86–89, 205, 208, 232–238; gaming tutorials, 219–224. See also Community

Zaslow, Emilie, 263n6
Zayas, Luis, 76, 265n8
Zermatten, Jean, 67
Zinsser, Kate, 3
Zolyomi, 202

ABOUT THE AUTHOR

Jane Juffer is Professor in the Department of English and the Program of Feminist, Gender, and Sexuality Studies at Cornell University. She is the author of three books: *Intimacy across Borders: Race, Religion, and Migration in the U.S. Midwest* (2013); *Single Mother: The Emergence of the Domestic Intellectual* (NYU Press, 2006); and *At Home with Pornography: Women, Sex, and Everyday Life* (NYU Press, 1998).

Printed in the United States
By Bookmasters